The Perils of Nonviolent Islamism

The Perils of Nonviolent Islamism

Elham Manea

With a Foreword by Russell A. Berman

Telos Press Publishing
Candor, NY

Printed in the United States of America
25 24 23 22 21   1 2 3 4

An earlier version of this book was published in German translation as *Der alltägliche Islamismus: Terror beginnt, wo wir ihn zulassen* by Kösel-Verlag, Munich, a division of Random House, in 2018.

ISBN 978-0-914386-82-7 (paperback)
ISBN 978-0-914386-83-4 (ebook)

Library of Congress Cataloging-in-Publication Data

Names: Manea, Elham, author. | Berman, Russell A., 1950- other.
Title: The perils of nonviolent Islamism / Elham Manea ; with a foreword by
   Russell A. Berman.
Description: Candor : Telos Press Publishing, 2021.
Identifiers: LCCN 2020047753 (print) | LCCN 2020047754 (ebook) | ISBN
   9780914386827 (paperback) | ISBN 9780914386834 (ebook)
Subjects: LCSH: Nonviolence—Religious aspects—Islam.
Classification: LCC BP190.5.V56 M365 2021 (print) | LCC BP190.5.V56
   (ebook) | DDC 297.5/697—dc23
LC record available at https://lccn.loc.gov/2020047753
LC ebook record available at https://lccn.loc.gov/2020047754

Cover design by Amanda Trager and Erik Moskowitz
Cover photo by @mhrezaa on Unsplash

Telos Press Publishing
PO Box 811
Candor, NY 13743
www.telospress.com

Contents

Islamism, Ideology, and Lessons to Learn

Russell A. Berman

E LHAM MANEA IS a political scientist at the University of Zurich. Her scholarly publications focus on topics in the Middle East, especially women's rights, as well as regional politics in the Gulf with regard to Saudi Arabia, Oman, and Yemen. She has also undertaken research concerning immigrants from the Middle East to Europe, and the intersection between political ideology and religious heritage. With that additional specialization, she has served as a member and now the vice president of the Swiss Federal Commission on Migration, and she has testified as an expert witness for the Home Affairs Select Committee hearing on Sharia councils in the British House of Commons. Given that scholarly profile, she is well positioned to address the topic of this volume, the ideological underpinning of Islamism and more broadly the character of the relationship between religion and politics in contemporary Islamist radicalism. For American readers, she provides important insights into the ideological preconditions of Islamism, as well as the disturbing encounters European societies have made facing this hostile force.

Yet Manea also brings important personal experience to the table in the discussion of this controversial and difficult topic. Born in Egypt, with a half-Egyptian, half-Yemeni mother and her father a diplomat from Yemen, she grew up with the cosmopolitan horizon of a well-traveled family. Her father educated her to humanism and to a liberal tolerance, but—as she recounts here, interweaving autobiographical reflection with political scientific analysis—she underwent her own period of Islamist radicalization, from which she fortunately emerged, chastened but wiser. This book benefits from that direct experience with Islamism, as it integrates the memories and psychological motivations with astute observations on the cluster of category problems that confront any analyst: How much is Islamism a political phenomenon, or is it more the outgrowth of religion? Is it a matter of psychological vulnerability, social alienation, and discrimination, or does it result from the economic disadvantage of the individuals attracted to radicalism? Manea plunges head-on into the debate between those who emphasize the "social problem" that shifts attention away from origins in Islam, Islamism, and the interpretations of the religious legacy and, on the other hand, the proponents of the claim that it is all ultimately about the religion.

This volume shows that each of these two approaches can lay claim to some validity, although ultimately Manea places the emphasis on the defining impact of part of the religious heritage. Yet the book should not be reduced to that one narrative strand. Instead it is vital to recognize how the author combines genres—part memoir, part critical self-reflection, a dose of autobiography, and some forceful polemic surrounding the core social theoretical and political scientific thinking about Islamism. Her own story is as important as her conceptual analysis and explains why her account, as someone from within the Muslim experience in Europe, can speak with a particular authority, and certainly greater credibility than those non-Muslim Western scholars, including scholars of "postcolonialism," who claim the right to tell her and other Muslims what they should be experiencing in Europe or the United States. We learn that it is vital to distinguish between the real experience of migrants, in Europe or elsewhere, and those adversarial academics who self-promote via their radicalism from the safe comfort of the ivory tower.

Manea leads us into the interrogation of Islamism by asking us to join her on her own path. She begins her narrative with her early youth in Rabat, where her father was posted in the diplomatic corps. The memories are unambiguously positive, as she recalls "the freedom we enjoyed and my ability to be focused in spite of it. It was the late 1970s and early 1980s. At the time, Morocco had still not been touched by the conservative religious wave that we see today all over the Arab and Islamic world. We were kids of privileged backgrounds living in a bubble. We did not grasp the reality of other people living in poverty and deprivation—neither in Morocco nor in our own countries. Instead, we were preoccupied with ourselves—with our classes, parties, dancing, music, and being kids our age." Add to that cultural setting the description of her family, especially, her father as not emphatically religious. While he insisted on her attending a school where Arabic was the primary language, and although he emphasized the importance of the Islamic cultural heritage, Ramadan for example was treated as a joyous annual family celebration, with no observant practice of fasting.

The diplomatic life is one of always circling back home, and after four years, the family returned to Sanaʻa. From Morocco to North Yemen: two Arab countries, two Muslim countries, but a world of difference between them, especially from the vantage point of the young daughter of the diplomat. "So you can imagine my shock on arriving in Yemen. It is not that I did not know what to expect there. But all the same it was shocking. I travel back in history when I travel to Yemen.... [It feels] as if you have left one time zone and entered another—except that you are now entering a parallel world with another social order." From Morocco, or at least a particular segment of it, to Yemen amounted to a step out of one version of modernity into a stringent, rigorous, and traditionalist society, just as it puts on display the variety of cultural forms within the Arab world, the rich diversity that has again and again been the target of homogenizing forces, from pan-Arabism to pan-Islamism. For Manea's analysis, this particular binary of Rabat and Sanaʻa plays a structuring role: both sites have tenacious claims on their Muslim identities, but their antithetical cultural choices point to divergent paths, two different ways to live Islam. Their separation eventually becomes central to her analysis of Islam and its potentials today.

(A further difference between Morocco and Yemen is of interest to current U.S. politics regarding Executive Order 13769, superseded by E.O. 13780, which placed limitations on entry into the country. Critics attacked it as a "Muslim ban," although that formulation obscures important distinctions. While travel from Yemen, deemed a security risk, was affected, it did not apply to Morocco, nor was there ever a ban on travel from the countries with the world's largest Muslim populations, Indonesia and India. The designation "Muslim ban" has instead functioned as a tendentious misrepresentation. Muslims as a whole were never banned from entry into the United States.)

Manea describes the implications for the young girl, who left Morocco behind, with its tolerance for casual relationships between men and women, only to discover very different norms of behavior in Yemen. "Morocco was more relaxed about women and social mores, at least in the circles I was moving in, and that was a big contrast to the North of Yemen. You certainly did not see women with headscarves in Rabat in that period. It was only elderly women who wore traditional *jalabyia*, and they were colorful. In Sana'a, girls wore headscarves and later they took on the *sharshaf*, the two pieces of black cloth that cover the woman from head to toe, along with another one that hides the face. I was spared that by my father. He did not believe in any of that and made it clear to his family. In Rabat young men and women kissed when they greeted. In Sana'a, a young woman seen with a male stranger can cause a tribal war and earn herself a severe punishment. Society is segregated. When you enter a house, you will not see a female face unless you are moving in circles with less conservative mores."

It was in this context that she underwent radicalization. At first, she merely complied with the obligation to wear a headscarf in school, quickly removing it once she left the premises. Yet it was in the same school where she fell under the influence of what turned out to be a Muslim Brotherhood cell, offering young people a sense of belonging and purpose while in fact grooming them to become cogs in the Islamist machine. The organization knew how to manipulate youthful idealism by appealing to the budding recruits' basic understanding of Islam as a message of goodness and ethical behavior, but the fundamentalist doctrine gradually took over. Discipline grew stricter, the hijab became mandatory, not voluntary, and a programmatic anti-Semitism was disseminated, a hatred of Jews as such, based on Quranic verses, by no means only the modern State of Israel.

Manea reports eventually breaking with the movement because of her own familiarity with the more tolerant and welcoming Islam she had known in Morocco, but also because of the Islamists' demand that she break with her own family. In a chilling anecdote, she relates how she was receiving instructions from an older woman, higher up in the Islamist hierarchy: "She was telling us about the importance of obeying our husbands. For women, the way to heaven is through fulfilling their marital duties. The Prophet once said that if it was not for the fact that only God should be worshipped, he would have suggested that wives prostrate themselves to their husbands, as they would when praying. But it was what Bushra said next that broke the camel's back. She repeated a saying attributed to the Prophet about a woman who ignored her husband's order not to visit her sick father. I was told the Prophet said, 'The angels are cursing her now, for she defied her husband's order.' That afternoon, I left our meeting knowing I would never return. Who should be cursed here? I asked myself. The woman who wants to visit her sick father or this bloody husband, who has no mercy in his heart?"

The passage is important not only because it marks the end of Manea's brief infatuation with Islamist fanaticism. It also sets up the complexity of the overall argument in the book. The autobiographical reflection introduces a moment in which the political operative appeals to the authority of religion, in one of its ancient texts, in order to pursue the construction of a very disciplined and profoundly illiberal order, one that Manea does not hesitate to designate as totalitarian. Manea's book is very much about Islamism, but it is also a meditation more generally on the instrumentalization of a premodern religious tradition in order to construct a highly modern—or perhaps better, because of the systematic illiberalism, postmodern—apparatus of domination.

Describing this space between religion and politics, Manea enters a rhetorical field that has itself been highly politicized. In the decades since 9/11, many Western liberals and leftists have rejected descriptions of terrorism emanating from the Middle East as having anything to do with Islam or Islamism, leading to grotesque circumlocutions especially during the Obama administration, which labeled it simply "violent extremism." On the other hand, on the far right the argument is made that terrorism is the necessary and inevitable result of Islam, just as in a similar vein, the movement of modern atheism, in principle hostile to all religion, denounces the religion of Islam because of its purportedly inescapable violent consequences. Manea describes all these accounts in order to carve out a space between them and to make a more complex argument. Her approach maintains the relationship between politics and religion without however reducing one to the other. Thus her reference to "nonviolent Islamism" means that the repressive political movement of Islamism, instantiated in the Muslim Brotherhood and similar organizations (and with a parallel in the Shiite world of Iran), does genuinely draw on Muslim sources, but it relies excessively on the bellicose and authoritarian substance of the Medina portions of the Quran, and much less so on the Mecca portions. That binary inherent to the holy scripture itself—such is her argument—maps onto the difference between the tolerant Islam of Rabat and the dogma of Sana'a.

Manea's own pursuit of a Muslim spirituality of tolerance includes, as she reports in the course of her narrative, leading prayer services in Switzerland in an open mosque, for a mixed gender congregation, and without head covering. Such is one of the possibilities of contemporary Islam. But a major point of her book is that "nonviolent Islamism," i.e., the ideological roots that empower violent actors, cannot be treated as absolutely different from Islam, neither from its past nor from its present. Islamism really does have something to with (part of) Islam. She warns us against the comforting illusion that extremism thrives only on the margins. She shows instead that it is a consequence of widely shared beliefs in the Arab world.

On this latter point she directs us to an important document, an opinion piece from 2014 by former Kuwaiti Minister of Information Saad bin Tafla al-Ajami, entitled "We Are All 'ISIS'!" Al-Ajami's point was hardly solidarity with ISIS but, to the contrary, the recognition that despite widespread condemnation of ISIS terror in the Arab world, much of its ideology had become commonplace and well embedded in popular opinion. No matter how the public that considers itself moderate and modern rejects terrorist violence, it shares the ideological precepts that have motivated the terrorist actors themselves.

In other words, Islamism is very much anchored in parts of the Muslim legacy. It is a specific reading of the religion, one that is impalatable to modern sensibilities, and it is certainly not the only possible reading, although it is undeniably one credible reading of genuine sources. It is therefore simply a matter of intellectual laziness for Western liberals to assert that ISIS is only a "perversion" of Islam, as President Obama once put it, as if it were up to him to determine which Muslim is the genuine Muslim. (Ironically that very claim to denounce counterfeit Muslim identity—to decide which is the real Muslim—is the hallmark of the extremists who regularly target those other Muslims, whether moderates or traditionalists, Sufi or Shia or others, all deemed apostates.) Nor is Islamism a consequence of European colonialism, American imperialism, or Israeli Zionism—the stereotypical explanation from the ideological left. Rather, it draws on narrowly selected elements from within the ancient religious tradition itself and implants them in a modern political agenda. It also draws on values and stereotypes tolerated or even embraced by the modern Arab world. Al-Ajami is therefore insistent that contemporary Arab culture bears considerable responsibility for ISIS atrocities because it participates in the same value structure. It is vital to hear his own words:

الحقيقة التي لا نستطيع نكرانها، أن "داعش" تعلمت في مدارسنا وصلّت في مساجدنا، واستمعت لإعلامنا، وتسمّرت أمام فضائياتنا، وأنصتت لمنابرنا، ونهلت من كتبنا، وأصغت لمراجعنا، وأطاعوا أمراءهم بيننا، واتبعوا فتاوى من لدنا، هذه الحقيقة التي لا نستطيع إنكارها. "داعش" لم تأت من كوكب آخر.

(The undeniable truth is that "ISIS" was taught in our schools, prayed in our mosques, listened to our media, was seated in front of our satellite channels, listened to our platforms, drank from our books, listened to our references, obeyed their leaders among us, and followed fatwas that came from us. This is a reality we cannot deny. "ISIS" did not come from another planet.)[1]

Manea points us to al-Ajami's statement because it is important for her own argument for several reasons. It recognizes that some of the cultural and intellectual limitations that beset today's Arab world are self-inflicted, a consequence of a heritage that has not undergone critical scrutiny because of restrictions on skeptical inquiry. The teaching of history, he decries, does not integrate مبدا الشك, the principle of doubt, vital to any professionalized humanities inquiry. Furthermore, the modern and moderate elements of society have made an indolent peace with extremist thought, tolerating its dissemination throughout cultural, religious, and educational institutions. All this runs counter to the familiar litany of the Middle East exclusively as victim; on the contrary, it has participated in its own victimization, and ISIS is the result.

Recognizing that participation in the construction of its cultural world is a statement of responsibility, al-Ajami and Manea reject the rhetoric of victimization in order to underscore agency. No matter what the external forces, one cannot understand social phenomena without investigating the subjective role of the internal actors. Here one more time is al-Ajami in a tone that could not be clearer:

باختصار، نحن جميعا "داعش"، نحن الذين خلقناها وصنعناها وربيناها وعلمناها وجندناها وشحنّاها
وعبأناها ثم وقفنا حيارى أمام أهوالها التي صنعناها بأيدينا.

(In summary: we are all together "ISIS," it is we who created it and manufactured it, taught it, instructed it, recruited it, shipped it, packed it, and then we stopped, in front of its horrors, that we made with our own hands.)

This insistence on the human construction of the cultural world is profoundly modern. In the context of the discussion of the Middle East, it stands in stark contrast to the paradigm popularized by Edward Said, who diminished modern Arab society by treating it as exclusively the victim of Western Orientalism. That narrative of the passive victim, which minimizes endogenous agency, appeals to an affect of resentment in the region, just as it finds eager recipients among Western critics of the West. Manea offers valuable insight into the latter, as she reports on how she encounters this anti-Westernism in European politics and universities.

The primacy of human agency has an additional importance for Manea's argument. As noted, as much as she is a critic of Islamism, both its violent practice and its ideological foundations, she makes it clear how much she retains an attachment to Islam. In the background, one can surely detect reverberations of her childhood memories of the difference between Morocco and Yemen. That geographic binary overlaps with her textual distinction between the Mecca and Medina strands within the Quran. Yet she does not simply act as steward of that distinction, reifying the legacy of the past. Rather she performs a religious, or if you prefer, spiritual, identity that actively chooses its points of reference and invents new forms of liturgical practice. Humans make their world, including their understanding of spiritual pathways. The divine becomes an expression of human expression. In terms of the history of

Critical Theory, Manea is engaged in the interrogation of orthodoxy and the discovery of the human content of divinity that played out in the course of the European nineteenth century, as early as in Hegel's early theological writings but especially in the works of David Strauss, Ludwig Feuerbach, and of course Marx's *Theses on Feuerbach*. Reclaiming the humanity of religion, and the urgency of religion for humanity, has once again become necessary today, in the face of both religious extremism, on the one hand, and the extreme animosity toward religion in contemporary atheism and liberalism, on the other.

Al-Ajami's title, "We Are All ISIS," كلنا داعش, presumably echoes earlier "We are all..." formulations, most famously "Nous sommes tous américains" in *Le Monde* after the 9/11 attacks (itself an echo of Paris 1968 and the cry of "Nous sommes tous juifs allemands"). Al-Ajami's 2014 usage predates the phrase's return after the attack on *Charlie Hebdo* in January 2015. There is an interesting distinction insofar as the standard Western usages of the "We are all..." formula involve assertions of solidarity and unity, whereas al-Ajami deploys it to denounce the collective of shared culpability, and therefore simultaneously lays claim to responsibility and agency.

That rhetoric of responsibility and self-criticism—his critique of shared ideological illusions—points to another piece of fascinating textual evidence to which Manea introduces us. Describing her youthful radicalization, she recalls the efforts undertaken by the Muslim Brotherhood to build up a sense of group membership, especially through song. Her own favorite utilized lyrics from the Palestinian poet Mahmoud Darwish that emphasized death, resurrection, and resistance, but she singles out another song as particularly popular, entitled "A Conspiracy Targeting the Youth." In contemporary Western centrist political discourse, labeling an allegation as a "conspiracy theory" is tantamount to a denunciation, a suggestion that disparate facts and fictions are being woven together inappropriately in order to fabricate an elaborate falsehood, the conspiracy. In the arsenal of the Brotherhood, however, the presence of a massive conspiracy is treated as a self-evident truth. It underscores the imminence of the threat faced by youth, by Muslims, and by the nation, against whom enormous nefarious forces are conspiring. That external threat justifies the need to police an internal identity and to maintain uniformity. Difference is prohibited.

"The conspiracy that targets the youth," or مؤامرة تدور على الشباب, is a widely disseminated Islamist text that exposes the substance of the political culture of the movement. The goal of the conspiracy, so the song claims, is to disarm the youth in order to render it prey to the enemy. The lyrics therefore appeal to the youthful participants to be vigilant in order to protect themselves against those external foes. Across different versions of the song, some of the enemies remain constant, crusaders, i.e., Christians, and Jews, يهود صليبيون, but others change. At times the enemies are Communists, الشيوعيون, but at other times the target becomes the Shiites, شيعيون. The orthographic proximity of the two terms in Arabic, separated by just one letter, only highlights the absurdly Orwellian suddenness in the designation of the enemy: change one spelling, change the adversary. The invocation of conspiracy and threat—no matter what the threat—in order to create internal solidarity is indicative of the totalitarian spirit of the movement. Islamist ideology operates with mechanisms reminiscent of the discourse of encirclement with which the Bolsheviks tried to suppress internal dissent, as well as the Nazi combination of external conspiracies and the need for internal homogeneity. This one-dimensionality is what was captured by the term "Islamofascism" in recent years, although the ideological production has as much in common with communism as it does with fascism.

Manea's narrative moves between the Middle East and the operations of Islamist movements there and their impact in Europe, both in migrant communities and in parts of the academic and political establishment. Aspects of her account of the European experience, in Switzerland, Germany, Belgium—her description of the Molenbeek section of Brussels is especially striking—the United Kingdom, and Sweden in particular, will be familiar to American readers, especially the sorts of political correctness and speech restrictions that have become standard in the American academic world. However, another and important part of her topic is very different from developments in the U.S. Of course, there has long been immigration into the U.S. from the Middle East, but the numbers are proportionately smaller than in Europe. In addition—and ultimately more significantly—the integration strategies in much of European society have failed dismally, leading to the growth of minority ghettos and an extensive sense of alienation among Muslim youth "with an immigration background," as the phrase goes, i.e., those whose parents or grandparents immigrated into western Europe but who still feel foreign and are treated as such. They live in separate worlds in Europe, while the tendency to develop a similar "parallel society" has been much less pronounced in the U.S. One might attribute this to a different and—despite all the polemic of recent years in the U.S.—a much more open relationship to legal immigration than in Europe. It also reflects a differently structured economy that facilitates immigrants' entry into American society and economy more effectively than in Europe. For an American reader, therefore, Manea's book is important both for the insight it provides concerning Islamism in the Middle East and as a cautionary note concerning the contradictions of European multiculturalism that have contributed to a fracturing of society there. The notion of a European unity that the European Union attempts to project from above cannot correct for the fraying of European society at the base.

This book is also of important for readers of *Telos* and others engaged in the tradition of Critical Theory. Manea's study adds to Telos Press's list of books addressing Islamism and multiculturalism more broadly, especially Matthias Küntzel's *Jihad and Jew-Hatred* and Jens-Martin Eriksen and Frederik Stjernfelt's *The Democratic Contradictions of Multiculturalism.* Across these volumes and in different ways, social tensions in the age of identity politics are examined especially with regard to questions of religion. Despite a contemporary liberal sensibility to wish religion away, it retains a durability and therefore continues to deserve attention. *Telos* is committed to its exploration of the important and complex overlaps among religion, ideology, and politics. No doubt, religion can become ideological in the sense of a "false consciousness," but it can also respond to currents of spirituality that play important roles in social life, and by no means solely as deception. While Manea points out that the Islamist claim to represent the one and only legacy of Islam is simply not tenable—one can interpret traditions in multiple ways—neither can one sever Islamism from Islam absolutely.

Analogous claims can be made about other world religions. Christianity too has its share of radical adherents whose views many might reject: both the extremists on the far right who couple an eccentric reception of the Gospel with Aryan racism and, a mirror image to be sure, the liberation theologians on the left who try to make Christianity compatible with communism, despite all the violence that communism has unleashed on the world during the past century. One could argue as well that even liberalism in the wake of Locke was grounded, at least initially, in Christian faith, and the role of the African American church in the success of the civil rights movement provides another prominent example of the engagement of religion in political spaces. Mainstream rabbinical Judaism has a long tradition of opponents stretching back to antiquity, whether among traditionalist zealots or, today especially on the left, progressive ideologues treating the spiritual legacy solely as a stand-in for political conformism.

Obviously, these political agenda as well as the religious resources that allegedly provide political foundations vary enormously. One can argue over the specific political platforms, just as one might scrutinize the validity of the interpretations of the sacred sources. At stake however is the common denominator: all are efforts to establish approximations between religion and politics. In that sense, Manea's case of Islam and Islamism provides just one more example of a fundamental social theoretical problem concerning legacies of faith and aspirations for political power. Ideology marks the point of the intersection between politics and religion, the potential mobilization of the passion of faith in the name of a political goal, but also the equally potential instrumentalization of faith—as ideology—in the pursuit of political goals at odds with the interests of the adherents. Political religion can amount to deception and manipulation. It can however have a very different standing, as a source of civic loyalty informed by spirituality. Political theology remains important as an ongoing, potential source of commitments and an appreciation of human worth, a pre-political grounding of the possibility of liberty—always a possibility, but never a guarantee.

While the parallel societies that Manea describes in Europe are largely unfamiliar in the U.S., aspects of the repressive ideological formation that she associates with Islamism are unfortunately increasingly present in North America, albeit not at all necessarily with a particular Islamic coloration. Her account of the ideological preconditions of ISIS, the nonviolent foundation for an ambitious political agenda that ultimately leads to violence, is uncannily reminiscent of the narrowing of allowable speech and thought in the context of what has come to be known currently as "cancel culture." Her description of the Islamists efforts to police language, thought, and everyday behavior echoes aspects of the creeping repressiveness around us. Is there an underlying affinity between Islamism and this cancel culture?

Manea describes for instance the appeasement and self-censorship that many otherwise liberal Westerners showed in the wake of the *Charlie Hebdo* murders. One could also look further back and recall how many liberals jettisoned their principles when Salman Rushdie's *Satanic Verses* was condemned by the Islamists in Tehran. For Manea there is no room for compromise in the defense of hard-won rights. One can of course disagree with *Charlie Hebdo*'s taste in publishing the Muhammad drawings, and one might engage in good faith literary criticism of Rushdie's novel, but it is, in her view, urgent to defend liberty: "There is no room here for cultural relativism. Without freedom of expression, there is no freedom at all. And this freedom should be protected." Precisely this line in the sand is under pressure today in the U.S. in schools, in universities, in editorial rooms, and in corporate boardrooms. Viewpoint diversity is disappearing.

The analogy to Islamism goes even further. As Manea narrates, one of the key steps in indoctrination involves instilling a sense of guilt in the young recruit, forced to believe that he or she has strayed from the path of religious purity, from genuine Islam. Indoctrination depends on the condemnation of deviation, but also on the association of that deviation with a sense of betrayal and ultimately of sinfulness. Dissidents must confess that being wrong is a sign of being evil, which in turn requires expiation. It is a passion play of sin, confession, and absolution. From this perspective, contemporary cancel culture reveals itself—like other eruptive political movements—to have an inherently religious character. Instead of offering a clear set of political program goals, subject to rational evaluation, the contemporary protest movement is difficult to nail down in any specific detail. Instead of policy debate, we witness ostentatious displays of righteousness—virtue signaling—side by side with iconoclasm—statue toppling—and ritualized public acts of liturgy, replete with kneeling, while reciting the name of the dead, in the pursuit of a collective redemption. Cancel culture is our Islamism.

Obviously, the violence associated with the contemporary social disorder in the U.S. does not by any means match the atrocities that took place under the reign of terror of ISIS. Not yet. But as Manea has shown us, that terror depended on a set of ideological preconditions: we are witnessing the spread of similarly repressive habits of the mind in the U.S. today. "We are all ISIS," wrote al-Ajami. If American society continues to succumb to an obligatory political correctness, a vilification of dissent, and the insistence on the infinite guilt of the West, we should expect the real-world consequences of this ideology soon to become clearer and rougher. That is the crux of Manea's message: repressive belief structures can turn into repressive practices. Long ago, the German poet Heinrich Heine wrote presciently that a country that starts with the burning of books eventually burns people. So far, the protest movement has attacked statues in the way that ISIS attacked shrines. We cannot however discount the prospect that the protestors in their self-righteousness will eventually attack people too, targeting proponents of political positions that they regard as anathema. For this reason as well, and not only because of its insights into Middle East political culture, Manea's critical theory of Islamism is important. This book sounds an alarm. It can happen here too.

1

Introduction

WE HAVE A PROBLEM, a global problem, and it has a name: Islamism. But we are unable to deal with it because we are either unable to speak about it or busy fighting an ideological battle.

Islamism tends to divide people in European and North American societies. Talking about it makes many people here feel uncomfortable. Not because they do not have an opinion about it. They just do not know how to talk about it.

Some are afraid to talk because they do not know much about the issue. They have an opinion but do not want to tread into uncharted territory; they prefer to leave the talk to those they think know more. Very often, the religious identity of those other people qualifies them for the task. And very often, those who are most organized in talking about Islam and Islamism are none other than Islamists themselves.

Others actually do know more about the issue, and are worried about it, but they are also afraid that if they speak up, they might offend Muslims. They certainly do not want to offend them. So they hold their tongues and end up censoring themselves out of an odd sense of respect.

Finally, you have those who are haunted by fear. Ordinary people. They too love their countries, their traditions, and their heritage. They see changes taking place in their societies. They do not like these changes; they know something is wrong, so they seek an explanation.

But the issue is so blurred and confusing. When they talk, they tend to be angry, lashing out, in fact expressing a sense of loss—a loss of identity.

What complicates the matter is how it is being shaped by the ideological battles of the left and right.

The left tells us there is no problem to talk about in the first place. Yes, there are jihadists blowing up themselves—and others—in Paris, Nice, Berlin, London, and Stockholm. But they are just disoriented, marginalized youths. Poor souls. We have isolated them in our societies. This is *our* doing. We—with our foreign policies, our discourse of discrimination, and our media that paints Islam as an angry violent religion—we are the ones who should be blamed for creating these jihadists.

In this ideological camp, you have those who acknowledge the existence of a problem, but who are very worried that taking the necessary steps to address it will only supply ammunition to their far-right opponents with their us-versus-them discourse. They will be damned if they will let that happen. Instead of differentiating themselves and taking concrete action, they prefer to bury their heads in the sand.

Their fear may be understandable given the discourse of the far right. In every person of Islamic faith, the far right sees a potential terrorist. Muslims, Islam, Islamism, and terrorism: to them, these words are synonyms; they stand for the same thing. They blame foreigners, migration, and immigrants for all the problems in their societies, and they end up exploiting Islam as a rallying cry for their racist demands.

Many who consider themselves part of the right side of the ideological spectrum shun these views or even oppose them vehemently. They are in the mainstream and cool-headed. They may see the issue but are hesitant to take the painful measures necessary to fight it. Too complicated, too expensive. And it will certainly hamper their governments' trade and economic relations with some of their best allies—think of the Gulf nations. Here, money does much of the talking.

On both sides of the spectrum, the focus is on the violent form of Islamism, on the jihadists, the terrorists, those who are committing acts of violence. They are not concerned about the nonviolent forms of Islamism: the ideology and its religious message that pave the ground for this violence. But that lack of concern complicates the matter enormously. And complex is not what they need. They need simple answers and simple solutions. It is not cancer we are dealing with. It is a simple headache. Just swallow this tablet, and you will feel better. End of discussion!

But that won't do. Simple answers and solutions are the formula for disaster. They will only encourage the polemics of the far right. The ideology of Islamism is the core of the matter. *It is what matters.*

So I repeat. We have a problem, a global problem, and it has a name: Islamism. But we are unable to deal with it because we are either unable to talk about it or busy fighting an ideological battle. This clouds our judgment and makes us complicit, directly and indirectly, in mainstreaming Islamism, a totalitarian ideology. While we are busy bickering with each other, we fail to notice the slow changes taking place in our societies and how they are gradually eroding the major achievement of Western society: the liberal and universal norms and values that protect the dignity and rights of the individual.

We Are ISIS?

Every time a terrorist act is committed, we hear a chorus of self-denial. We are told that religion has nothing to do with what ISIS is doing. We are told that Islam is a religion of peace and tolerance, and that we are dealing with a group of sick people who have twisted the message of Islam and are committing these atrocities in the name of religion. These terrorists are lone wolves. They are disoriented and manipulated.

Certainly the young men and women who have joined the ranks of ISIS have been manipulated. But just don't tell me that religion has nothing to do with it. That is incorrect.

Many of those insisting that "Islam is a religion of peace" are of Islamic heritage and are truly convinced of their opinion. After all, they are the genuine embodiment of that peaceful practice of their religion. They are citizens of their European and North American countries; they contribute to their societies and, just like others, are afraid and angry. They abhor the atrocities committed in the name of their religion and condemn them vehemently. So they end up engaging in a defensive discourse to dispel the "bad image" of Islam, caused, as they believe, by "biased media coverage" and, of course, by those misguided sick people twisting Islam for their purpose.

But there is a paradox here. These European and North American citizens of Islamic faith—and they are many—are often left alone when they try to organize and do something about it. The main Islamic orga-nizations—i.e., the organized arm of their faith in their societies—shun them.

That was clear in the peace march in Cologne on June 17, 2017. The organizers of the Liberal Islamic Union wanted to send a clear message against the recent atrocities committed in many European cities—in Manchester, London, Stockholm, Paris, Berlin, and Brussels. "Not in our name": that was their message. The organizers expected to have tens of thousands of German Muslims participating. Then the main Turkish Islamic Union (DITIB), which represents 896 local Muslim communities in Germany, decided to boycott the event. Only a handful, roughly a hundred people, showed up, leaving the organizers bitterly disappointed.[1]

How did the DITIB explain its position? By acting the victim, once again turning to the well-worn playbook of such Islamic organizations. The DITIB had the audacity to say that the Muslim peace march—not those committing these atrocities and killing children and civilians, but this very peace march—"stigmatizes Muslims" and "narrows interna-tional terrorism to them, their communities and mosques."[2]

The DITIB's excuse is hypocritical. Its discourse of victimhood is part of the problem. Blame the others; we have nothing to do with this. But ISIS is our product. I said that in Arabic and German, and I am now saying it in English.

It would be easy to insist that ISIS does not represent the correct teachings of Islam. It would be very easy to do that. And yes, I do believe that Islam is what we, humans, make of it. Any religion can be made into a message of love or a sword of hatred, depending on the people who be-lieve in it. And yes, there is a peaceful reading of Islam, and many people follow it. But the fact remains that the actions of ISIS were ideologically mainstreamed long ago in mosques that curse "Christians, the Crusad-ers," "Jews," and "unbelievers" in every Friday sermon.

And they were mainstreamed by religious figures and preachers, who greet us everyday through satellite TV programs, preaching a mes-sage of hatred and intolerance against the "other," regardless of who that "other" is. And they are mainstreamed in schools and Quran schools that teach us that the penalty for converting from Islam is death; that we should stay away from the "unbelievers"; that Christians and Jews are "protected people," who should pay a tax to be left alone or else face war and slavery. In other words, if they do not comply, they, and their children and their positions, would be legitimate spoils of war and targets of looting for Muslims. We learn that in our schools and Quran lessons! The fate of members of "other religions" is left untold, but we can read between the lines. In these classes we were never taught that a citizen has the right to choose his or her religion, or that a citizen is equal before the law regardless of religion or beliefs.

Little wonder that we see the face of this extremism clearly manifested today: in the girls still kidnapped and sold by Boko Haram in Nigeria, in the face of Yazidi women held as slaves by ISIS, in the members of the diverse Iraqi and Syrian minority groups, fleeing for their lives because of an ideology that treats them as subhuman and inferior on account of their religious affiliation. We see its face in laws in Islamic countries that violate citizens' rights and human rights with impunity and uphold religious beliefs by force. We see it spreading like a cancer in failed states all over the MENA region and South Asian countries. And we see its face in the closed communities in European societies and the radicalization of young men and women within Western societies, turning them against their new homelands. We see it in the way it is changing our societies wherever it gains a foothold.

ISIS is the product of a religious discourse—a mainstream discourse. Ignoring the problem will not do, not any longer. We have to act, we have to call the problem by its name and tackle it by whatever measures necessary. It is we—people everywhere—who are paying a high price for the inaction in dealing with this extremism.

We are all in this together, like it or not.

I am sure you are aware that the majority of victims of violent Islamic extremism live in Islamic countries. Five countries—Iraq, Afghanistan, Nigeria, Syria, and Pakistan—accounted for three-quarters of all terrorism victims in 2016. In Iraq and Afghanistan alone, 14,339 people died in terrorist attacks.[3] The numbers declined over the last four years, but the Muslim-majority countries remained the main targets for terrorism.[4] But this does not seem to raise an alarm. We only scream when it hits us near home. Remember our outcry after the *Charlie Hebdo* massacre? I posted one of the magazine's Muhammad cartoons on my Facebook wall in solidarity with its victims and their right to freedom of expression. I did not like their cartoons, but I thought it necessary to say that what offends me is this massacre, not these cartoons.

Millions went to the streets in Paris in solidarity with the *Hebdo* victims, and rightly so. But it does seem odd that the same respect and solidarity was not extended to the Nigerian civilians whose sixteen villages were razed to the ground in the same week by Boko Haram—burned to nothing in a matter of days! The same week! Their numbers are estimated in the hundreds—some say as many as 2,000.[5] Did we see any solidarity actions honoring their memory? Our silence was very loud.

I am not trying to make you feel guilty here. From a psychological perspective, this reaction may be normal. We identify with those closest to us. One master's student said that to me, in a course I give on Islamism, when we discussed the Paris attacks of 2015: "I see myself in these victims of the club and cafés." They were spending their evening doing what he would have been doing: enjoying a late weekend activity. It could have been him. Of course he relates to their tragedy more than those in distant Nigeria—the distance here is not only geographical.

But their deaths should remind us that this violent extremism, and most importantly its ideological and religious roots, must be *our* concern. All of us! There is no *we and they* here. We are all in this together, regardless of our faith, color, or nationality.

This is a global threat and we have to address it, together.

Nonviolent Islamism

I told you that the ideology of Islamism is the core of the matter. I added that what concerns me is not the violent form of Islamism but its nonviolent form. Perhaps it is time to explain what I mean. I see Islamism as a spectrum, and its violent form lies at the furthest extreme. Young men do not just wake up in the morning and decide to blow themselves up and commit atrocities. They have been indoctrinated in a process that socializes them into a worldview and a narrative of victimhood and convinces them that what they are doing is an act of defense—a legitimate act. Not all of those affected by this ideology commit terrorist acts. Only a small percentage acts on it. My argument here is that focusing on the violence alone is not enough. Our first priority should be its ideological and religious roots, and those who promote this form.

The ideology has two components: political and religious. That is why I said religion is also part of the problem. Nonviolent Islamism is not just a totalitarian political ideology that seeks domination; it is also the religious interpretation of Islam that legitimizes this domination and sanctions its action. Consider this example. When ISIS started to take Yazidi women and sell them in slave markets, it was interesting to see how many prominent religious figures were silent on the issue. Of course you had those who clearly said that slavery is an ancient practice and cannot be revived as Islamic. But al-Azhar, located in Cairo, perceived as the highest Sunni authority and long infiltrated by the Salafi reading of Islam, did not issue a condemnation of this action by ISIS. It condemned its violence strongly, and said ISIS did not represent Islam, but it did not utter a word about taking women as slaves.

Why? The reason is simple. From al-Azhar's perspective, taking women as sex slaves during a war can be accepted when the circumstances are right. It does have to be a legitimate war. This position was clearly articulated in a *fatwa*, a religious edict, issued in 2014 by one of al-Azhar's leading female scholars, Professor Suad Saleh. On a TV program she said that "Muslims who capture women in a legitimate war against their enemies may own them and have sex with them as slave girls…in order to humiliate them."[6] The enemy she referred to in her talk was Israel. The timing of that fatwa raised eyebrows in Egypt.

Similarly, after ISIS atrocities, when some Saudi intellectuals called for a clear fatwa prohibiting slavery, they got a swift reaction from the main Saudi sheikhs. Many hurried to use the words of Sheikh Saleh al-Fawzan, a member of the Council of Senior Scholars and the Permanent Committee for Islamic Research and Issuing Fatwas. Years ago, he was recorded as saying that Islam did not "forbid taking women as slaves" and that "those who are calling for the prohibition of slavery are ignorant, unbelievers, or atheists. This is God's rule."[7] You should know that al-Fawzan wrote the religious curriculum that is used today for Saudi children.[8] He publicly said that taking slaves is part of *jihad*, Islamic holy war.[9] Now if you think what he says has nothing to do with us here in our European and North American societies, think again. His books and fatwas are being taught and promoted in Saudi-funded schools, madrasas, and mosques.

So ISIS was not acting out of a script written by aliens when it decided to take women and children as slaves. Its actions have been mainstreamed by a fundamentalist interpretation of Islam, and that interpretation is based on religious scripts and religious history.

Nonviolent Islamism propagates an ideology of political Islam *and* a radical interpretation of Islam. Later in this book, I will talk in depth about it and its different forms. Suffice now to say that it divides the world into two camps: believers and unbelievers. The believers should raise the banner of Islam and spread it, if not by violence then by *dawa*, preaching. According to this view, Islam is not merely a religion. It is both state and religion. Religious laws should be applied, and those who deviate from this religion and its laws should be harshly punished. God, accordingly, is the ruler. This view insists that Islam is destined to rule over the world and that jihad, holy war, is the tool to achieve this goal. There are times to use violence, of course. But the concept of jihad is not disputed at all. People are divided into categories and treated accordingly: Those who believe enjoy their rights. Those of other religions, beliefs, or different Islamic denominations will suffer. Throughout its preaching and work, the discourse of victimhood is a key message that shapes all its narration of history and current affairs: Islam is being attacked, and Muslims are a persecuted group.

A complex web of organizations and movements actively promote this type of Islamism. They control mosques, schools, madrasas, charities, and social work and economic institutions. It is an international web, connected around the world. Of course, one can find stark diversity among these groups and movements, and they very often compete against each other. But when they agree, they agree on two things: Islam is under attack, and the West is the enemy.

In Western democracies, their organizations and movements claim to be the sole group speaking for Muslims in the West. They insist that Muslims be treated as a "homogeneous group," they assert that human rights is a "Western imposition," and they present their own Islamist demands as those of all Muslims. Often, Western policy makers oblige and treat these organizations as "representatives of all Muslims." This in turn has ramifications, as the Islamists' stipulations undermine the secular human rights–based order of Western democracies. Doing so puts into question the greatest achievements of Western democracies, especially those concerning the separation of state and religion, women's rights, and the freedom of expression. The reluctance of mainstream politicians to defend these norms and values, combined with the white man's burden, which haunts leftists and liberals alike, has allowed these movements to spread their ideology within Muslim communities. They control Quran schools, youth activities, and mosques, and in the process they succeed in separating Muslims from their broader societies, transforming them into closed communities with their own parallel rules and norms.

This type of Islamism provides the main ideological framework and worldviews of violent Islamism. This is the type of Islamism we must pay attention to.

The White Man's Burden

Earlier I said that the liberal and leftist Western intellectuals are very often part of the denial chorus. They are shaped by what, in another book, I called the "essentialist paradigm": a way of thinking that reduces people of different nationalities to their religious identity, treating them as one homogeneous group, in the process essentializing their cultures and religion.[10]

If that sounds abstract, here is a clarifying example. An essentialist will not see me as a woman of dual citizenship, an academic, or a human rights advocate. He/she will only see in me the religious person. To the essentialist, I am a *Muslim* woman; my religion is what marks me. I may not be religious at all—in fact, I may be an atheist—but that does not seem to occur to him/her. If your religion is Islam, then you are a Muslim, and Muslims are religious: they all want halal food, they do not drink alcohol, they do not engage in sexual activity before marriage, they all want to wear a headscarf, they all want to pray in their schools, and they all want to apply Sharia law in their lives.

It is a racist way of seeing a person and very similar to the racist attitude of their far-right counterparts, but it has a different motivation. What motivates them is not hate or the desire to harm; it is the urge to protect.

They are haunted by the "white man's burden": a strong sense of justice intertwined with a strong sense of guilt and shame over the Western colonial and imperial past and its way of conducting politics. That burden creates the desire to protect the rights of minorities or people in former colonies. But in their desire to protect, they end up becoming the unwitting allies of Islamists, whom they consider the authentic voices of their communities. So they start supporting the demands of these Islamists and frame it as support for the "civil rights of Muslims."[11]

Worth mentioning here is that unlike their Western counterparts, many Arab intellectuals, from Morocco to Saudi Arabia, have become vocal in their critique of the fundamentalist religious roots of terrorism, for example the Salafi interpretation of Islam, and its nonviolent ideology, for example that of the Muslim Brotherhood. They insist that it has been mainstreamed in their societies for far too long. I will elaborate more on that later in the book.

If some liberal and leftist Western intellectuals are essentialists in their worldviews and are haunted by the white man's burden, then this situation leads Western politicians to tread a very fine line. Of course, they can be opportunistic and cynical in their choice of Muslim partners. Working with Islamists in their societies can guarantee them a vote, given the ability of these groups to organize themselves and deliver results.

But other politicians are fearful of a racist anti-Muslim backlash and eager to gain the support of their citizens of Islamic faith, along with entire Muslim societies, in their campaign against radicalization and ISIS. Hence, they focus on the violent extremism and stay away from its ideological and religious roots. Former U.S. President Barack Obama was famous for his refusal to use phrases such as "radical Islam" or "Islamic terrorism" in his speeches, most pointedly in February 2015 at a White House conference on combatting violent extremism. When asked why, he explained that "they are not religious leaders; they are terrorists. We are not at war with Islam. We are at war with people who have perverted Islam."[12] While I respect his motivation, it is worth mentioning that many Arab Muslim commentators would disagree with his view and give ample evidence to the contrary. Religious sheikhs with their discourse and narrative of hatred and victimhood breed the terrorists in their communities.

Others recognize the role of ideology while trying to stay away from the religious side of it. Theresa May, then British prime minister, articulated this position after the terrorist attacks in Manchester and Westminster in June 2017. She said that what connects them is "the single evil ideology of Islamist extremism"—an ideology that is a "perversion of Islam."[13] May was right to say that security measures are not enough to defeat this ideology. It will only be defeated, she said, when "people's minds are turned away from this violence."[14]

As I listened to her speech, I wondered what these measures would be. Would they include looking at the type of Islam preached in British mosques and Quran schools, the mainstreaming of Salafi and Deobandi fundamentalism Islam in the closed communities of British Muslims, and the proliferation of Sharia councils in these communities? Or would all that be conveniently ignored? And while we are talking about appropriate measures, it was truly odd that she withheld the publication of a Home Office study on the Saudi role in fostering extremism in Britain. But then the economic ties with Gulf countries often dilute such resolve in fighting extremism.[15]

I hope by now you have realized that I am not interested in a polemical discourse. I am interested in finding solutions for a problem that we have ignored for far too long. We need to name it, and define its roots, so that we can understand the phenomena we are dealing with. Otherwise we will continue to move in circles and allow this extremism to take hold of our youth, change our societies, and undermine their hard-won universal rights, norms, and values.

My task here is to clarify and explain. I have seen how this type of Islamism changes societies and destroys social cohesion—both in countries where I have lived and those I have visited for field research. My research over more than twenty years, in Arab, Islamic, European, and African countries, has allowed me to see the different forms of Islamism in different countries from different angles: how they change their behavior and rhetoric according to their contexts, and how state elites mainstream their ideology and religious discourse out of a cynical politics of survival. I have seen how they eradicate local culture and history, divide families, change social behavior, and persecute those who do not share their worldviews. I have seen how they propagate a sick, sexualized image of women and how they incite hatred against minorities and segregate Muslim communities from their larger societies.

I also have personal experience with this type of Islamism: I was radicalized at age sixteen. Perhaps it is better to start with that personal experience to show you how easily it can happen.

2

Radicalized at Sixteen

REMEMBER THE 1980s? Not only was it a different decade in a different century. It represented a distinct historical and political era. Allow me, therefore, to start by taking you back to this period.

The Cold War was at its zenith. It was "the least safe time to live on earth," to quote Micah Zenko of the Council on Foreign Relations.[1] At the time, Ronald Reagan was the U.S. president. He was convinced that the Soviet Union, with its communist ideology, was an evil to be fought. So he continued the covert CIA operations started by his predecessor Jimmy Carter after the Soviets invaded Afghanistan in 1979. But he was intent on a more assertive policy that would go beyond containment, in the process articulating a doctrine that took on his name: the Reagan Doctrine. His aim was to counterbalance the doctrine of the Soviet leader, Leonid Brezhnev, who proclaimed in 1968 that the Soviet sphere would only expand. Reagan's doctrine, on the other hand, called for direct support to those "freedom fighters" who were "risking their lives on every continent from Afghanistan to Nicaragua to defy Soviet-supported aggression."[2]

Newspapers in that decade were filled with smiling pictures of the photogenic Reagan welcoming into the Oval Office the Afghanis he called "freedom fighters": Islamist *mujahideen*, plural for the Arabic term *jihadi*. These pictures serve as testimony to something we seem to have forgotten. During this time, the United States worked with Islamists and with conservative authoritarian Muslim and Arab states—think of Pakistan, Saudi Arabia, and Egypt. They were united on a mission: defeat the Soviet Union and its communist ideology. Osama bin Laden was also a product of that era. Influenced by Islamists rallying to the Afghan cause in Saudi Arabia, he went to Afghanistan and helped finance, recruit, and train those so-called freedom fighters. He was also crucial in sending Arab fighters—from Egypt, Algeria, Lebanon, Kuwait, Turkey, and Tunisia—into Afghanistan to battle against the Soviet forces deployed to support Afghanistan's communist government.[3]

Terrorism was also a problem in that decade—but back then its motivation was radical leftist or nationalist ideologies. Gruesome terrorist attacks and kidnappings were committed by organizations such as the Red Brigades, the Baader-Meinhof group, the Palestinian Fatah under Abu Nidal, and the Irish Republican Army. On this side too, such organizations worked in concerted effort with radical authoritarian Arab states—think of South Yemen, Libya, Syria, and Iraq—together with Soviet Bloc states.[4]

This was the decade that saw Israeli troops completing the Sinai withdrawal and dismantling Jewish settlements in accordance with the Camp David Agreement. Egypt's President Anwar al-Sadat, who signed that agreement, paid for it with his life; he was killed by militants of the same Islamist groups he helped revive after coming to power. And it was the decade that saw Israel invade South Lebanon in retaliation for a PLO splinter group's attempt to assassinate Israel's ambassador to Britain, along with a PLO rocket bombardment of Israel's northern border towns.[5]

~

Aside from the Israeli invasion of Lebanon and the assassination of President Sadat, I was oblivious to all of these political developments.

When we left Rabat, Morocco, and returned to Sana'a in the Yemen Arab Republic (North Yemen), I was sixteen. The year was 1982. My father, a North Yemeni diplomat, had just finished four years of service in Morocco. Following the normal procedure, we went back to Sana'a for two years before moving elsewhere.

I loved Morocco. It was the first time in my life that I lived for four years in a row in one country. Before that, we were moving, always moving, from one country to another. One year here, two years there. The longest periods I had in a country were in West Germany and Iran, three years each. I loved the change and learned early on how to cope with the goodbyes. Embrace the country you are in wholeheartedly, love your friends deeply, but do not look back after saying your goodbyes. Just look forward and the pain will eventually dissipate. Over the years one gets tired of this cycle. But back then I was still young.

Those four years in Morocco allowed me to feel something I never knew before: being attached to a place. I only got to know this feeling again after living in Switzerland for more than twenty years. Finally, this was a place to call home.

Of course I lived in a bubble—the Arab diplomat kids' bubble. My father, a unique man, insisted that my brother and I should go to schools that taught Arabic as their first language. He did not follow his best friends' practice of sending their kids to American schools—but not because he had a thing against the English language or the United States. Not really.

After flirting with communist ideology in his early youth, he encountered its totalitarian side when he studied in East Germany. He came out of that experience cursing despotic ideologies, convinced instead of the need for enlightened humanism. So what motivated him was not a rejection of Anglo-Saxon culture. He was simply convinced that if you did not know yourself, you would not be able to embrace others. "Learn your language, master it, and you can learn other languages after that—but know yourself first. Your language is your door to your own cultural heritage." That is how he explained it to us. The man was a proud Yemeni humanist, and he instilled that pride in us.

In Morocco, I ended up in an Iraqi school in Rabat, supposed to be one of the best. Arabic was the language of instruction, with English coming second. That would do. Many Arab diplomats sent their children there: it was known for its excellence and yet offered its services for free. There were political reasons for this generosity, but they are irrelevant here. Besides, Moroccan schools were teaching many subjects in French, which posed a problem for many Arab kids, so we wound up together.

That school had a deep impact on me. In it, I learned an important lesson: there is nothing special about boys. I was used to mixed-gender classes. Except in Yemen, all of my schools, kindergarten through primary, had offered mixed-gender education. But in this Iraqi school, the difference was profound: in the first year of secondary level I was the only girl. We were thirteen pupils, all boys except for me. The early months of that year were very tough. Two boys, the Yemeni ones, decided I was fair game for bullying. They tried to taunt me—making fun of me, silly girl. They also made a bet that I would never be as good in the class as one of them—and he was an excellent pupil. They managed to turn the other boys, of other nationalities, against me. It was very difficult to be the bullied girl among the boys in the first months. But I never cried in front of them. Not once. Of course I cried alone in my room, at night. But in front of them, I stood my ground, fought back, and studied hard. My grades settled the bet in my favor—I was the best in my class and continued to be for the rest of my school years.

Though these months were so difficult, they had a deep and lasting impact on my relationship with the boys. Somehow, I earned their respect. The bullying stopped, and over the years they trusted me enough to be their best female friend. Boys were not intimidating. That is what I learned from this experience. You just have to fight back. They can be friends too, and, yes, I discovered how insecure they were in reality.

Something else marked these four years in the Iraqi school in Rabat: the freedom we enjoyed and my ability to be focused in spite of it. It was the late 1970s and early 1980s. At the time, Morocco had still not been touched by the conservative religious wave that we see today all over the Arab and Islamic world. We were kids of privileged backgrounds living in a bubble. We did not grasp the reality of other people living in poverty and deprivation—neither in Morocco nor in our own countries. Instead, we were preoccupied with ourselves—with our classes, parties, dancing, music, and being kids our age. In that period, sex, alcohol, and drugs were all common. I stayed away from most of that—tried alcohol, of course, and smoked cigarettes, but that was as far as I got. Of course I would have loved to fall in love and have a boyfriend. But the boys saw me as their friend, their buddy. That was the downside of earning their respect.

Other than that, I was focused. Yes, "focused" describes how I have been since childhood. Focused on my school and studies, reading every book I could get my hands on. That was something ingrained in me by my father. "Education is your way out." He did not need to say those words out loud; his life was a testimony to it.

Like my mother, he came from a poor background. His father died when he was six, and he had to work several jobs while going to Sana'a's only school. His mother, a remarkably strong woman not in the habit of showing much affection, told him dryly: "Your half brother and sister have a father. You have your school." Words like needles that pierced his soul for good. He was driven. He would wake up every day at dawn to go to the mosque to study. It was the only place in Sana'a that had electricity. His aunt would not let him use the lamp in the evenings; the oil cost too much. His dedication earned him a scholarship. He was one of the "famous forty," the first forty North Yemeni students to leave the country to study abroad. I did not need a reminder of the importance of education. It was the way out. Besides, I was a girl, and Yemeni girls who don't thrive in school get married. Some get married despite their excellent records in school. Luckily, neither my father nor I thought marriage was a good idea.

You must have noticed by now that I did not say much about my mother. I do not want to talk about her here. I will perhaps do that later in this book. But somehow talking about her now pains me. It was during these four years in Morocco that she started to be mentally ill. I was twelve when it became clear that the loving mother I once had was no more; she was trapped elsewhere. Hate is a word I seldom use in describing a feeling I have. But I hated her sickness and still hate it today. It took her away from me. Most importantly, it represents everything concerning women that I want to see changed in Arab Muslim societies. The sickness did not come out of the blue—it was a symptom of the profound social diseases we have in our societies. I will not talk much about her now. Suffice to say, I was struggling with her illness during those four years.

So this was my background when I arrived in Sana'a in 1982, leaving behind a country, school, and friends I loved. Free-spirited, focused on studying, struggling with a mother with mental illness. My family was a privileged one—educated. My father set the tone in our family with a humanist view of the world. We were secular, I would say. He himself was an agnostic freethinker, who did not think much of religion—all religions, but especially Islam. My mother started to be religious when she got sick. But her upbringing also shaped her; she was raised in Mahala al-Kubra, Egypt, in a religious but tolerant way. It was from her that I learned about religion, from her and my private tutor, Sheikh al-Shawadfy. I will talk about him later.

Other than that, we were not religious at all. Ramadan was a tradition to celebrate, but we did not fast. My brother and I tried, but it was more of a test of will that lost its appeal over time. Mother was the only one fasting. It must have been lonely for her. But we all respected the tradition—we ate small snacks, trying to be discreet—and waited patiently for the *iftar* dinner when we would break the fast together.

So you can imagine my shock on arriving in Yemen. It is not that I did not know what to expect there. But all the same it was shocking. I travel back in history when I travel to Yemen. I do not mean that in disrespect. I love Yemen. Along with my mother, Yemen is my wound—I carry the pain of knowing how it could have been but never had the chance to be. But it does feel as if you have left one time zone and entered another—except that you are now entering a parallel world with another social order.

Morocco was more relaxed about women and social mores, at least in the circles I was moving in, and that was a big contrast to the North of Yemen. You certainly did not see women with headscarves in Rabat in that period. It was only elderly women who wore traditional *jalabyia*, and they were colorful. In Sana'a, girls wore headscarves and later they took on the *sharshaf*, the two pieces of black cloth that cover the woman from head to toe, along with another one that hides the face. I was spared that by my father. He did not believe in any of that and made it clear to his family.

In Rabat young men and women kissed when they greeted. In Sana'a, a young woman seen with a male stranger can cause a tribal war and earn herself a severe punishment. Society is segregated. When you enter a house, you will not see a female face unless you are moving in circles with less conservative mores.

The school was different too. All girls. Segregation was a mode of life, so even a glimpse of a person of the opposite sex was exciting—hysterically exciting. I remember my amazement when I saw a group of teenage girls crowding into a corner over a balcony, giggling and whispering to each other. When I looked down to where they were staring,

I saw a young man who had entered the schoolyard and was waiting for something or someone. Boys and men were not anything special, remember? But to these laughing teenagers, he might as well have been an alien coming down from Mars, and even the alien might have paled in comparison to what this young man represented. Social control was certainly suffocating.

We had to wear headscarves in the school. I complied. But outside the gates of the school, I always took it off. It suffocated me.

～

It was in the first months of my return that I had my experience with radicalization. My father was still in Morocco. My mother and I came back earlier so that I could enroll and start my school year, and we stayed temporarily with relatives. Our new house in Hadaa City was not yet ready for us.

In that school, I was radicalized.[6]

Now you have to understand the context here. It was 1982. There were two Yemens at the time. The North, where I come from, run by a conservative tribal military regime, was a satellite state of Saudi Arabia. The South was the only communist regime in the Arabian Peninsula. It was working closely with the Soviet Bloc states and intent on exporting its "revolution" to its Yemeni northern sister and the Gulf states. North Yemen was considered the gate stopping the tide of the communist South. To counter the communist ideology, Saudi Arabia supported the northern regime using an established method at the time: it exported its line of Salafi Islam, a harsh and uncompromising interpretation of a fundamentalist movement created in the eighteenth century.

Religion was considered the antidote to the communist ideology. But it was not just any religion that was used. It was an extremist version. The religious curriculum of the country's formal schools was changed in the late 1970s, an outcome of systematic efforts by Muslim Brotherhood and Salafi functionaries at the Education Ministry. Instead of the earlier one hour a week of ethics, now students spent eight hours with Salafi readings on religion. With the support of Saudi Arabia, a parallel religious educational system was created. Thousands of institutions for both genders, called the Scientific Institutions, were created to indoctrinate young Yemenis. Mosques were erected with imams preaching this

Sunni line of Islam, slowly changing the denominational demographic in the North. Young men were urged to join the holy jihad against the Soviet infidels in Afghanistan. Thousands were recruited. The Muslim Brothers were working hand in hand with the Salafis of Yemen, and the kingdom generously supported both. At that time there was a clear alliance between the Yemeni state and the Islamists: a convenient marriage that continued despite some hiccups until the first decade of the twenty-first century.[7]

That marriage was reflected in my school. Our teachers were Egyptians and Syrians. Many of them were members of the Muslim Brotherhood who had fled their own countries. They taught us religion, and it was not tolerance that we learned from them.

Tellingly, young Yemeni Salafists and members of the Muslim Brotherhood were allowed to preach openly in the school. This is how I came to be involved with them. Every day, a circle of young students, with a charismatic leader whom I will call Nadia, would sit in a circle in the middle of the schoolyard during the school's long lunch break. I got curious, asked a classmate about them, and was told they were pious religious sisters talking about religion. So I sat with them and was embraced with open arms.

At the beginning, Nadia's message was one of kindness, of thoughts on how to be a good Muslim. You should smile at others. If you see something that could harm others in the middle of the road, you should pick it up. When you are greeted, answer with a better and longer greeting. Be a good neighbor and a good daughter. When you do, you will be rewarded generously in the afterlife—a good deed is always rewarded sevenfold.

Of course, you should be a good Muslim. Apparently, Muslim societies, including Yemen, were not really Islamic. They were practicing a corrupted version of Islam. To understand what I mean here, we have to go back to the true way of Islam: a way that is detailed, heavily structured, and fully laden with rituals. Now we were told about the mercy of God. Nadia explained to us that the moment we enter into Islam, all our sins will be washed away. Islam erases all that you have done during your pre-Islamic way of life. Whatever wrongs we have done will be forgiven. We will be born-again Muslims. But first we have to follow the right way of Islam.

The right way of Islam was introduced to me in small booklets, given to me for free.

They taught me how to pray: not only the five prayers but also what you say in them, and which prayers you can add to them—several, it turned out. It is also how you fold your hands when you pray and how you position your feet when prostrating yourself. Later I learned about the sectarian significance of the hand folding: if you pray with your hands stretched out at your sides, you will be following the Shiite tradition of prayer—not one they advocated.

These booklets told me what prayer to say when I would leave the house, travel, or enter the bathroom. Which foot to use when entering the bathroom—the left—and which hand to eat with—the right. Satan likes to eat with his left hand, so we should not emulate him. You use your left hand or foot when you do things that are not clean—what you do in the bathroom is not clean.

They even specified how to relieve yourself in the bathroom. You should lean to the left, as there is significant scientific evidence of the health benefits of the Prophet's way of relieving himself. It never occurred to me to inquire about these health benefits—they knew better, of course. Plucking your hair from your body or face, using nail polish: all of these were frowned upon. Naturally you should not try to emulate the other sex in their behavior or clothing; trousers were not welcomed.

I told you that, up until now, I mainly knew religion through my mother and my private tutor Sheikh al-Shawadfy. My religion classes in the other schools were simply boring, with their repetitiveness and their frowning God. My mother's way of Islam was simple and very spiritual in nature, despite its traditional clout. You pray, fast, and love God—and God will love you back.

In Rabat, I was lucky though to be taught by the Egyptian Sheikh al-Shawadfy. Four years of weekly private lessons. My father, the agnostic humanist, heard about him—he taught Arabic language and religion to Prince Hisham, the nephew of King Hasan. So my father contacted him and tried to convince him to teach my brother and me. The sheikh refused. He did not believe in paid private lessons. My father persisted and pleaded with him that he should meet us first and decide for himself whether teaching us was worth the trouble. The sheikh finally agreed to meet us and indeed changed his mind. Yet he refused to be paid for the classes. I remain grateful to him for his devotion.

I always respected him as a man of integrity and great knowledge. His way of teaching was focused on the richness of the Arabic language, giving me a strong basis in Arabic poetry during its various historical phases. He taught us religion but not in the ritualistic way I learned in Yemen. It was about the basics but with a general understanding of Quranic stories and their morals.

It would be an exaggeration to say he was liberal. I still remember the expression on his face when he heard about a book I was reading, one given to me by my father: *The Days*, the memoir of the famous Egyptian intellectual Taha Husain (1889–1973). Husain was a critical thinker, strongly opposed to the al-Azhar religious institution; in his writing he suggested that the Quran should not be taken as an objective source of history.

The look on his face was clearly one of disapproval. But he did not say a word against Taha Husain. He merely suggested that I might benefit more from reading other books. Despite his disapproval, he did not talk badly about him. Just like my mother, his approach to religion was certainly different from that of the missionary group at my school in Sana'a.

And yet, despite this background, the missionary sessions fascinated me. There was something very reassuring about them. For a teenage girl, searching for her identity, the message was mesmerizing, and at the beginning I embraced it wholeheartedly.

You see, with them, I did not have to choose. The choice they gave me was clear, undivided, and not confusing: you are Muslim. One. That is your identity. You do not have to choose between two nationalities. Religion is your identity. And identity was very important in this whole context.

"Who am I, grandmother?" I asked that repeatedly in my first Arabic novel, *Echo of Pain*.[8]

Who am I indeed?

Half, half. That is how it felt at that time. I was called half-caste, *muwallada*: an expression in North Yemen reserved for those of mixed blood. Born in Egypt, to a mother of mixed Egyptian-Yemeni origins,

I was never allowed to forget that I did not really belong. In Yemen I was the tall Egyptian, and in Egypt I was the Yemeni. I also did not know how to sort out all of these other countries and their memories: Germany, Iran, and most importantly Morocco. Where do they fit in me? Too many places, too many nationalities, and too many identities. Together they made me the person I am today. Whole. But at that time, it was very confusing. Who am I indeed, grandmother? With Nadia and her group, I did not have to choose. It was simple. I am a Muslim, full stop. This is the identity, total and complete.

The changes in me were gradual. It started with everyday language. Instead of greeting others with "good morning" or "good evening," as we used to, I began using only what they called the salute of Islam: *assalamu alaikum*, peace be upon you. Later I would learn that this salute is only reserved for Muslims—real Muslims. "Do not use it with non-Muslims," I was told. "We are not at peace with them. If you say it to them, you will commit hypocrisy."

My days took on a rigid religious structure, starting with the dawn prayer and moving to the evening prayer. Part of the night was dedicated to worship, and reciting from the Quran was a must. It was strict, but simple and clear. A way of life far from the one I had had in Morocco. The rituals were comforting. Your whole day was tightly organized. And the belief—that strong belief that you are in good hands, that God is always on your side—was intoxicating.

One incident illustrates the strength of the belief I am describing here. In 1982 North Yemen had a devastating earthquake. It was a strong one, measuring 6.2 on the Richter scale, and 2,800 people died. I was in school when it happened, and it was frightening. After the first earthquake, many people decided to stay outside their buildings and homes, fearing aftershocks. Not me. I went to my uncle's apartment, where I was staying at the time, took out my prayer carpet, and kept praying. I felt pity for those poor souls, fearing death that way. I was sure that if death came now, I would go straight to heaven. Why should I be afraid? I took up the true religion, and my sins were already erased. That is how I felt.

I was told that from now on, I would have to call the members of the circle "sisters." We were "sisters in God." We did not see the "brothers." But the men who belonged to the group, I was told, should also be called "brothers." We, those who believed, were brothers and sisters, united in our belief. It was our family now, a bond that must transcend my blood relations. We should follow the lives of Muhammad, the Prophet of Islam, and his companions. They too were brothers and sisters working together against the infidels of the time. They had to sacrifice their lives, families, and belongings for the Islamic cause. They should be our role models.

"You have to wear the hijab," they told me. "Hell will be filled with women hanged by their hair because of the way they seduced men with their beauty," and "you will make these men commit sins by showing your feminine side." Guilt was a feeling I had constantly during this period. I had to aspire to be a better Muslim—all the time—and the more I did, the more I was required to do.

They did not ask me to wear the *sharshaf*. Even the Salafis do not ask Yemeni women to wear the traditional *sharshaf*. They want women to wear the Saudi *niqab*—their uniform. Similarly, the Muslim Brothers group insisted on us wearing their distinctive uniform at the time: a long headscarf that covers the whole body, leaving the face and hands free. I was not willing to take on that uniform. But I complied nevertheless, covering my head with a hijab and wearing a long coat over my body. I hated it despite my love of God. It suffocated me. But if this was the price for God's love, how could I object?

But their message grew to be troubling, and questions began to stir in my mind. I was told that all those around me, including my practicing loving mother, were living in *jahiliyya*—the state of ignorance and false belief that prevailed before the time of Islam. I was just like the companions of Muhammad: if my family asked me to forsake my new belief, I would have to renounce my parents and their society.

I started to feel uncomfortable but said nothing.

I was told that everything that made up civilization was forbidden: painting, sculpture, art, music, poetry, and philosophy. All of these were part of *jahiliyya* and prohibited by Islam. I grew up surrounded by paintings, sculpture, and music. I recited poetry and read books that glorified philosophers. Why should beauty, life, and wisdom be forbidden?

The more I embraced their message, the more I was drawn away from my family and most importantly from my father. When he finally arrived from Morocco, he realized that something had gone wrong. He met a changed daughter. The outgoing, laughing, inquisitive daughter he knew was now very subdued, quiet, and covered. She was trying, kindly, to convince him to follow the path of Islam. Something had happened in his absence, and he did not like it.

He objected to my wearing the hijab. "Your hair is beautiful, why do you cover it?" He objected to my narration of Islam and the world. He kept talking to me, telling me that it is normal for a teenager to seek answers, and sometimes religion might seem to be the answer. But I should be careful about the type of religion I was embracing. I started to get angry and spoke louder. "This is Islam," I insisted. "It is fundamentalism you are embracing," he would reply, always calmly. Somehow he knew he should remain calm in the face of my anger.

I think at this stage I began to tear at the shrouds of my hypnotization. You see, the alarm bells I heard when they said my mother was involved in *jahiliyya* grew louder when they switched to target my father. He was no longer my father, they said; he was an enemy of Islam.

When I complained to my group about our arguments, they repeated the message about the companions of Muhammad and how sometimes they had to fight their own family members, even on the battlefield. Some of them had to go so far as to kill their own fathers and sons for the love of Islam. That is what the companions did; that is how strong their belief was.

By this time, our meetings were no longer in the school but in the homes of young members of the movement. Regular sessions. Older women were talking to us now. The message became political, in essence sanctioning violence. It is jihad, they said, and it is meant to spread Islam.

They said that killing was acceptable. I was given a booklet about the life of Khaled Eslamboli, the army officer who planned the assassination of Egypt's President Sadat in 1981. Eslamboli was called a "hero of Islam." Sadat, they said, was a pharaoh who made peace with Israel, who worked with Jews intent on destroying Islam. He deserved to die.

Short booklets served the purpose of providing clear and direct messages. In addition to the booklets that preached about praying, women's behavior, and the beauty of martyrdom, there were also short versions of important books written by radical Islamist thinkers such as Hasan al-Banna, Sayyid Qutb, and Abul A'la Mawdudi. But one book was given to me in its entirety: *Milestones* by Sayyid Qutb, considered the manual for violent jihadist Islamists. He kept repeating in his book that all Muslim societies are living in ignorance, and to create the Islamic state it is legitimate to fight these ignorant Muslims.

In all the booklets, literature, and preaching sessions, hatred of the Jews was a common thread. Pure hatred. And please note that the core of that hatred was not the state of Israel, although it was always mentioned as a target for ultimate destruction. No. It was the Jews themselves, their Jewishness.

God had cursed the Jews and turned them into pigs and monkeys. Quranic verses were used to support that argument. Accordingly, Jews today were the descendants of these pigs and apes. That hatred was laden with an epochal religious doomsday dichotomy: good and evil. At the end of time, when the final Islamic victory comes, even the trees and the stones will tell on the Jews, calling on Muslims to come and kill the Jews hiding behind them. That saying of Muhammad was used here to support this belief. Hatred. Jews are subhumans conspiring with other forces against Islam. Jews, communists, and crusaders: these are the forces trying to destroy Islam. While communists were heavily denounced for their atheism, Jews had a special place in the dichotomy of us versus them: the forces of evil par excellence. The taste of that hatred was bitter. I did not like it.

"War is deception." Only when I started to research Islamism did I realize the implications of this saying, attributed to Muhammad, which was constantly repeated in our religious sessions. They told us detailed stories of early companions of the Prophet. They converted to Islam, and Muhammad told them not to reveal their conversion, as a means to deceive their own people during the time of confrontation between belief and disbelief. War is deception, they said, and it is all right to deceive the infidels in order to raise the banner of Islam.

It was not just the militant dimension of their message that finally made me realize that something was fundamentally wrong with this group. It was the gender aspect. The moment of recognition came during an afternoon session led by an older woman I will call Bushra. She was telling us about the importance of obeying our husbands. For women, the way to heaven is through fulfilling their marital duties. The Prophet once said that if it was not for the fact that only God should be worshipped, he would have suggested that wives prostrate themselves to their husbands, as they would when praying. But it was what Bushra said next that broke the camel's back. She repeated a saying attributed to the Prophet about a woman who ignored her husband's order not to visit her sick father. I was told the Prophet said, "The angels are cursing her now, for she defied her husband's order."

That afternoon, I left our meeting knowing I would never return. Who should be cursed here? I asked myself. The woman who wants to visit her sick father or this bloody husband, who has no mercy in his heart?

Remember my mother? She became mentally ill because of patriarchal notions about how to treat a girl and later a woman. I was too young to articulate that in words or to make the connections. But as I heard Bushra utter that sentence, the anger inside of me tipped the scale of my doubts and settled my struggle. I knew then that the God this group worshipped would not bring me salvation.

With a sigh of relief my father witnessed the end of my short flirtation with Islamism. As the first sign of the end, I took off my headscarf.

But I was lucky. I was raised in a context that provided me with the tools to question everything I was told, not to take things at face value. Others are not so lucky and remain entangled in a web of radicalism.

It was necessary to share this personal experience with you so that you could have a glimpse of the type of indoctrination that takes place. At the time, the ideology, structure, and system behind this indoctrination were not clear to me. I thought it was Islam they were preaching—and yes, it was Islam, but a politicized extremist version of it. Many youths in European and North American countries today do not question what is given to them, thinking they are embracing religion.

Over the years, I would come to see this type of ideology and other forms of it in countries I lived in or visited for field research. In the next chapters I will take you on a journey through Islamism, showing how we have mainstreamed it in our daily lives and the consequences of this mainstreaming. What we call the "moderates" are in fact extremists promoting a political ideology—in essence an ideology of hate.

But before we move to the next chapters, it is important that you keep the following remarks in mind.

First, what happened to me was a radicalization—a cognitive radicalization. It was not a teenager going through a harmless religious phase. If radicalization is a spectrum, the last stage of which is the act of violence, the indoctrination I experienced prepared the ground for such an act of violence. We were never asked to commit violence, but violence was considered more than legitimate. It was part of a world order, part of a narrative about a world divided into two camps, one of them a victim under attack, fighting against forces of evil. Certainly dying for the defense of Islam is glorious—an act that would be rewarded generously in the afterlife.

Second, we are dealing with an ideology that uses religion to gain power. The ideology will exploit any device available to support and further its narrative of victimhood and war against Islam. And of course, grave policy mistakes by leaders such as George W. Bush and Tony Blair are very useful to their narrative. But it is not the foreign policies of Western democracies that brought this ideology into existence. There was no Iraq War to blame for my radicalization. It was the 1980s when my story took place; at the time, my group considered Americans to be the good guys. Still, we were already hearing the narrative of a dichotomy between believers and nonbelievers. Islam was under attack then just as today, and the site of this attack was where communism controlled people. The main focal points of confrontation were Afghanistan, Kashmir, and Israel. There was a logical disconnect in the way they preached: the enemies were Jews, communists, and crusaders—in that order. The crusaders were the Christians, but at the time they had to be tolerated grudgingly, as their American friends were helping defeat their communist enemies in Afghanistan. At the same time, they repeatedly attacked the "West" as morally corrupt.

If you are thinking that Israel is a painful grievance responsible for the rise of this ideology, it is important to understand that the Muslim Brotherhood was created in 1928, long before the Cold War—and long before the State of Israel was created in 1948. The Brotherhood's founder, Hasan al-Banna, made clear in his tracts and writings that Jews are a people not to be trusted and are enemies of Islam. The man was in fact a big fan of Hitler.[9] It is hatred of Jews and their Jewishness that is a driving force in this ideology.

Al-Banna's words are being quoted and used today in the Muslim Brotherhood's teachings and are published in broad daylight in various publications, forums, and websites, such as its own Islam Online. Under the heading of "The Muslim Brothers and Jews," the site quotes al-Banna as saying this: "The Jews in the current history are the children of their fathers, the misfortune of sedition, the stoves of evil, the food of revolutions, and the vaccine of intrigues; for in any strife in any state or revolution in a nation, you will see the hands of the Jews behind them, fueling them…as if they want to retaliate against the whole world for the loss of their dignity, humiliation, and materialism."[10]

Similarly, the Salafi Islam, the Saudi strand of Islam, which was also represented among my Yemeni group, was created in the eighteenth century, before the creation of Israel—and yet the hatred of Jews is ingrained in its worldview. I will come back to this point later.

Third, some leftist and liberal intellectuals and policy makers insist that young Muslims are becoming radicalized because of poverty, marginalization, and the current discourse of Islam. But this does not capture the core of the issue. In fact, it can be very misleading. If poverty is a factor, why are not other marginalized minorities of different faiths in the UK or France engaged in their versions of jihad?

Going back to my experience, I came from an upper-middle-class background, privileged and educated. Poverty was not a factor at all. But I was young, confused, and searching for my identity in an Arab and Muslim-majority society. While personal crises and the search for an identity are crucial factors in the radicalization of youths in our societies, the ideology behind it and the group propagating it are core factors we should also consider. Plenty of studies show that poverty is not all that crucial a factor in radicalization, and they testify to the core role played by the social context and the indoctrination of the ideology. I will say more on this later.

Fourth, I did not realize it at the time, but the regular weekly meetings I attended were part of a meticulous organizational structure within the Muslim Brotherhood. It starts with a small unit called the "family." The family has a leader, and his/her role is to follow the progress of its members in their religious training. In the family, the members are introduced to the political literature of the Brotherhood. The leader makes sure that during the week the members have fulfilled their religious duties and read the Quran. He/she also makes sure that they stay away from writings or individuals whose ideas are deemed secular, deviant, or un-Islamic. They should only read what the Brotherhood's leaders sanction as good reading.

There is a hierarchy in the membership of the Brotherhood. One goes through different levels of membership and is only accepted after a process of vetting and testing. To be formally accepted by the Brotherhood after the preliminary stage, the new member has to take an oath of allegiance, promising loyalty and obedience. I was still in the preliminary stage when I left the group after seven months and hence never took the oath. The organizational structure spans from neighborhoods to cities to states into an international network that includes European and North American cities.[11]

Fifth, in addition to their huge financial resources, which I will talk about later, Islamist movements are supported by a myriad of publishing houses around the world. The small booklets I described getting as a teenager continue to be produced in various cities worldwide. These religious publishing houses are generously supported by different financial sources: individuals, governments, and missionary civil society organizations. Sometimes those publishing houses cater to a group of these movements; sometimes specific houses cater to a specific religious line of the Islamist movement: Salafi, Deobandi, Muslim Brotherhood, Jamaat-e-Islami, etc.

I think it was clear from my story that these booklets and other literature were preaching a fundamentalist version of Islam and an extremist political ideology. And yet go to any library in a big mosque in any European or North American city and you will find them. They are distributed free. And they are found not only in mosques and religious institutions. The societies that work with youth are of course laden with them. I even found them in a museum in Switzerland, in La Chaux-de-Fonds. In 2016, with another journalist I visited the first museum on Islam in Switzerland, created by a group affiliated with the Brotherhood. The project is supported by a very generous donation from Qatar.

Guess what I found in the literature available at their library! Yes, my old booklets—the small missionary and political booklets of writers like Qutb, al-Banna, and Mawdudi.[12]

Sixth, I am afraid there is no politically correct way to say this, but religion is very much part of the problem. The issue goes beyond the way these movements use Quranic verses or sayings of the Prophet Muhammad or his companions to support their political ideology. No. It is the religious indoctrination that comes with it, the *dawa*, missionary, work that provides a strong uncompromising religious foundation. This brings me to the question of the next chapter: Is Islam the problem?

3

Is Islam the Problem?

"THERE ARE OFFENSE JUNKIES out there who just love being offended; they can't have enough of it," said Richard Dawkins, the famous British evolutionary biologist, "and I think this is partly fed by a kind of dogma...spread in the academic world. It is the idea that feelings are what really matter. It does not matter what is true, what is objectively true, but *how do you feel about it*. Well I do not give a damn how you feel about it; I care about what is true."[1]

It does not take much for Richard Dawkins to grab your attention, and he did just that at a recent conference. I was trying, at just that point in his talk, to decide whether I should feel offended, but his statement made me laugh—and think. He does have a point, I told myself, even if he seems to believe that anyone who has religious beliefs must be "stupid." Every time he used the word "stupid," I flinched. Some of us who were invited to speak at this conference on Free Expression and Conscience do have religious beliefs, including me. Does that make me stupid?

Still, the problem is not Dawkins and what he says, even given his intellectual arrogance. Rather, it is those who are so intent on suppressing and silencing his voice. We are on the same side, I reminded myself. He is fighting for universal human rights—and freedom of speech is core among them. Besides, I like the man.

But Dawkins certainly has every right to feel frustrated. The latest attempt to silence him occurred in July 2017, before the conference, when KPFA Radio in Berkeley, California, canceled a scheduled event on his latest book because of what it described as an "abusive speech against Islam." His tweets are bold, and yes they may be offensive, but they remain pointedly accurate.

The cancellation is part of a growing trend to stifle freedom of speech, not only in Berkeley, known as the home of the Free Speech Movement in the 1960s. In fact, it is becoming normal for far-left protesters on campuses to successfully silence speakers and academics with whom they disagree.[2]

Somehow it is startling to see how much behavior these students share with Islamists, who often do the same on campuses in the United Kingdom. What is more alarming is that feminist and leftist student organizations often support the disruptive actions of Islamists.[3] Something is wrong with this picture.

"They are very happy about me bad-mouthing Christianity, but when it comes to Islam, the rules of the game change,"[4] Dawkins commented on the cancellation of his event.

His comments are a good starting point to discuss the question I posed at the end of the last chapter: Is Islam the problem?

You see, what I find amazing in this whole debate in European and North American countries is our inability to discuss this issue without being afraid to the point of paralysis; we fear we will be censored or accused of being racist or Islamophobic. Islam tends to evoke very strong emotions—the attempts to silence Dawkins demonstrate that plainly. Most of us feel very uncomfortable when the issue is raised. We stutter and search for words, and when we are afraid of what we are actually thinking, we resort to the comfortable position of watching silently as people from the two camps argue with each other.

The first camp says Islam is not the problem: it is a religion of peace, so you cannot blame it for those fanatics committing atrocities around the world. The second insists that Islam is indeed the problem: it is a religion of violence. The first avoids taking responsibility and therefore applying the necessary and painful measures to tackle the problem. Meanwhile, the second insists that any measures will be futile; after all, you cannot change a religion, can you? But until we challenge its ideological basis, Islamic extremism will not go away. It will persist within our societies, Western and Islamic alike.

While those two groups fight from their separate corners, a third group is speaking more loudly. Not surprisingly, most of these people come from Arabic-speaking and Muslim-majority countries. I belong to this team. We take a middle ground, candidly articulating the problematic sides of the Islamic religion while highlighting how it is being utilized and exploited by political and religious elites. Of course religious reform is crucial, we say. But meanwhile, remember the institutional structures that helped mainstream this reading of Islam worldwide

This discussion may sound theoretical, but it has clear ramifications. You see, among academics a debate is raging about radicalization. Some insist that what we are dealing with is nothing new; we have had these disoriented youths before—remember the leftist radicalization of the 1970s? Hence what we are dealing with is an Islamization of radicalization. Others disagree: you are comparing apples to oranges, they say. These types of radicalizations are not similar—for one thing the ideology is different and religion is very much part of it. Therefore, what we are facing today is a radicalization of Islam. Both groups, while screaming at each other, may be ignoring the obvious: their positions complement each other. This makes it imperative to comprehend what we are dealing with. If we keep looking at cancer and calling it the flu, we will not be able to treat a sickness that is metastasizing. Allow me therefore to start by discussing the first position: that *Islam is not the problem.*

Islam Is Not the Problem; It's a Religion of Peace

One cannot but sympathize with the mission of the first camp, intent as they are on sending the message that *Islam is a religion of peace,* and convinced of it as well. One group within this camp captured headlines all over Europe: the March of Muslim Imams against Terrorism, beginning on July 8, 2017.

Around sixty imams, mostly Francophone, from several European countries, went on a bus tour of cities hit by Islamist terrorism. The tour kicked off in Paris with a prayer at the site on the Champs-Élysées where, in April, an Islamist militant had shot and killed a police officer and wounded two others. A day later they reached Berlin's Kaiser Wilhelm Memorial Church, where in December a terrorist had targeted a crowd, killing twelve people and wounding dozens more. The imams were unequivocal in condemning terrorism committed in the name of Islam. *Not in our name*, they insisted.[5]

Taha Sabir, imam of a mosque in Berlin, told a reporter he was participating to spread this point: "there's no such thing as Islamic or Muslim terrorism.... This is a fascist ideology that misuses Islam."[6]

But just like the march against terrorism in Cologne on June 17, 2017, few European citizens of Islamic faith showed up to support the imams in the European cities they visited. The German international public broadcaster Deutsche Welle counted more journalists covering Sunday's event in Berlin than spectators who turned out for it. Why this lack of enthusiasm? Explanations varied. Among them: not enough publicity, Muslims work on Sunday (seriously!), and going to demonstrations is just not part of Muslim culture.[7] Or maybe they are just busy with their lives, thinking this has nothing to do with them—after all, it is terrorists committing these atrocities, not real Muslims. In fact, some European Muslims may consider this a valid justification.

In fact, the real story lay elsewhere. Hocine Drouiche, vice president of the association of Muslim imams in France, fought back tears as he explained. He told reporters that people within the Muslim community had threatened him, and his family, because of his liberal views. He added that some of the imams taking part in the march would lose their jobs for expressing their views. "The majority of Muslims don't accept our speech," he told Deutsche Welle. "We're afraid for our wives and children. It's a very difficult problem."[8]

Here was a sobering reminder that the problem is deep and widespread. These imams deserve great praise for insisting that their reading of Islam does not condone violence; meanwhile another reading of Islam has become so mainstream that a culture of extremism is silencing dissenting voices within Muslim communities across the world.

This mainstreaming of an extremist interpretation of Islam has seeped into our consciousness, and our behavior, in a way that sometimes takes away from our humanity. Consider this example. Abdul Hussain Abdul Ritha, a beloved Kuwaiti comedian, died on August 11, 2017. While his admirers were mourning, a popular self-styled Salafi preacher tweeted this: "Muslims are not allowed to pray for [the soul of Abdul Ritha] because he is a Shiite Persian and Allah forbids Muslims to call for mercy and forgiveness for polytheists."[9] In fact this preacher, Ali Alrabieei, used the word *rafidi*, a derogatory expression for followers of the Muslim Shia denomination. Kuwaiti intellectuals quickly condemned the tweet—which gives us reason for hope. Still, it is disheartening to see that this Dr. Alrabieei has more than a quarter of a million followers on Twitter.

One often hears such messages of hatred in the Gulf countries, excluding the Sultanate of Oman, and they have contaminated countries that used to have a moderate form of Islam. Rabab Kamal, an Egyptian journalist and a staunch defender of civil rights in Egypt, observed that every time a terrorist act targets Egyptian churches or Copts, she hears empathetic condemnations of such action. But if she calls for mercy and forgiveness for the souls of those killed, these very same people would reply, "Oh, but we cannot call for mercy for them. They are not Muslims!" They never notice the contradiction in that reaction.[10] The very interpretation that tells the jihadists to kill the "unbelievers" is the one that tells those condemning this terrorism not to pray for the victims' souls.

This double bind is clear in the argument stating that Islam is a religion of peace. Two groups espouse this position: one uses religious texts to highlight the peacefulness of Islam, and another alludes to external factors, such as Western foreign policies, to justify the indoctrination and violence that are being committed. Both are intellectually dishonest; both avoid taking responsibility for a problem that they could address.

In 2014, 120 of the world's top Muslim leaders and scholars (all men, of course) wrote an open letter to Abu Bakr al-Baghdadi, the leader of the Islamic State. This letter is one example of the first group's position. Among those who signed were top Muslim clerics from Nigeria, the United States, Canada, Pakistan, and Indonesia, in addition to the former and current grand muftis of Egypt. The letter was meant as a theological rebuttal to ISIS and its fighters, telling them that they are in fact deviants distorting the message of Islam.

Reading the text in two versions, Arabic and English, I could not help but think that the current shape of Islamic theology makes the rise of ISIS all the more logical. The theology has yet to truly and unreservedly respect the dignity and rights of a human being—not just in words but also in deeds. Its mentality belongs squarely in the Middle Ages. It simply does not contain such concepts as unconditional equal citizenship, freedom of religion and conscience, or wholehearted rejection of violence.

Consider three issues raised in their letter.

Freedom of Religion, Thought, and Conscience: Responding to the ISIS declaration that many people living under their rule are in fact "apostates" and "non-Muslims," the letter maintained that "it is forbidden in Islam to declare [a person] non-Muslim *unless he (or she) openly declares disbelief.*"[11]

In other words, if someone decides not to believe in Islam, or to convert to another religion and *openly declares* his or her new belief, then it is acceptable to pronounce that person an apostate. So we see that the freedoms of religion, thought, and conscience are not acceptable within the established religious interpretation of these religious leaders. This fact has grave ramifications for many critical thinkers, intellectuals, and scholars living in Muslim-majority countries.

These leaders even direct this lack of tolerance toward those in their own religious ranks. Some of the religious establishments to which the signatories belong have openly engaged in persecuting and silencing religious scholars for simply providing an alternative reading of the religious texts. According to them, blasphemy means deviating from their own reading of Islam. In al-Azhar in Egypt, the religious scholar Sheikh Mohammad Abdulla Nasr was sentenced to five years in prison for questioning the rationale behind following the *Sunna*, the written corpus of sayings and deeds of the Prophet of Islam—which was written two hundred years after his death.

Abdulla Nasr also dared to come up with a different interpretation that disputed the concept of corporal punishment. He said that what the Quran was addressing was not the physical cutting of the thief's hands. Rather, the real meaning was that society should provide the thief with a dignified means of livelihood that would stop his hands from stealing. This interpretation can be described as humane, especially as it seeks to avoid injuring a person's hands, and thus creating a disability. But it was not convincing in al-Azhar, where several members had signed the letter. Instead, it led to a vicious defamation campaign against Sheikh Nasr that led to him being imprisoned.[12]

It is not surprising that the letter itself does not consider corporal punishment (*hudud*) to be an outdated form of punishment. No. These *hudud*, which include the chopping off of hands, the cutting of legs and arms, and stoning, can still be applied, but they must follow the *correct procedures*, whatever that means.[13]

Equal Citizenship. When you look at how ISIS treats Syrian and Iraqi Christians, are you reminded of the pogroms committed against Jews? I certainly am. ISIS marked their homes with paint to single them out, then looted those homes and property, destroyed their churches, and engaged in a campaign of terror; many have died, and survivors fled. Those who remained were given three choices: pay *jizyah* (poll tax), take up the sword (go to war), or convert to Islam.

Notice how the letter responded to these mentioned atrocities:

> These Christians are not combatants against Islam or transgressors against it; indeed they are friends, neighbours and co-citizens. From the legal perspective of Shari'ah they all fall under ancient agreements that are around 1400 years old, and the rulings of jihad do not apply to them.[14]

The expression "co-citizens" was used in the English translation of the letter. The original Arabic text used an expression we know quite well in the MENA region: "partners in the nation." It is a vague term that avoids acknowledging that Christians and Jews also deserve full rights as citizens. Islamic law refers to them as people of the book, i.e., also readers of scripture, and they are perpetually relegated to second-class status. Those who belong to other faiths, such as the Bahá'ís, are not even granted this courtesy. They are plainly persecuted by the very religious establishments whose members signed this letter.

The letter did take a clear position toward the enslaving of the Yazidi minority, saying that it had been prohibited for one hundred years. This statement should be strongly commended, especially as other sheikhs hesitate to speak out wholeheartedly against slavery. That said, in order to provide a religious argument for protecting the Yazidis, the letter tried to convince ISIS to treat them as people of the book and not think of them as *Satanists*.[15]

Tellingly, the letter went into some detail on how to treat the people of the book and the three choices given to them: *jizyah*, the sword, or conversion. It described the appropriate type of *jizyah*, how it should be levied, and when to use the sword and against whom.[16]

Most tellingly, it never questioned the legitimacy of these choices. To these religious leaders, these are not practices from antiquity that have no place in the twenty-first century. Instead, they see them, just like corporal punishment, as valid practices that should be applied, as long as the circumstances are correct and "legitimate."

Naturally, these beliefs influence the way religion has been taught over generations. Even today, children learn these three choices in Islamic religious classes. They learn about Muhammad's raids against the infidels in the last ten years of his life, and about the Islamic conquests after his death and the three choices his followers gave to the populations of the invaded territories. They are told, just as my generation was, how merciful Islam is. After all, it gave these people a choice: believe or we will kill you, and if you choose neither you can pay us to protect you. Logic does not seem to be a strong quality of these lessons. The concept of equal citizenship has never been mentioned in these religious classes.

Jihad—the Use of Violence: A similar pattern appears around jihad. The use of violence is not rejected outright. No, it is considered the duty of every Muslim. Hence, the letter says "all Muslims see the great virtue in jihad."[17] But that "great virtue" should be used—yes, you guessed it—under the *right circumstances*. Hence, "Jihad in Islam is defensive war. It is not permissible without the right cause, the right purpose and without the right rules of conduct."[18] It should not be used against Muslims—they do make that clear. Targeting non-Muslims is legitimate, but again only under the *right circumstances*.

Reading one passage in the letter, I got the impression that the signatories harbored a certain fascination with the ISIS fighters. Misguided, yes, but certainly true fighters for Jihad:

> In truth, it is clear that you and your fighters are fearless and are ready to sacrifice in your intent for jihad. No truthful person following events—friend or foe—can deny this. However, jihad without legitimate cause, legitimate goals, legitimate purpose, legitimate methodology and legitimate intention is not jihad at all, but rather, warmongering and criminality.[19]

There is a word for the conduct of these religious leaders: hypocrisy. It applies to the crisis of Islamic theology today: rigid, uncompromising, and literally living in a bubble of medieval history. Most importantly, this reading of Islam shares with political Islam the conviction that Islam is both religion and state—no separation is possible. It should control every aspect of our lives; moreover, Islamic law, Sharia, the corpus of jurisprudence that was developed between the seventh and tenth centuries, should govern society as well. These leaders only disagree on the *right circumstances* to implement all this.

A second group is also involved in the denial discourse. These people use external factors to justify violence and radicalization. They play on the sense of guilt embodied in the white man's/woman's burden in order to promote a narrative of victimhood. According to this viewpoint, everyone is to blame except for Islam itself and Muslim communities.

Consider an article published in *Foreign Policy* in 2015 debating the question of whether the wave of violence sweeping the Islamic world could be traced back to the religion's core teachings. Manal Omar, an associate vice president for the Middle East and Africa Center at the United States Institute of Peace in Washington, DC, wrote a response to an article by Ayaan Hirsi Ali with the title "Islam Is a Religion of Violence." Omar's article had the counter-title one would expect: "Islam Is a Religion of Peace."[20]

Omar argues that it is individuals who commit acts of violent extremism, which is not fundamental to Islam. She states that the issue is complex, the product of complex political and social circumstances. She is certainly correct to point to the role of states, domestic power struggles, and government dysfunction across the Middle East. The problem is the way that she presents this complexity, as if to legitimize the violent extremism. She points to the failures of states, which are not limited to economic needs but also include "lack of political inclusion, freedom of expression, and the right to live with dignity," and says that they "have been primary drivers of youth radicalization and violence."[21] Does this mean that the authoritarian grip of Egyptian President Abdel Fattah al-Sisi justifies bombing churches and targeting minorities? People could, after all, choose nonviolent means of opposition. Egypt has a strong peaceful opposition, fighting to reverse all the problems Omar mentions, but they never resort to violence and never say that it is justified. They are the first to condemn every terrorist act.

Omar's article summarizes an argument that plays masterfully on the problem of the white person's burden, maintains a stance of victimhood, and has become beloved by Western liberal and leftist intellectuals: *blame the West*. Doing so begins with colonial legacies and artificial borders, and moves on to the role of Western states and their military interventions, and U.S. polices on Israel.

When intellectuals like Omar point fingers at colonial legacies to excuse Islamic extremism, the whole scene reeks of double standards and intellectual dishonesty. To begin with, they do not seem to grasp the full picture of that legacy. For example, the Gulf countries, except for Saudi Arabia, which was not colonized, were protectorates of Britain. Some of them actually sought that protection to chart their path toward independence from the hegemonic Ottoman Empire. All of them have Britain to thank for their creation and survival. They never fought Britain for their independence. Considering the privileges they often enjoy, their citizens rarely question the legitimacy of these states. They want to reform them, yes, but not to topple them.

These very apologetic intellectuals never bother to look at the legacy of the Ottoman Empire, its imperial role in the region, and its policies that left these countries deformed. I have good reasons for using the word *deformed*. For example, consider the problems facing greater Syria today—those created by Ottoman policies, not by France or Britain. The Ottomans persecuted minorities and instituted a hierarchy of citizens with Muslim Sunnis at the top; this created group consciousness throughout society. Then, when these minorities had the chance to take control, they used the same oppressive methods they had experienced.[22] Some of these countries, like North Yemen, engaged in continuous wars against what they saw as their colonizers: the Ottomans.

But looking at this history, it is hard to blame the West: the Ottomans are hardly westerners, and they are clearly Muslims. So where is the fun in this history lesson? Might as well ignore it.

I also find it very revealing that arguments about colonial legacies are never used in considering the history of China, Singapore, Japan, or South Korea. They have all been colonized or controlled for various periods, just like Middle Eastern countries. And Japan colonized many countries in Asia, including Korea. But do you see them moaning today? No. They are flourishing. China is now a world power, and many see it replacing the United States as the next global leader. These Asian countries are not playing the role of the victim. They have not forgotten what happened, but they have moved forward. They are busy building a future. Nor do the apologists use this argument about the Hindu nationalist extremism that is disturbing Indian political life lately. Why not blame that on the West as well?

Colonial legacies have played negative roles in many regions, but that has not stopped these countries in East Asia from standing on their feet and building their own nations. So, why cannot Middle Eastern countries stand up and do the same?

It is also true that we should consider the role played by the United States—but which one? Certainly some members of ISIS are former Baath functionaries and recruits from the Iraqi Army, as Omar reminds us. No one disputes that. But did America create the ideology and religious interpretations that let ISIS take Yazidi women as slaves? We cannot ignore the ideological foundation. Imagine looking at the Nazi movement without looking at its ideological foundation of social nationalism and race theories! The policies of the United States, as foolish as they may be, did not create that ideological foundation.

It is interesting that Omar did not mention another role the United States played: during the Cold War, it collaborated with Islamists and Muslim countries in using a dogmatic version of Islam to fight communism. She would not mention that, because doing so would highlight the role of religion in this equation, however much it may have been exploited. Besides, with all due respect, the 9/11 terrorist attacks took place before the United States invaded Iraq in 2003—so we cannot blame George W. Bush, as short-sighted as that invasion was, for these terrorist acts.

This brings me to Israel, the scapegoat used to explain every problem in the region. Certainly the Israeli–Palestinian conflict needs to be resolved. And yes, the Jewish settlements are illegal, and of course Arab Israelis are treated as second-class citizens, especially when it comes to land distribution and state services. I will never defend the indefensible. But how does this situation explain Islamic extremism?

All the different forms of Islamic extremism agree on the hatred of Jews and the need to "eliminate Israel." They use the word *elimination*. They are not talking about a dispute to resolve through negotiation. No.

They see it as an apocalyptic religious conflict that will only be resolved by eradicating Israel from the face of earth.

Again, I ask, can we explain Islamic extremism by pointing to the Israel–Palestine conflict? Can that explain the atrocities committed during the creation of the Kingdom of Saudi Arabia? That country was created against the will of Britain. In fact, during the mid-nineteenth century, the British missed no opportunity to impede Saudi encroachment upon adjacent territories. They tried to stop the kingdom's rise, but they failed. By the second decade of the twentieth century, they faced reality and grudgingly acknowledged the kingdom. Simply put, the kingdom's founder, King Ibn Saud, and his army of Ikhwan—tribal religious fanatics not unlike ISIS fighters—were stronger than the British. The atrocities committed in the eighteenth and early twentieth centuries against the Shiite population in Arabia's Eastern Province provided a template for ISIS atrocities in 2014. Ibn Saud and the Ikhwan enslaved women and children, destroyed religious shrines and monuments, and looted and killed.[23] Israel did not exist in the time of Ibn Saud. So, how do we explain that violence?

Let's return to the present and consider the expulsion of a local Ahmadiyya minority from an island province in Indonesia. Does the Israel–Palestine conflict explain that? In early January of 2016, this minority community received a letter from the local government of Bangka regency, located off the east coast of Sumatra in the province of Bangka-Belitung Islands, demanding that they either convert to Sunni Islam or face expulsion from Bangka. Human rights groups have pointed to the strength of extremist Islam in this area. This minority used to live in peace with other Muslims—but no longer. Indonesian Islam is being eroded and replaced with an Arabized Salafi form of Islam.[24]

And does the Israeli factor explain the Taliban's killing of children in schools? Surely you remember the 2014 school massacre in Peshawar, Pakistan, when 148 people were killed, all but sixteen of them children.[25] How can you explain massacring children who are simply going to school? Does blaming Israel make sense here? Does it explain why Boko Haram has kidnapped Christian girls, why Shia mosques are targeted all over the Muslim-majority countries, or why the Bahá'í minority is persecuted in Iran and Yemen?

You cannot discuss all of these developments and atrocities without discussing the ideology and the religious dogma that legitimize them. Religion is very much part of it, I am afraid.

Take Israel out of this. Do solve the problems there. Please! Address the unjust situation created by the occupation and settlement, of course. Look at both sides of the conflict and force them to negotiate and settle for peace. But please stop using Israel as a justification for Islamic extremism. It is Israelis who are being targeted by this extremist violence today, and that should be condemned just as we are condemning the violence targeting Western and Muslim-majority countries.

It is also crucial to debunk the "blame the West" argument—because it distracts us from addressing the roots of the problem. And if we do not do that, we will not be able to come up with the right policy measures and certainly will be wasting our time, efforts, and resources. If it makes you feel good to blame the West, well, good for you; it is just not the answer to the problem we are facing.

Islam Is the Problem: A Religion of Violence

Maybe you thought I would start this section with Ayaan Hirsi Ali's article "Islam Is a Religion of Violence." But no, she does not belong to this category. She belongs to the middle-ground team, and she does offer a nuanced position despite the title of her article. Read it before you condemn her.

The second argument insists that religion is a force of destruction, that Islam as a religion is a *bad/evil* religion, that what ISIS is doing is a true manifestation of the spirit of this religion, and that Muslims are either (a) disoriented and blinded by their religion or (b) inherently extreme and incapable of being trusted.

Among those who espouse such opinions are a group of freethinkers and hard-core atheists who consider religion, any religion, a force of domination and ultimately destruction. Faith, using the words of Jerry A. Coyne, is "belief in the absence of convincing evidence, and hence isn't true or false, but simply irrational."[26] Irrationality aside, we must candidly address the type of violence that is haunting our time. Coyne, therefore, is forthright on the source of ISIS actions:

> Well, if ISIS is not Islamic, then the Inquisition was not Catholic. The fact is that there are no defensible criteria for whether a faith is "true," since all faiths are man-made and accrete doctrine—said to come

from God, but itself man-made—that becomes integral to those faiths. Whatever "true faith" means, it doesn't mean "the right religion: the one whose God exists and whose doctrines are correct." If that were so, we wouldn't see Westerners trying to tell us what "true Islam" is.[27]

While intellectuals of this type are vehement in their critique of Islam, they are also steadfast and unwavering in their support of human rights, freedom of expression, gender equality, and, yes, freedom of religion as well. Hence, their critique is motivated by a genuine outrage at the grave violations committed in the name of Islam.

Sam Harris, a star in the New Atheism movement, puts it this way:

> ...the truth about Islam is as politically incorrect as it is terrifying: Islam is all fringe and no center. In Islam, we confront a civilization with an arrested history. It is as though a portal in time has opened, and the Christians of the 14th century are pouring into our world.[28]

He has harsher words for Muslim immigrants, who "often show little inclination to acquire the secular and civil values of their host countries, and yet exploit these values to the utmost—demanding tolerance for their backwardness, their misogyny, their anti-Semitism, and the genocidal hatred that is regularly preached in their mosques."[29]

Despite these clear opinions, Harris was unequivocal about Donald Trump, whom he described as "displaying the anarchic grandiosity, callousness, and ineptitude of which he seems uniquely capable." And he insisted that the travel ban against nationals of some Muslim countries is a terrible policy: "Not only is it unethical with respect to the plight of refugees, it is bound to be ineffective in stopping the spread of Islamism."[30]

The last sentence, using "Islamism" rather than "Islam," indicates a modification in his position, something that becomes obvious on reading his dialogue with Maajid Nawaz, a British activist, radio host, and author of *Radical: My Journey out of Islamist Extremism*, in their co-authored 2015 book, *Islam and the Future of Tolerance*.[31]

I cannot discuss this group without mentioning Richard Dawkins. He is famous for his clear words on Islam. While he thinks that all religions are bad, he warns us about the temptation "to say all religions are *equally* bad because they're not. Looking at the actual impact of different religions on the world, it is clear to him that at present the most evil religion in the world has to be Islam." But he also insists that Muslims are the first to suffer from its impact. Hence, "they suffer from the homophobia, the misogyny, the joylessness which is preached by extreme Islam, Isis and the Iranian regime."[32]

No surprise, Dawkins is equally vehement in his critique of Donald Trump's policies. Because while it is important to address what he sees as a major evil in the world, "we don't do what Trump did and say all Muslims should be shut out of the country. That's draconian, that's illiberal, inhumane and wicked. I am against Islam not least because of the unpleasant effects it has on the lives of Muslims."

Dawkins always says in his interviews that he is talking about Islamism. His words often show that to him it is the same as Islam—and he is entitled to his opinion. You should read and hear what he says about Christianity—he is not very fond of that either. I defend unequivocally his right—and that of others—to express opinions about Islam, and to criticize it and even shred it into pieces. After all, freedom of expression includes the right to offend. But I am not sure that their line of argument is helpful as we pursue solutions to the problem we are facing today.

Their argument about religion is accurate when religion, any religion, becomes the basis for a political and legal order, that is, when religion and politics merge and intertwine in a political state and shape the social order. So of course the impact of such an order is evil. However, these fine intellectuals tend to ignore the fact that faith, however irrational it may seem from their perspective, has a spiritual dimension, which is crucially important to many people on this globe. For these intellectuals to ignore the perspective of believers is to undermine the very plurality they cherish so much. I have to add as well that religiosity is not synonymous with extremism. I dare say, and I insist, that being a devout Muslim is not and should not be equated with extremism or fundamentalism.

Moreover, to contend that Islam is all fringe, or all extremist violence, ignores the fact that one could say the same about Christianity in the Middle Ages, when it launched religious wars, crusades, and an inquisition. We cannot say that about Christianity today, though modern Christian fundamentalists are trying to make inroads into politics and education. Christianity is mainstream today because it went through a necessary process of reformation, which led to an enlightenment that paved the ground for *a separation of religion and state*. Islam has yet to go through a similar reformation. In other words, just as Christianity needed to be *tamed* and brought back to the private domain of the individual, so does Islam.

Further, this type of argument tends to fall into using identity language, a practice that these intellectuals are the first to criticize. If you insist on treating 1.5 billion individuals as one category (Muslims), you disregard their nationalities, traditions, diverse religious orientations, diverse economic and educational experiences, divergent ideological backgrounds (liberal, secular conservative, left, right), and more. In doing so, you turn religion into a category similar to color and race. No one can change their color, but we can change our religion, however difficult that may be in Muslim-majority countries.

Most importantly, the prism used by this group tends to ignore the rising tide in Muslim-majority societies of intellectuals and activists, many of whom are of Islamic faith, who stand at the forefront against Islamic extremism. They often pay a high price for their courage, sacrificing their lives and liberty. Karima Bennoune correctly described their endeavor in her much-acclaimed book *Your Fatwa Does Not Apply Here* as the "most important—and overlooked—human rights struggles in the world."[33]

Notice that Islamists use a similar argument when they insist that there is only one type of Islam: their type. There is no room for diversity in their argument. And when they start their *dawa* preaching in new areas, they make sure their Muslim listeners hear that the type of Islam they have known all their lives is a corrupt one—it is not a real one, because it is tainted with local deviant traditions. To be a real Muslim, you have to follow the *one Islam*. Once they are in power in the new area, they immediately start to destroy any signs of diversity or local Islamic tradition.

So I know that this group of intellectuals is fighting for the right causes—at this level, we stand on the same side—and I defend their right to express their opinions without any form of censorship. But I have yet to hear them offer one constructive measure that would help us face this Islamism. Just repeating that "religion is evil" and that we should get rid of it is not the solution. Not to the issue we are dealing with here.

Before concluding this part, for the sake of accuracy and complete-ness, I must mention another segment of society that supports the total-ity of the argument that Islam is evil and Muslims cannot be trusted: far-right groups. These people should not be conflated at all with the previous group. What motivates them is an ideology of racism and a belief in the superiority of their own race/religion. Just as they are anti-Muslim, they are also anti-Jew. They see people of different faiths and colors as inherently different and inferior, and believe their presence only corrupts their own societies. Their aim is not rationality, enlight-enment, or the protection of human and civil rights—just the opposite. If they had lived during the Holocaust, it is obvious which side they would have fought on. I mean persons such as the Dutch politician Geert Wilders, president of the Party for Freedom, and the American Steve Bannon, former White House chief strategist and again the execu-tive chair of Breitbart News, a far-right website.

Yes, Religion Is a Problem, but Why Is It Relevant in the First Place?

The middle-ground position acknowledges that religion is part of the problem but considers its political context and maintains that context is significant.

In 2006, when I started to conduct field research on women's rights in various Arab countries, I went there convinced that Islam was the cause of the miserable conditions for women. What I saw and heard compelled me to revise my position and ask the question: Yes, religion is part of the problem, but why is it even relevant? The outcome was a book on the trap of authoritarian governance in the MENA region. Once you formulate the question this way, the political dimension of the issue becomes clear.

My argument therefore is twofold. First, it highlights the politi-cal nature of the mainstreaming of fundamentalist Islam and political Islam. Second, it insists that reforming Islam in a must—but this ref-ormation must go beyond simple cosmetic measures. It has to start by considering the human nature of religious texts, including the Holy Quran, and must distinguish between two sides of the Prophet of Islam: a messenger of universal peace and a tribal warrior. A reformed human-istic reading of Islam orients itself toward the first side of Muhammad.

Let me illustrate the first side of the argument with an example. To one 29-year-old Mauritanian blogger, the issue was slavery. But he ended up in prison for blasphemy. His name is Mohammad Cheikh Ould Mkhaitir. His case embodies the marriage of politics and religion in Muslim-majority countries.

You probably are not aware that slavery is still practiced in Mauritania—a hereditary form of slavery. While estimates of the numbers vary, most slaves are descendants of individuals who were captured centuries ago. Although they are not bought and sold, they can be given away as gifts. They work as cattle herders or as domestic servants, and their offspring automatically become slaves too.[34]

Young Mkhaitir is part of the strong anti-slavery movement in Mauritania. In 2014, boldly critiquing the practice in his country, he wrote an article that was construed as a harsh critique of Muhammad, the Prophet of Islam. In reality, he was simply pointing out the obvious. He said that the religious texts and narrations of the life of Muhammad taught in the country provided a justification for slavery. In the schools, children are taught about the Prophet's conquests and the slaves captured during them. Mkhaitir maintained that if the authorities were serious about fighting this enduring practice, they should begin by dealing with these texts.[35]

The harsh reaction of the Mauritanian authorities revealed the alliance between the political establishment, the owners of slaves, and the clergy. At first, they wanted to execute him, but thanks to an international campaign they backed off. He remained in prison until released in 2019.[36]

The alliance in Mauritania between the political establishment and the clergy can be found everywhere in Muslim-majority countries. In the case of Mauritania, the alliance that served to maintain the privileges of a small stratum of the society also helped maintain a classical orthodox reading of Islam that was left untouched and unquestioned, and in essence has provided a legitimization for continuing slavery.

Likewise, Arab and Islamic states and leaders, in their Machiavellian approach to the politics of survival, have helped mainstream an ideology of extremism. So while I agree that religion is part of the problem, as I will discuss in the next section, it is also important to address this political role. Without states and governments making a radical reading of Islam mainstream in their societies, we might be in a very different situation today.

In a context where unscrupulous Arab/Islamic leaders rule without legitimacy, the Islamist/Islamic card has become the tool to compensate for that deficit.

Starting in the 1950s, the MENA region was divided into two camps. The first, led by Egypt, advocated for a leftist pan-Arab nationalist ideology; the second, led by Saudi Arabia, advocated for a pan-Islam, including more Western-oriented yet conservative regimes. Saudi Arabia and the Gulf countries used the Wahhabi teachings of Islam and the ideology of the Muslims Brothers as an important tool to fight the leftist ideology of pan-Arabism that threatened their monarchies. Using their newfound oil money, they spread it first in the Arab region and then worldwide.[37]

Some semi-secular Arab states also used the Islamist/Islamic card. In Egypt in the 1970s, President Sadat was the first to exploit the Islamist card to face his leftist opponents: he released Muslim Brotherhood leaders from prison and gave them a free platform to spread their politicized Islamist message in the education, religious, and media sectors. He worked hand in hand with the Gulf monarchies. Pakistani political elites did the same; since the country was established in 1947, they have exploited a mixture of political and fundamentalist Islam as a cheap method of gaining the legitimacy that guarantees their survival. The outcome was a mainstreaming of their ideology and interpretation at the expense of other strands and readings of South Asian Islam. Pakistan was a crucial part of the Gulf alliance.

The United States joined in, seeing Islam as a means to fight the Soviet Union and its socialist allies in the region. Put simply, religion was a tool in the Cold War rivalry, but what the United States propagated was not just any religion—it was one of the most reactionary fringe readings of Islam. But Washington did not create this reading; it is important to understand that so we do not end up in the blame-the-West syndrome. This reading of Islam and its political form were already in existence and were exploited by Arab and Islamic countries.

In 2009, Hillary Clinton, the former secretary of state, made this U.S. support clear in her testimony to Congress, saying that "the people we are fighting today we funded 20 years ago. And we did it because we were locked in this struggle with the Soviet Union." At the time, it seemed like a good idea to work with the Pakistani military, to recruit the *mujahideen*, and to bring some of them into Saudi Arabia and other places and import their Wahhabi brand of Islam. At the time it looked like a clever strategy, one way to beat the Soviet Union.[38] And it worked. Except that it backfired, and the ghosts it unleashed have come back to haunt us today.

The Machiavellian role played by Western governments and think tanks, such as the Carnegie Endowment, did not end with that episode. During the Arab Spring and its aftermath, these groups endorsed another wave of mainstreaming, this time against the will of the Gulf states, except Qatar. With the support of this tiny emirate, flush with oil money, they started to promote what they described as "moderate Muslims": radical Islamist movements such as the Muslim Brotherhood and the Tunisian Nahada. This type of schmoozing had a purpose, Karmia Bennoune reminds us. These Islamists "look like what Muslims are supposed to look like" and "say what Muslims are supposed to say," but they "do not ask embarrassing questions about the global economy as their secular nationalist and leftist opponents [do]. Instead, they talk about God and 'tradition.'"[39] How convenient. The mainstreaming did not spare Western societies though, something I will discuss in another chapter.

The fact that Islamic theology has yet to go through any process of reformation has made it an easy target for political manipulation, changing according to political contexts and leaders and the zeitgeist of a given era. In the 1960s, theology was becoming less important than individual practice in countries like Egypt. But once states began mainstreaming political Islam, this ideology of domination started to shape religion, which was then brought back to the public sphere and used as a tool for legitimizing political beliefs. Slowly the ideology developed into a series of hegemonic messages that seek to shape the political, social, and legal orders of each society. Instead of a subdued spiritual message, it became a message of jihad, of hating others and seeing Muslims as supreme—and then a call to establish a theocratic Islamic state.

Since 2004, I have been writing about this marriage between politics and religion and the mainstreaming of Islamism, in both Arabic and

English. Scholars like the late Egyptian Nasr Hamid Abu Zayd and the Sudanese Mahmoud Taha did that before me in the 1980s and 1990s. Both paid a high price for their work. Abu Zayd was forced into exile in Egypt, and Taha was executed in Sudan for blasphemy. The silence that engulfed the region for a while was deafening.

In 2004 I thought I stood alone with my analysis. Today I know am part of a growing movement. The loud voices are coming not only from countries such as Egypt (Rabab Kamel and her 2017 *The Imam's State*) and Tunisia, where Professor Amel Garami struggles unwaveringly to expose the Islamization taking place there after the Jasmine Revolution of 2011. These voices are echoing from none other than the Gulf region.

It is dawning on people in the region that this is a time of reckoning, and the rise of ISIS is a sobering catalyst in that realization. Former Kuwaiti Minister of Information Saad bin Tafla al-Ajami embodied that moment of reckoning in August 2014 when he wrote an article with the title "We Are All 'ISIS'!"

He was not celebrating the Islamic State of Iraq and the Levant (ISIS) or the atrocities it is committing against civilians and minorities in Iraq and Syria. Instead, he was reminding his readers that while the majority of Muslims condemn ISIS, it is the product of an Islamic religious discourse that has dominated our public sphere in the past decades—a mainstream discourse! ISIS "did not come from another planet," he said. "It is not a product of the *infidel West* or a bygone orient," he insisted. No, "the truth that we cannot deny is that ISIS learned from our schools, prayed in our mosques, listened to our media...and our religious platforms, read from our books and references, and followed fatwas [religious edicts] we produced."[40]

What he said has been repeated in different forms by a chorus of Arabic-speaking intellectuals from the Gulf and elsewhere. For example, when Iraq announced it had defeated ISIS in Mosul, the famous Saudi writer Turki al-Hamad tweeted that the military victory is not the end of the story. He called ISIS "a germ that lies in our schools, our universities, our institutions, our families, and all around us. Waiting for the opportunity to revive again as long as the legacy of Ibn Taymiyyah and his disciples [remains] among us."[41]

Al-Hamad has more than 200,000 followers on Twitter and was referring to Ibn Taymiyyah, the controversial medieval Sunni Muslim theologian, whose teachings inspired the modern fundamentalist Islamic movements of the eighteenth century, such as the Wahhabi Salafi Islam.

It is interesting that while liberal and left-leaning Western intellectuals are busy beating their own backs, blaming the West for the rise of Islamism and ISIS, many Arab intellectuals are looking elsewhere. Conspiracy theory is naïve, as the famous Kuwaiti intellectual Aziz Alqenaei told me. "We cannot really blame the 'other,' because the main responsibility can be traced to our [religious] references, history, mentality, and heritage."[42]

He is correct.

It is time to look at religion and the necessity of reforming it.

Reform Is a Must!

I admit that I'm confused.

I look at the personality of the Prophet Muhammad, and I get the impression I see two persons, not one, with two different natures, personalities, and visions of life.

One man was calling peacefully for monotheism, social justice, and tolerance, and was married to one wife. This is the Prophet who stayed in Mecca for thirteen years.

The second man is different. I do not mean to offend anyone by saying this, but he is more of a warlord and tribal leader, with many wives. He engaged in tribal raids and conquests, distributing the spoils of war—which included women and children—among his supporters. He had no problem sleeping with a woman after he had killed her father or husband or marrying the wife of his adopted son after the son divorced her. This is the personality of the Muhammad who lived in Medina for ten years.

We are talking about two men—not one. The first is a prophet preaching a message of love and social reform, and the second is a tribal warrior. Their different personalities and their different behaviors are reflected in the verses of the Quran, taking them in two contradictory directions and reflecting the nature of each side of Muhammad.

Some will say there is nothing to be confused about. It is a natural development. During his Mecca period, the Prophet was using a discourse of the weak, preaching a new religion, which was facing strong opposition. He had to use a language that appealed to the majority he was trying to reach. Once he gained power and established his small state, he changed course, and discourse; now he used the discourse of power.

Some might even ask this question: Imagine if Jesus Christ had not been crucified but instead lived until he became the king of a small state. Would his message have remained one of love and peace? The answer remains entangled in a future that was never to be. But this is not our issue here.

A humanistic Islam builds its interpretation on the personality and conduct of the Prophet during his Mecca period and disregards his conduct during his Medina period. It does not see that latter time as a source of inspiration. It is a historical period, but it is not fit to provide us with the inspiration to reform Islam.[43]

I wrote all of the above in Arabic in a 2012 article—part of a series on the human nature of Islamic scriptures—in my popular blog: over two million readers have visited it.

I did not invent what I said. Anyone who knows the life of the Prophet will acknowledge that what I described is accurate. The contradiction was never articulated or explained in any religion class I had. Muhammad was the most tolerant and kind person, we were told. Even when he slept with the Jewish woman who would later be his wife, he was very kind to her. "Being kind" had a different meaning when I heard it then. What he did during the raids was explained as showing his endurance and success in defeating the infidels, who certainly deserved everything that happened to them. Only my father, who found the Medina period repugnant, highlighted its graphic details.

There are two sides to the Prophet, reflected in the religious scriptures, and we have to reckon with this fact if we are to move forward from the current religious stagnation.

I also reiterated then that this reform should not be cosmetic. It should be undertaken with much love and respect, but it should not avoid entering the *forbidden areas of thinking*: the human nature of our holy scriptures. I call them holy because we hold them dear as part of our heritage, but I highlight their human nature because we should not be held hostage to their contradictory messages. We should have the courage to say what the passages from Medina truly are: historical and ghastly by today's standards.

The key question, Ayaan Hirsi Ali said in her 2015 article "Islam Is a Religion of Violence," is not whether Islam is a religion of peace but rather whether Muslims follow the Muhammad of Medina.[44]

I agree with her. You see, on a personal level it may suffice to simply confine us to the Meccan side of the Islamic message. Many religious Muslims are doing just that. But this approach is not sufficient if we are looking for a process of reformation, especially at a time when the Medina version of Islam has become so mainstreamed, thanks to Gulf money.[45] If I choose to ignore the Medina side, someone else will choose to embrace it and use it for his or her political purposes. We have already seen that. While the imams on their "anti-terror" tour were citing religious scripts to emphasize the peacefulness of Islam, ISIS and its fighters were citing other verses that justified exactly the opposite behavior. Unless we acknowledge that the contradictory messages of the Quran are the product of a human process—that is, the Quran is the spoken words of the Prophet, gathered and written by humans—we will continue to go around in circles. The Quran in this sense is the Church of Islam, treated as synonymous with God. It is as if daring to question the nature of the Quran is questioning our faith in God—and at the same time we declare our rejection of Islam itself.[46]

Therefore, the real challenge is to build a reform process based on the peaceful message of the Meccan Muhammad, to acknowledge the two faces of the religious scriptures, with their human and historical nature, and to maintain that Islam, just like all other religions, should return to its normal sphere: the private spiritual sphere. Reform is possible.

"The religion as we see it today in many Arabic and Islamic countries, and in closed communities in the West, is not one of peace, and it has its own seeds of extremism in it,"[47] Kacem El Ghazzali, a brilliant young secular Moroccan blogger, told me. He was speaking from experience. Many in the Arab region know his story. He created a blog, using a pseudonym, and on it he criticized Islam and declared his atheism. The blog became very popular and drew attention to him. Before he knew it, Islamists had exposed his identity. He was harassed, stoned, and attacked, both at school and at home. The local imam called for a boycott of him and his family. Eventually he was expelled from school with an administrative order stating that "his ideas about Islam represent a threat to the belief of pupils" and accusing him of "foreign support to destabilize the faith of believers."

He was not even seventeen at the time.

He had to flee for his life from Morocco, considered a moderate Muslim state—certainly in comparison with Saudi Arabia. Moroccan human rights organizations did not support him, and the police, who were supposed to protect him, were looking for him to question him about his "ideas."

His story showcases the dilemma facing many young men and women living in Muslim-majority societies. Those who are critical do not take no for an answer and insist on criticizing the social order in their societies, including religion, the religious establishment, and its discourse. But they are living in states that behave as guardians of religion and enforce "believing" by oppressive measures; and they are moving in societies that once embraced the Meccan Islam, only to be infiltrated by the Medina Islam, turning individuals into fanatics who think they should force a sixteen-year-old to believe in Islam against his will.

The task of reform is certainly daunting. I know that, and still I insist it is possible. My optimism is not naïve. The rising tide of men and women, willing to defy extremism and Medina Islam in their own Muslim-majority societies, provides reason for hope. But a key question arises here: Which Islam is being mainstreamed in Western societies?

Radicalization of Islam or Islamization of Radicalization?

The question about Islam—whether it is violent or peaceful, in its two sides of Mecca and Medina—is not theoretical. It is directly relevant to our fight against violent extremism in Western democracies. Are we dealing with a radicalized form of Islam—the Medina Islam? And if so, how do we address its violent message while respecting freedom of religion?

Given the sensitivity of the issue, it has become a heated subject for academic debate with important policy ramifications. To explain what I mean, let me describe a public intellectual fight between two renowned French experts on Islamism.

Gilles Kepel and Olivier Roy—two distinguished French academics—need no introduction.[48] Both have worked on the broader phenomenon of Islamism and have offered valuable insights into violent radicalization in Europe. Both have worked within the tradition of French sociology on radicalization and have lists of books to their names, along with years of on-the-ground experience in the Middle East, Central Asia, and the Paris suburbs. And they were colleagues and friends over the course of their careers—but that friendship ended abruptly with a messy public confrontation.[49]

At the heart of their differences are their differing analyses about what is paving the way for ISIS to radicalize and recruit French citizens from migrant backgrounds. Simply put, they disagree on where to place the blame for the spat of homegrown violence that has gripped France in the last couple of years. Can it be attributed to a radicalization of Islam, the Medina Islam making inroads into closed communities in the French suburbs (*banlieue*)? Or do we look to an Islamization of radicalization, that is, disoriented youths looking for a reason to rebel who find it in ISIS?

Within their tradition of French sociology, Kepel and Roy have influenced the study of radicalization by describing its overall cultural and socioeconomic context. Both have identified the marginalized dysfunctional French *banlieue* as the pool from which second- and third-generation migrants are being radicalized. And in essence, both agree that the radicalization of these youths is a process in which they seek to reconstruct a lost identity in a world they perceive as hostile and confusing.[50]

But what sets them apart is their explanation of how and in which context this radicalization takes place. That difference was leaked out of academic circles and publicly splashed on newspaper platforms.

More than a week after ISIS terrorists massacred 130 people in Paris, Roy, who teaches at the European University Institute in Florence, Italy, published an op-ed in the newspaper *Le Monde* with the title "Jihadism Is a Generational and Nihilist Revolution." He argued that the young French Muslims who committed this atrocity "did so less because they were Muslim than because they were young." Radicalized French youth recruited by ISIS are seeking "a cause, a label, a grand narrative on which to slap the blood-stained signature of their personal revolt." To Roy, the real threat to France and the rest of the West is not ISIS, "which will sooner or later disappear like a mirage"; instead, it is "the nihilistic and revolutionary reflexes of a certain cross-section of alienated youths." They are rebels seeking a cause, and hence what France and the rest of the West are facing is "not the radicalization of Islam, but the Islamization of radicalism."[51]

Kepel, a professor at the prestigious Institut d'Études Politiques de Paris (Sciences-Po), reacted to Roy's arguments with an article in *Libération* titled "The King Is Naked," playing on the meaning of Roy's name in French.[52] In strong language, he suggested that Roy should first visit the suburbs from which these terrorists emerged—which have turned into hothouses for Salafism. Kepel argued that Roy was just echoing the analysis first proposed by American specialists who, "knowing neither Arabic nor Arabs, declared that these acts of terrorism were the product of ruptures with their dominant societies."[53]

The school of thought that Roy represents sees ISIS militants as no different from the members of the Red Brigade in Italy or the Red Army Faction in West Germany during the 1970s: "The same rebellion, the same rupture, the same rupture with violence." Kepel thinks this is utter nonsense. To him, the mantra of "radicalization" signifies "the absence of analysis." He insists that Roy did not "hear the actual words pronounced by Salafist preachers in the suburbs, just as he had failed to read the tweets and tracts they were broadcasting." Kepel argues that Salafism must be taken seriously—even if that leads to accusations of Islamophobia.[54] "If you want to comprehend their functioning, you have to understand their background; you have to understand the intellectual resources of Salafism," Kepel commented to a *New York Times* journalist.[55]

Polarized as these two positions are, I think the clash is overly exaggerated. In fact, the two arguments complement each other.[56] Roy would like policy makers to focus on the behavior and psychology of the jihadists who committed these atrocities: individuals alienated by their society. Kepel, while not at all disputing the alienation dimension, wants to expand the focus and look at the ideological/religious roots that radicalize these youths: Salafism and its religious structures and tools. To him, the atrocities committed in France and Belgium are an expression of an Islamist radicalization that took shape over decades, festering in the segregated Muslim communities. In other words, Roy would like to focus on the individual and local drivers, while Kepel would like to expand our scrutiny of a global factor: the transnational jihadi Islamism that feeds on these local drivers. Roy's position provides a politically correct way to discuss a delicate issue, while Kepel would like to get to the bottom of it, even if that would offend the sensitivities of some liberal and leftist academics in the West.

And Kepel should be heard. In fact, many Arab intellectuals support Kepel's position. When the former Kuwaiti minister mentioned above reminded his readers that the Gulf monarchies had mainstreamed Salafi Islam, he was in fact stating quite clearly that their tactics for political survival led to none other than a *radicalization of Islam.*

Now I think it is time for me to explain what I mean by nonviolent Islamism: a political ideology based on a fundamentalist reading of Islam (the Medina form).

4

Forms of Nonviolent Islamism

I TOLD YOU IN CHAPTER 1 that nonviolent Islamism is not just a totalitarian political ideology that seeks domination. It is also the religious interpretation of Islam—the Medina version of Islam—that legitimizes this domination and sanctions its action.

So we are talking about two forms of Islamism. The two, while they draw from each other, are divided into many different and often competing groups. The first form is *neo-fundamentalism* (*societal Islamism*), and the second is *political Islamism*.

The first form preceded the second. *Neo-fundamentalism* (*societal Islamism*) is a set of extremist movements that sprang up in the eighteenth century, promoting the Medina form of Islam; in essence they were created as a reaction to the challenges of modernity. Wahhabi Salafi Islam is an example of this form; Deobandi Islam is its South Asian sister. The second form is *political Islamism*, basically a political ideology grounded in interpretations of neo-fundamentalism. Hence the Muslim Brotherhood, which is the prototype of political Islamism, is Salafi in its religious creed. Jamaat-e-Islami and Millî Görüş are the twin sisters of the Muslim Brotherhood, in South Asia and Turkey respectively.

The two forms work openly in Western democracies. The first can be described as *hard-core Islamism*, blunt and direct in the way it declares its objectives. It does not attempt to look pretty. It just is what it

says and does, defiant, sullen, angry, and sarcastic: "Islam will dominate the world, and multiculturalism will help us make that happen."
Full stop. The message is one of outright segregation: do not mix with
the nonbelievers and hate them in your heart. And it is repeated in their
mosques, preaching, Quran schools, and Islamic schools. Their focus is
on the everyday social behavior of the communities they work in.

The second form is *soft-core Islamism*: well-mannered, smiling,
shaven, articulate, in love with multiculturalism, and engaging with the
authorities. "We are *the* representatives of the Muslims, and this is how
Muslims should practice Islam. This is what the Muslims want. Respect
our difference."

The demands they articulate pave the way for segregated communities—for they insist that Muslims should be treated as a "group," not as
individual "citizens." These communal demands lead to de facto special
treatment and segregation. Their aim is to control the Muslim communities, preaching their Medina Islam and creating their small enclaves.
Smiling patience is the motto: "Of course Islam will dominate the world,
in this society as well; just give it time."

Both insist there is only *one Islam*, their Islam. Diversity in Islamic
denominations and traditions is not only frowned upon, it is detested.
Remember what my school group told me about my Yemeni Muslim
society and my parents? Other forms of Islam are always deviant. Some
are not only deviant—they are heretics, polytheists (such as the Shia,
Sufi, and Ahmadiyya forms of Islam), and deserve to be actively persecuted. Just remember how many Shiite and Sufi shrines have been
targeted in the last decade in Pakistan, Afghanistan, Iraq, and Syria.
Then consider how the Ahmadiyya have been treated and persecuted
in Pakistan and Indonesia, and defamed and boycotted in South Africa
and England.

When these two forms of Islamism take hold within societies, persecution and violence follow, legitimized and sanctioned by their religious interpretation.

Both forms propagate and work as sects, seeking to create what I
call the *new super Muslim*. Both agree on one objective: Muslims should
be allowed to apply Sharia, Islamic law, in Western societies. The first
form applies Sharia anyway, without waiting for any recognition from
the authorities, imposing it in the areas they control. And the second is

using every possible means to make it happen in democratic contexts. Again, the strategy is patience and lots of deep breaths.

Another important element brings the two types of Islamism together: they both start with the woman and control of her behavior and body in their preaching about an ideal Islamist world, a point I will return to later.

It is these two types of Islamism that should be our main concern; this is what we need to challenge and confront. And our policy makers should stop providing them with the platform to define what "Muslim needs" are. Look more closely and you will see they are setting the stage for segregated communities, defined by a Medina form of Islam, undermining social cohesion in Western democracies, and paving the way to radicalize young people.

The next two sections will give substance to what I just outlined above, starting with the first form: neo-fundamentalism.

Neo-Fundamentalism (Societal Islamism)

I was trying to understand what had just happened. This well-mannered man would not say that it is wrong to take women as slaves.

It is in the Quran—that was his argument.

And yes, it is in the Quran. Several verses allude to men having wives and slaves, reflecting the social reality in the era when the Quran was written. Two examples suffice. In chapter 23, *Al-Mu'minun* (The Believers), verses 5 and 6 praise the believers who are chaste in their behavior and sleep only with their wives and slaves. In chapter 4, *Al-Nisaa* (The Women), verse 3 tells men who want to deal justly with orphaned women that they can have four wives. If they fear that would not be just, they can have one wife in addition to those they own as slaves.[1]

Why are you surprised, I asked myself—after all, you know his ideology. Why should he think differently? Yet somehow I could not stomach his argument. Not now, when ISIS was making headlines with its slave markets and its enslavement of Yazidi girls and women. What he was saying was no longer theoretical. It has clear ramifications. He must have known this, and still he was adamant—it is in the Quran.

In his late thirties, he was pious in a good sense, eager and earnest, looking as one would expect him to, in a white tunic and with a long beard. Throughout our interview he was giving me ample evidence that whenever he is involved in arbitration on family affairs, he tries to take the side of the women. And he meant it.

We were in Johannesburg, South Africa, in a Deobandi mosque. Mosque is an understatement. This was a center with sections to handle specific tasks: Quran and religious education for children, a section for family and women's affairs, and a hub meeting place for community members. It was summer 2015, and I was conducting some fieldwork on women's lives under Muslim law in South Africa.[2]

You probably never heard of the Deobandi movement. It is named for Deoband, a town in northern India, where the seminary of Deobandi (Dar al-Ulum) was established in 1867. If you don't know of it, that's OK. Not many do. But I am sure you know of the Taliban or have at least heard of them? The Taliban in Afghanistan bases its religious interpretation on Deobandi teachings.

We always mention the Wahhabi Salafi when we want to talk about fundamentalist Islam and forget its other fundamentalist relatives. Both the Wahhabi Salafi and Deobandi Islam are modern puritanical reformist movements of the eighteenth century. One originated in the heart of Najd, today Saudi Arabia; the other, the Deobandi, started in India. While they follow different schools of jurisprudence, they were both inspired by a controversial thirteenth-century religious scholar, Ibn Taymiyyah (1263–1328). You can call him the father of an extremist reading of Islam.

The Deobandi movement is often described as the branch of the Wahhabi movement on the subcontinent, despite its distinct origins. It advocates for a strict Sunni orthodoxy, it frowns upon the Sufi tradition of Islam, considering it a form of polytheism, and it insists on a separate Muslim identity and application of Sharia law. Experts today emphasize the recent convergence between Salafi theology and Deobandi sectarian political ideology—which came about as a result of Gulf oil money. And yet the two movements compete against each other. This should not be confusing. In fact, it is a feature that shapes the relationship between many different branches of Islamist movements.[3]

The Deobandi movement was and still is instrumental in emphasizing orthodox Islamic behavior and engendering a separate communal identity within some South Asian communities in India, the UK, and South Africa.

I came across this movement and its Tablighti[4] missionary branch in 2013 when I was conducting research for my book on Sharia councils in the UK. It was there that I began to see the dots merging into a worrisome picture. My field research in South Africa only deepened my sense of alarm.

The Deobandi approach is rather quiet and bottom-up—it does not engage with the state. It prefers to be left alone and work silently with the masses. Ghaffar Hussain, an expert on extremism and Islamism in Britain, who as a youth was a member of a political Islamist movement, described to me the Deobandi approach in the UK:

> They are powerful as well, but they were very, very quiet. They did not want to make a noise or be noticed by the mainstream society; they wanted to do their work in the mosques, hidden away in mosques. So when we speak to them as [political] Islamists, they would say: you guys are trying to change the system from the top, but we are like lots and lots of ants that are eating away at the system slowly. What they think they are doing is slowly converting everybody, and they will automatically be Islamists. So they are not opposed to the idea of enforcing Islam through the state, but they just do not believe in political revolution and political engagement.[5]

The approach entails separation, decreeing religious rules that would form the basis of a closed community identity, and creating ghettos in many areas, such as Leicester, England, where the movement has a strong presence. Leicester's lack of integration is not only "striking," it is considered the "most conservative in Europe"—according to a cable leaked via WikiLeaks. Farah Pandith, the U.S. State Department's senior adviser for Muslim engagement, visited the city in 2007 and wrote those words. In a local bookshop, she had seen texts in English that seemed designed to "segregate Muslims from their wider community...playing up the differences between Islam and other religions...and feeding hate of Jews to the young."[6]

Many among the Deobandi population will "voluntarily submit themselves to the authority of the Deobandi ulema [sheikhs]," observed Innes Bowen in her book *Medina in Birmingham*. "A local sharia council helps to settle disputes between adherents." She also observed a new phenomenon that is increasing not only in Leicester but also in many areas with a Muslim minority: women veiling their faces. Although it was once unusual among Muslim women in Britain, it is now the practice of a substantial minority.[7]

~

This development can also be seen in Johannesburg. Ten years ago, I was told, you would have been hard-pressed to see a woman in *niqab*, a burka. Today you see them popping out of their houses in closed communities. Many women actually believe that what they are doing is God's command. Many others are forced to cover themselves.

Given this background and the fundamentalist nature of the Deobandi teachings, the position of my South African interviewee was not at all surprising. He reads the Quran literally, and if it tells him that men can have slaves, then he cannot condemn it—even if slavery has been abolished today as an abhorrent and antiquated violation of human dignity.

This literalistic behavior makes it difficult for this movement in the era of ISIS. While they share ideological roots with ISIS, they insist that the ISIS reading of Islam is shallow. Mainstream Deobandi leaders would criticize ISIS for declaring the Caliphate prematurely and for launching armed jihad without waiting for approval from Muslim leaders. Again, we see the issue is waiting for *the right circumstances*. Hence, in 2015 when ISIS criticized the Deobandi *ulama*—the body of religious scholars—for being "anti-jihad," their answer was swift and simple: of course we are pro-jihad.

Radio Islam, an Islamist radio station in South Africa (I am consciously using the word *Islamist*), asked the Deobandi *ulama* to respond to this question, and I quote it here: "There have been allegations by ISIS propagandists that South African Ulama are anti jihad, which is a Quraanic injunction. Is this slander?" The written answer of the *ulama* was very telling.[8]

The statement is clear. I have deliberately quoted some of it in the endnote so that you can read it yourself and see how they argue—and for that matter they are not doing a good job of it:

> Our surrounding society is an ungodly system; we are not satisfied with it; we aspire for an Islamic state with a system of shari'a governance; and yes of course, we are pro Jihad, which is a duty of Muslims;

but we reserve the right to use violence and bear arms in times of "oppression" of the *umma* [the whole community of Muslims worldwide
bound together by ties of religion]. Until then, we are for co-existence
with other people.

You almost have to feel sorry for them because they know they are
cornered by ISIS—which is taking what they are preaching and implementing it literally in reality. ISIS is both words and deeds. The *ulama*,
on the other hand, stand accused of being hypocrites. They use only
words. But words can be dangerous, especially if they are repeated in a
religious discourse that ultimately leads to our young people becoming
cognitively radicalized.

The Deobandi mosques in South Africa, along with their Tablighi
missionary arm, and their Quran schools and *dar-al-ulums*, the seminaries responsible for training their imams, play a major role in shaping
the worldviews of Muslim youth in South Africa.

The same can be said about Britain. I did not tell you that the Deobandi movement in the UK, together with the Tablighi missionaries,
controls almost half of the mosques in the country. Over the last thirty
years it has established twenty-five *dar-al-ulums*. The annual output of
graduates from these highly conservative literalist Deobandi seminaries does meet the British government's demand for English-speaking
imams, but it fails to support the humanist values of equality, tolerance,
liberty, and religious pluralism.[9]

I hope by now you understand my alarm.

Wahhabi Salafism: Hard-core Islamism

The Deobandi movement is not that well known outside of the South
Asian context. It is often confused with its twin sister, the Wahhabi Salafi
movement. The latter is the face of *hard-core Islamism*—an extremist
reading of Islam. I think by today many are aware of its existence and its
disruptive role.

Salafi Islam is a fundamentalist interpretation of religion that seeks
to implement Islam as it was observed during the Medina time of Muhammad and his *salafs* (companions, followers, and forefathers—hence
the adjective *Salafi*). It emerged in a coherent form in the thirteenth century through the writings of Ibn Taymiyyah, the controversial religious
scholar I mentioned earlier. His ideas were revived in the eighteenth

century through various movements including the Wahhabi movement in the Arabian Peninsula. Starting in the late 1960s, during the reign of the Saudi King Faisal (1964–1975), it became mainstreamed, using oil money.[10]

I had a bitter experience with its teaching through my late uncle, a professor of agriculture who earned his PhD with honors in Germany. In Bonn, when I was three years old, he would carry me around on his shoulders. I adored him. He also had a wonderful sense of humor, and we would have a good laugh when I came back from Morocco and stayed with him in Sana'a. By then he had converted to Wahhabi Salafi Islam—in Germany. After Yemen was unified in 1990, he became an enthusiastic member of the Islamist Islah party, made up of three currents: Muslim Brothers, Salafis, and tribal sheikhs.

In 2005, I started to write my series on a humanistic Islam, and something began to break between the two of us. The more publicity my writing attracted, the more he distanced himself from me. It pained me, but I did not mind. I thought it was only natural and his right to disagree with my opinions. But I did not expect that he would issue a fatwa in public, saying that my writings constituted blasphemy and I should be killed for them. "The punishment for blasphemy is clear," he said.

It was not just pain I felt hearing this. No. It was utter disappointment in his sense of decency and humanity. "I was your baby niece. Remember? You loved me just as I adored you—we cracked up laughing at your jokes. And yet you shun this relationship, this love. You throw it away, telling others it is OK to kill me because I read Islam differently from you? What kind of God do you believe in?"

My brother responded quickly. He recognized how serious this was. I traveled constantly to Yemen for work and to see my father, and some in Yemen might act on his words. So he sent him word through relatives that he should be careful about what he was saying. He and my father stood behind me.

My uncle did not have a PhD in Islamic studies—he had studied agriculture. And yet he felt confident he could give his religious opinion and call for others to carry it out. This should remind you of the self-proclaiming Salafi sheikhs we have in Western democracies. They are converts—all of them. Even if they grew up in Islam, they remain converts. Remember what their reading of Islam tells them: "The way you practiced Islam before was corrupt. Now you are following the true Islam."

This lack of a profound scholarly religious background is not surprising. After all, their role model, the founder in the eighteenth century of modern Salafi Islam, Mohammed ibn Abd al-Wahhab, was also known for his rudimentary religious training. His father was a known religious scholar in Najd, Arabia's central region, the heart of today's political and religious powerbase. But al-Wahhab himself was no scholar.

He also had limited exposure to the outside world—no Western colonial influence to blame here. Najd was never colonized. His travels were limited to Medina, Basra, and Hasa, the Shiite eastern province of today's Saudi Arabia. There he was confronted with the Islamic traditions of the Sufi orders and Shiite Islam—a profound experience, we are told. He returned convinced that what was being practiced in his time was *jahiliyya*, ignorance. It was corrupt versions of Islam, polluted by idolatry and innovation and the paganism of the tribes and common people.[11]

His teachings were not welcomed in Najd. That was not surprising. He rejected all the religious traditions of his time, branding the people of his time as heretics—even if they were applying Sharia. His father disowned him. Everywhere he went with his supporters, he was asked to leave after a while. His teachings were disruptive, creating conflicts and dividing families. Only when he went to Darayyia, the town of an aspiring political leader, did he find an opportunity for recognition. The leader there was Mohammad ibn Saud, the founder of the Saudi dynasty. His tribal lineage was not as strong as he wished, and he needed a source of legitimacy. He found it in the Wahhabi teachings. If not for this political factor, the Wahhabi reading of Islam might have vanished after its leader's death. The first Saudi state was established in 1744, based on the alliance of the two men. They pledged to create a state based on Wahhabi principles. The same pledge was reinstated by Ibn Saud a century and a half later and provided the foundation of today's modern Saudi Arabia, created in 1932.[12]

What made his message different were the dogmatic tools he provided in his teachings. Not only are people living in *jahiliyya*, ignorance. In addition, they do not know how to believe in God. The belief in the Oneness of God—*tawhid*—is the first duty of the Muslim, even before prayer. But one has to know how to perform it.

All people, including non-Muslims, believe in a common form of monotheism. Al-Wahhab called it *tawhid al-rububiyya*, the belief that God alone is the creator, owner, and controller of everything. God gives life and death. But it is the second form of monotheism that distinguishes real Muslims from the rest of humanity. In every act of worship, you have to single out God alone. Only God should be the addressee of prayers, sacrifices, and other forms of God. People must not take anyone or anything else along with God, worshipping them or seeking nearness to them as they do with God. This doctrine he called *tawhid al-uluhiyya*.[13] The consequences of this distinction turned everyone but followers of Wahhabi Islam into unbelievers.

To al-Wahhab, Christians remain unbelievers, no matter how pious they are. They can worship God night and day, give alms, and live secluded from others in a monastery, but still they are "enemies of God and destined for perpetual fire because of their belief in Jesus and other Saints."[14]

Muslims would share the same fate if they were to pray to a being or object other than God. If they did, "their conduct took them beyond Islam and rendered their lives, property, and wives forfeit." It was *tawhid al-uluhiyya* that brought the believer into true Islam. Anything worshipped in place of God was an idol, *taghut*.[15]

Having created this distinction in how to believe in God, Ibn abd al-Wahhab was in a position to declare the rest of his society apostates—hence the concept of *takfir*, excommunication. It is not only those who convert from Islam to another religion who are apostates. A Muslim is not disqualified from being an apostate by merely performing the five pillars of Islam. One must also practice *tawhid* to avoid being an apostate. Otherwise, no one would punish the worshipping of idols, which would be a complete renunciation of Islam.[16]

Do you understand now why Sufis and Shiite Muslims, who adore their saints and visit their shrines and tombs, are considered polytheists in these Wahhabi teachings? They and their shrines are the first to be targeted by Wahhabi followers in any society they move into.

Jihad is part of the Wahhabi teachings. It is a core of its worldview. According to al-Wahhab, force was integral to *tawhid* and required the "unsheathing of the sword." "If God ordered jihad by word and deed against unbelievers and hypocrites, the believer had no choice but to wage it." The obligation to wage jihad was absolute, and it had to follow the right motive, not purely a desire to seek booty.[17]

Today, Salafis in different currents disagree on when and how to use violence. There are three types of Salafis.[18] One is called the *purists*. Just like the Deobandi form of Islam, they focus on propagation, purification, and education. They view politics as a diversion that encourages deviance. Within Muslim-majority societies, they ask their followers to obey the state's political leader in order not to commit *fitna*, discord and chaos. You can imagine why many leaders in Muslim-majority countries have turned to this type of Salafi Islam for support. But the support is always conditioned on the permission to spread their teachings in society.

A second type is called the *politicos*. They use political means to propagate their ideas and put them into practice. In this way they hope to create a society where God alone has the right to legislate. They should not be confused with the political Islamists of the Muslim Brotherhood or its relatives. This second type remains Salafi to the core.

The third type is the *jihadis*. They are no longer preaching. They are not waiting for any political process to bear fruit. No, they take a more militant position and argue that the current context calls for violence and revolution.

All three factions share a common creed but offer different explanations of the contemporary world and its associated problems and thus propose different solutions. That is why Saudi sheikhs may agree with all that ISIS is saying, doing, and preaching, but they will still attack it because it waged jihad without permission from the true "caliphate." The splits are therefore about contextual analysis, not belief or creeds.[19]

Ibn abd al-Wahhab introduced another dogmatic tool that has proved to be significant in our time. True Muslims, he said, do not only perform *tawhid*. They have to love and hold fast to everything that God commands and approves of, and meanwhile withdraw from, oppose, and hate everything God disapproves of and forbids. This everything includes behavior, customs, traditions, and humans. This principle is called *al-wala' wa-l-bara*, loyalty and disavowal.[20]

Hence, true Muslims have to be openly hostile to polytheists and proclaim their hatred of them; this prohibits any kind of friendly association with them. Either they separate themselves from the polytheists or they migrate to a place where true Islam is practiced. This concept of migration is called *hijra*.

These teachings have clear ramifications for the integration of minorities of Islamic faith in Western democracies. When this type of Islam spreads in a community, it turns it into a closed ghetto: it tells people to literally hate their surroundings and separate themselves from other non-Muslims (including non-Wahhabi Muslims!). They cannot socialize with them, hence no eating or going out together. They cannot imitate them—no celebration of Christmas, birthdays, or Valentine's Day. And when it is too much to live among the polytheists and unbelievers, it is their duty to leave and migrate to a land of true Islam. Why do you think many families, and single young women and men, left to join ISIS when it declared the establishment of the Caliphate? In their mind, they were performing *hijra*.

Gilles Kepel, whom I mentioned in chapter 3, was not exaggerating when he demanded that we look at what the Salafis are doing in closed areas in the French suburbs (*banlieue*). He was telling us that silence in the face of this ideology is a recipe for disaster.

It is a recipe for disaster because the Salafi sheikhs working in Western democracies never made a secret of their intentions. "Coexistence," as they call it, is only temporary, but the end result should be taking over, establishing the supremacy of Muslims, thanks to—guess what—multiculturalism.

Listen to the words of Haitham al-Haddad, a famous and controversial Salafi figure of Palestinian origin working in the Sharia Council in Leyton, England. On a talk show on the English-language Salafi Huda TV channel, al-Haddad said this, directing his words to the show's anchor, Jamil Rashid:

> Of course, as Muslims, we believe that this co-existence cannot take place unless they are living under the umbrella of al-Islam, under the system of al-Islam. But brother Jamil and brothers, we have to differentiate between a situation of a necessity that we are dealing with and the ultimate aim in an ideal situation. Now we are talking about minorities living in the West so we have to provide them with workable solutions in the short run. And as we said, these visions and strategies are meant to be for a short run, means within fifty years,

something like this. It is not the far ultimate aim of Muslims because the far ultimate aim for Muslims is to have Islam governing the whole world, Islamisation of the whole globe....

But we are not talking about that at the moment, we are talking about the immediate goals. So, in terms of immediate goals we need this peaceful co-existence and they claim that they are promoting it and we need to take it from there. And we need to tell them that this peaceful co-existence, in order to have real peaceful co-existence, then we have to talk about real multiculturalism, we have to talk about real pluralism.[21]

The moderator responded by asking him how he would react to those who say that while he is talking about multiculturalism, in reality it is about Islam taking over. Haddad's answer was matter of fact:

Even if we say that, what's wrong with that? Because this is our aim at the end of the day, and I don't want to react as so many Muslims reacted toward the issue of integration when they had this attack. They said, "No, no, no we are integrated." I don't want to say, "No, no, no we are not going to take over." Our ultimate aim is not a matter of taking over using this terminology, our ultimate aim as Muslims is to have, to see Islam spreading all over the world and to see the word of Allah dominant on the whole globe, because justice will never be achieved unless the word of Allah is dominant.[22]

Political Islamism: Smile, We Are Taking a Picture

He loved hearing the story—one he heard over and over, along with the other children in the Muslim Brothers mosque. He was ten years old, an Egyptian boy from a family of limited means. He was always eager to go to the mosque because there he had a chance to play football on a team. Other boys, from well-to-do families, could join a club to play sports. He could not. The mosque was his way to play. After playing, he would join the Muslim Brothers Cubs—young members of the group. Stories of the life of Muhammad the Prophet—the *sira*—were mandatory during those lessons. And this particular story was repeated constantly:

Once upon a time, there were two boys, Maaz and Mauz, two incredible young believers in Muhammad. They were boys in their early teens, but they were among the first followers of the Prophet of Islam—a decision they made when they visited Mecca in an envoy from Medina. One well-known companion of the Prophet, Abd al-Rahman ibn Awf, told of their courage in the Badr Battle, the first major battle between the Muslims and the *kuffar*, the unbelievers. He said he was standing at the side of the battle and saw the two boys joining in and was upset because they were so young. They had no place in such a battle, he thought to himself, and besides he would have preferred to have adult men fight on his side. But Maaz came up to him and asked politely, "Uncle, where can I find Abu Jahl?"

Abu Jahl was one of the most vicious "unbelievers" of Quraish [the tribe to which Muhammad belonged, which ruled Mecca]. When the Prophet was still preaching in Mecca, Abu Jahl took the lead in harassing and hurting him; he tortured and killed some of his followers. Ibn Awf was surprised by the question, and replied, "Why are you asking?" The boy answered "I heard he insulted the Prophet, and I swore I will not leave this battle until one of us dead." The other boy repeated the same pledge, enthusiastically. Ibn Awf complied reluctantly. He looked around and identified the man.

The two boys ran toward Abu Jahl and attacked him. His men surrounded him, but the boys were brave. Maaz hit at the leg of the horse, and it fell. With his sword he cut Abu Jahl's leg. It was torn from his body. Together, the boys—not rattled or afraid—continued attacking Abu Jahl despite his men's resistance, until they killed him. They ran to the Prophet Muhammad to tell him what they did. He asked them, "Which one of you killed him?" The two said they did. He looked at them and said, "You both killed him," and granted them the loot from the dead man.

End of story!

∾

There is a system to the way the *sira* is taught to the children in Muslim Brothers groups. The boy who loved that story is Ahmed Abo Elmagd, now a human rights lawyer who works as a trainer in the field of human rights and civil society in Egypt. He told me about it in 2012.[23]

A handsome man in his early thirties, he is wearing a T-shirt and navy jeans, and yet he is very serious for his age and clearly dedicated to his human rights work. His experience with the Muslim Brothers, which ended in his university years, gave him a first-hand taste of their methods of induction and indoctrination. And it is not moderate, as some of our policy makers like us to think.

The story is told in such a way that the child is pulled into the time of Muhammad, Abo Elmagd told me in 2017. He becomes part of that period, a witness to and a participant in an epic confrontation between believers and unbelievers: the *kuffar*. The *sira* is told in a way that makes the child eager to be a participant in that battle.

The more that child is embedded in that period, the more it shapes that child's views of the time he/she is currently living in. Abo Elmagd himself was always thinking, "I should be like Maaz, who killed the enemy of Muhammad, brave and a true believer."[24] He was also convinced that the society in which he lives is part of the *jahiliyya*.

What he described is no exaggeration.

The Muslim Brothers have a structured system for teaching the children and training the youth, for indoctrinating its members and propagating its ideology. Former members of the Brotherhood, like Abo Elmagd, and security experts working on the movement agree on this account. Even when Western governments review the movement, they recognize its dark side.

The British government review of the Muslim Brothers, commissioned in 2014 by former Prime Minister David Cameron and published in 2015, had this to say on the Brothers' educational system:

> From its foundation the Muslim Brotherhood organised itself into a secretive 'cell' structure, with an elaborate induction and education programme for new members. It relied heavily on group solidarity and peer pressure to maintain discipline. This clandestine, centralised and hierarchical structure persists to this day.[25]

You do not have to look further for evidence to support this statement. Just read what the Brotherhood's leading theorists have written, and you will see their design for a systematic indoctrination into an Islamist ideology: dividing the world into two camps, believers and nonbelievers, engaged in a confrontation where the Muslims are ultimately destined to dominate the world. The means to achieve this goal is to work patiently on those Muslims who are not yet Muslim enough.

One major book used constantly by the Islamists was written by a late president of the Muslim Brothers in Syria, Munir al-Ghadban:

The Kinetic Approach of the Prophet's Biography. In three volumes that stretch over 448 pages, al-Ghadban details the life of Muhammad and insists that it should be the manual for the creation of the Islamic state. He says, "In order for the preachers to take over earth, the kinetic approach to the *sira* should be compulsory in their jihad to establish the State of God on earth."[26]

When you read the book, you realize that he is talking to the young members of the Brotherhood. "Be patient," he tells them, and "trust your leaders." He reminds them that the Islamic state was not created overnight. It took several different stages and phases to create it, and they should be guided by the Prophet's "strategy" of first preaching in peace until he was strong enough to carry arms.

He specifies fives stages of *sira* that should inspire the creation of the Islamic state. In the first stage, the call to Islam and the organization were both clandestine. In the second, the call was made public but the organization remained secret. Then came the stage of creating the state, followed by one where its pillars were secured, and finally the last stage where "the call was spread worldwide."[27]

In the book, he kept repeating that there are lessons to be learned from Muhammad: times to make peace with the unbelievers and a time to eradicate them from the face of earth. The strategies and methods change according to the circumstances.

So yes, Abo Elmagd was correct to say that there is a system to the way the Muslim Brothers are teaching the *sira* to children and youth. Stories like Maaz and Mauz and how they killed Abu Jahl are not arbitrary. They are part of a system for inducting children and youth into a worldview.

Thus, the Muslim Brothers divide their curriculum according to the age and life stage of the members. They teach different topics: the Quran, the sayings of Muhammad, jurisprudence (Islamic law), the *sira*, and creed (beliefs), through various activities and songs. Children learn from a six-volume book called *Al Rashad for Cubs*. The *Principles* series is used for the secondary level (middle school), the *Rehab* volumes are for youths in high school and university, and the *Light* series is for graduates and "workers" in the Muslim Brotherhood. They all disseminate a Medina Salafi form of Islam caught in a battle for the survival of Islam. In all the series, the teacher is told which messages to emphasize.

So if we go back to the story of Abu Jahl, the children are introduced to his life in the second part of *Al Rashad for Cubs*. The story is told in a way that makes killing him at the hands of the "two Muslim children"—to use the words of the curriculum—only natural and just.[28]

Children are also led to hate specific figures in Islamic history and then direct that hatred toward a general category of unbelievers. For example, in part one of *Al Rashad for Cubs*, children are told the story of Abu Lahab, the uncle of Muhammad, who is condemned in the Quran as the enemy of Islam. The instructions in the curriculum tell the tutor to emphasize "I hate Abu Lahab because he was *kafir* [unbeliever], did not believe in Allah and the messenger (Muhammad), and he used to torture Muslims."[29] The instructions specify the following three lessons the children should learn from the Abu Lahab story. I am quoting directly here:

1. Allah will put the *kuffar* [unbelievers] into the fire of hell;

2. The Muslim hates the *kuffar* and loves the Muslims;

3. The *kuffar* hate Islam and hurt Muslims.[30]

Part 1 of this book, taught to children in the first grade, includes other detailed lessons from Quranic verses and stories of the life of Muhammad. The most important among them are that the Muslim obeys God and the Muslim loves jihad for the sake of God. Of course the Jews are also constant targets for hatred in the curriculum of the Muslim Brothers: "Jews are the enemies of God. The Muslim knows that the Jews are characterized by all evil, for they are cowards, and traitors and cannot be trusted."[31]

In Western democracies, the Muslim Brothers run many schools, kindergartens, youth camps, and Boy Scout troops. Let's pause for a moment and ask ourselves what these kids are being taught. Anyone who tries to raise an alarm is immediately defamed and forced into silence.

One recent example is the case of Professor Adnan Aslan of the Institute of Islamic Study at Vienna University, who published a study about Muslim kindergartens in Austria. He concluded that the majority of these kindergartens are run by Muslim Brothers and Millî Görüş, the Turkish branch of the Brothers, and that they indoctrinate children. Immediately after he published his study in 2016, a targeted and systematic defamation campaign sought to destroy his reputation.

In Sweden, when questions are asked about how the Muslim Brothers use the public money they receive for their educational organizations, the reaction is the usual victimhood outcry: "This is a racist question. You are Islamophobic." But seriously, what are these kids being taught in these schools and kindergartens? I will come back to the two cases of Austria and Sweden later in the book.

⁓

Even the songs taught to children and youth in the Brothers' classes are part of this system of indoctrination. The Muslim Brothers' songs, *anashied,* are performed without musical instruments. Only drums and flutes are allowed because these were the instruments used during the time of Muhammad.

Remember my story in chapter 2 about my teenage experience with these people? During that time when I was hypnotized, I also started to listen to these *anashied.* My favorite one read, "I came back from death to live and sing; let me borrow my voice from a burning wound; support me with a hatred that sows in my heart a goji berry.... The blow of the executioner taught me to walk over my wound, walk and walk and resist!" The lyrics were written by the Palestinian Mahmoud Darwish.

One of the most famous songs the Muslim Brothers teach to youth is "A Conspiracy Targeting the Youth." You hear it on Islamist satellite channels, and it is part of their mainstream, whatever their orientation. If you Google it in Arabic, you find it immediately. It tells the youth that there is a conspiracy against them. The aim is to prevent them from "embracing their swords": waging war and jihad for Islam. The conspirators are diverse: "Shiites stemming from the womb of Jews and Crusaders; and Communists stemming from the womb of Jews and Crusaders." But while these plotters disagree on everything, they "agree on us [Muslims], so we end up prey to dogs."[32]

Nor are their social activities designed in an arbitrary manner. Children and then youth go on trips and to camps. Some of these are purely entertaining. So Abo Elmagd went to Sharm El Sheikh, where he swam, ate, and had a really good time with the group. Other trips are different. The focus is struggle: you stay in a rough place and sleep on the floor, the food is horrible, and then you have the walks, the long walks in the heat of the sun, 10 to 15 kilometers, marching in columns. Abo Elmagd experienced these activities gradually: children walk less. The older he got, the harder it became.

These social activities, camps, and trips are a feature of Muslim Brothers organizations wherever they are. Shall we pause for a moment and demand control of what they organize for youth participants here in Western democracies?

An experience I had in Switzerland may help illuminate this point. Before I moved into academia, I was a journalist for Swissinfo—a multimedia platform for Switzerland. It was a time when I learned a great deal, and I still cherish it. In 2004, I covered the annual event organized by the Muslim League of Switzerland, a Muslim Brothers affiliate. In one activity on the stage, children of the Muslim Boy Scouts started to enthusiastically sing a song (*anashied*), of course without musical accompaniment. What were they calling for? The creation of an Islamic state.[33] The Arabic-speaking audience was not exactly impressed by the content of the song—which I saw as a good sign.

Just as the Muslim Brothers have a system for teaching the *sira* to children and youth, and engaging them in other activities, they also have a structure for pulling people into their ideology.

The UK government review called it a "cell." People I have interviewed and the literature of the Muslim Brothers, including that of its founder Hasan al-Banna, call it the "family." Cell or family, it is an organizational unit.

"You do not choose the membership of the Muslim Brothers. They choose you," several former members have told me.

They observe people. Those who seem to have religious tendencies or pious devotion or who are well-mannered will be targeted. Rabab Kamal, whom I mentioned in the last chapter, was going through a personal crisis after the untimely death of her fiancé. She turned to the mosque and devoted her early evening hours to prayer. She was asked to join a "religious lesson circle."[34]

But asking a person to join a religious circle does not automatically guarantee membership. In the 1990s, Moomen Sallam, editor-in-chief of the secular web magazine *Civil Egypt*, wanted to join the Muslim Brothers after reading the translated books of the Marxist Roger Garaudy, who claimed a conspiracy was plotting to destroy Islam. He wanted to stand up to the conspiracy—and what better way to do that than to join the Muslim Brothers?

They took him, of course, but kept him under observation, fearing that he might be a member of the security service. After a long period of scrutiny, he was asked to pledge his allegiance, to swear obedience, and he joined the cell. But he never moved further up in the organizational structure. He remained in the category of "worker." "I asked a lot of questions," he told me, half smiling.[35]

"People would think they are real members of the Muslim Brothers, only to discover that they were never really in," Abo Elmagd told me.[36] Some find themselves in the category of *al-muhib* (the loving), those who love and support the work of the Muslim Brothers. This category stands outside the organizational structure.

Joining the family means one is a "worker." Al-Banna's choice of the word "family" was not arbitrary. The family, composed of a number between three and seven people, is meant to become the person's real family. A mentor heads the family. Members and mentor meet once a week. The mentor asks them what chapters of the Quran they read during the week. Then did they pray? Most importantly, did they pray the dawn prayer at that time? Did they talk to others about Islam? Then the lesson starts, with its different components.

This structure separates people from their surroundings. A member can only play with other members of the "family," socializing only with them, and later marrying from among them. Contacts with nonmembers are only reserved for the *dawa* mission—the missionary propagation of the Brothers' form of Islam. The mentor decides what one reads: only publications sanctioned by the Brothers. At some point, the members find themselves embedded into the worldview of believers and nonbelievers. They are *the true believers* defending Islam and God's Messenger.

"When you fail in a task assigned to you," Abo Elmagd explained, "it is not the mentor you failed. No. You feel you failed our beloved Messenger—Muhammad."[37]

Abo Elmagd was a member of the family structure, beginning in primary school, moving to secondary school, and ending in university. The mentors changed as he grew, and at each level he was asked to work with a new mentor. Those the member gets to know through this process become his/her real social network, the real family.

Abo Elmagd started to question the group when he was exposed to different intellectual movements at the university level. At first he thought that he could debate the secular and leftist students and convert them to Islam. Instead, the debates opened his mind to other intellectual horizons—other sources of knowledge. When he started to share his questions with the mentor, the latter "ordered" him to stop seeing these students. When he did not and persisted with his questions, he was expelled.

Just like that.

It was a devastating experience to him.

Suddenly he had no "family." His best friend—also a member of the "family," whom he had known since childhood—cut off their relationship. No questions asked. Instead, he accused him of being an "unbeliever" and betraying Islam. Abo Elmagd could not believe that such a strong bond could be so easily erased.

"It is not physical pain you endure when you get expelled," he explained. "It is a psychological damage you endure."[38] You are left alone in the cold, deserted, and ostracized by the group and its members. They all join in a campaign of rejection.

The membership of the family structure remains wherever you are, even if you leave one country and move to another, Moomen Sallam told me. If you decide to migrate to Sweden, for example, you see a phone number on your cell. You are supposed to call it when you arrive. A new mentor will take care of you there.

I said Hasan al-Banna's (1906–1949) choice of the word "family" was not arbitrary. After all, he was a teacher. While jihad was a mandatory obligation of any Muslim, as he states in his tract on it, even more important was spreading the *dawa* using education and missionary work. The religious content of this *dawa* and education is based on Salafi Islam[39]—the Medina form of Islam.

You have to understand the influences that shaped this man's thinking because it can tell us a lot about the type of organization we are dealing with.

His father was a Sufi sheikh. From the Sufis he designed a system based on allegiance and obedience borrowed from the way a member of a Sufi order displays allegiance to his Sufi sheikh: "Like a dead body in the hand of the person washing it."[40]

The system is based on battalions (*kataib*), organizational units that consist of a group of families. In al-Banna's words, they are a group of the army of *dawa* and the Battalion of Islam, and their aim is to prepare the person for jihad.[41] The structure almost follows that of the Sufi order, except that the structure and the discipline imposed on the members are not meant for spirituality—this is a political mission for domination.

Al-Banna was also influenced by the structural organization of the communist movements present in Egypt at his time. From them he took the clandestine structure, the recruitment methods, and the induction of the members. He also took the idea of the vanguard of Muslims, who should lead the world to pave the way for the new Islamic order.[42]

And yes, I am afraid I must also report that he was inspired by the Nazi and fascist movements of his time. Hitler fascinated him. Both shared a dogged hatred for the Jews. Most importantly, Hitler was a leader who brought Germany from the verge of ruin and made it a leader among the nations. This was a leader to learn from. One cannot help but see the similarities between the two. Hitler was convinced of the superiority of his people by virtue of their race. Al-Banna considered Muslims to be superior because of their religion. Hitler thought in terms of race, al-Banna in terms of religion.

Remember Munir al-Ghadban? The one who designed the strategy of using the *sira* as a political tool for mainstreaming the Muslim Brothers' ideology?

Listen to what he tells his readers about working within a democratic context. Use every means available to you to spread the *dawa*, he says, even if that means exploiting a *kafir*, an apostate regime. He adds that while democracy is not Islamic, it is better for the Islamic movement than a dictatorship. That is because it "provides the appropriate environment to hatch the *dawa* and spread it." So, he continues, "while it is a *jahiliyya* system, it is better for the Muslims than any other type of *jahiliyya* system. For it usually guarantees the freedoms of expression, religion, and belief, or in other words, the freedom to worship and the freedom to *dawa*."[43]

There is no attempt here to hide his intentions: "Use democracy—the system of the *kuffar*—use it for our mission's sake."

He is not alone in this clarity.

Read their literature. You have to. Because only then will the magnitude and objectives of this ideology become clear. Kepel was correct to criticize Western scholars who, not proficient enough in Arabic to understand the seriousness of the type of ideology being spread, downplay it. He was talking about the Salafis, but his argument also holds for the Muslim Brothers movement. Without reading what the leaders of this movement are writing, it is easy to say that they are "moderate" or merely conservative pious people, who take their religion seriously. It is a religious far-right movement we are dealing with—a racist totalitarian ideology.

While they are all smiles, shaking hands and engaging in pro-integration and interreligious dialogues in Western democracies, what their theorists tell them is clear-cut: there are times to make alliances with the "unbelievers" and times for confrontation and war. Now is the time for the smiling pictures and *dawa*. Or using the words, in Arabic, of Sheikh Yusuf al-Qaradawi, the chairman of the International Union of Muslim Scholars and a well-known global spiritual leader of the Muslim Brotherhood movement: "I expect that Islam will conquer Europe without resorting to the sword or fighting. It will do so by means of *da'wa* [proselytizing] and ideology.... But, of course, the Muslims must start acting in order to conquer this world."[44]

5

How Nonviolent Islamism
Changes Behavior and Communities

HOW TO CONNECT THE DOTS? How can we see the picture in all its dimensions? When you look only at ISIS, al-Qaeda, and Boko Haram and their violence, you are taking a snapshot through the eye of a needle. The rest of the picture, the whole landscape, the other faces and actors: all that is left unexamined, safely ignored thanks to an absurd sense of political correctness.

In order to understand the violence, we have to recognize the role that nonviolent Islamism plays in both its forms: as an ideology and as the fundamentalist religious interpretation of Medina Islam. We have to see how it serves as both the foundation and the pillars of that worldview, and how it supports a narrative for that violence. Once we see all this, we will have to face the consequences of understanding: adjust our policies on anti-terrorism and de-radicalization so that we can address the work and narratives of these forms of Islamism.

We also have to acknowledge that integration, or rather the lack of it, plays an important role in the dilemma we are facing today. Over the last five decades, many Western democracies have been engaging in "integration policies" that focused on our differences rather than on what unites us. The outcome was not a true sense of multiculturalism that respects an individual regardless of his/her religion, race, color, or origin. No. What we ended up with are closed communities with a "plural monoculturalism": a society where different traditions live side by side, wary of each other, and never really meeting.[1]

The factors that led to the rise of this plural monoculturalism are diverse and differ from one context to another, but Islamist movements took advantage of the idea and used it to cement the separation between these communities.

But I am getting ahead of myself.

Let me set the stage for the discussion that will follow by presenting the profiles of some young jihadists, people we have lost to the violent form of Islamism.

Leila is an intelligent aspiring British South Asian university student in her twenties. When she entered the university, she was wearing the headscarf—something often imposed on women as part of the suffocating social control exercised by her closed community in the Midlands. But it didn't suffocate her. She was very religious to start with, and she wanted to wear the hijab. She would tell you it is part of her identity, her religious identity.

As a child, she would finish her regular school day and then go to a Quran school attached to her local mosque. She went for an hour every day.

By the time she entered the university, she was sure that Islam was superior to all other religions. If asked, she would tell you that Sharia is God's law but that she lives in an un-Islamic context and has to follow the law of the land. And she would tell you that there are different forms of jihad, one of which is a person's internal struggle to be a better Muslim. The form of jihad that means waging war is only allowed in specific conditions.

She was very shy but a bright student. Her teachers expected her to graduate with honors. During her first year of university she joined an Islamic society. At the university you have several of these Islamic societies. It would be more accurate to call them Islamist, as they often advocate an Islamist political agenda. Security officials notice the difference. They know that university campuses are often a recruiting field for Islamists. The relationship between extremism and the social deprivation among British Muslims is not one of simple cause and effect; a government report on youth extremism made that clear. The report's case histories suggest that the British Muslims who are most at risk of being drawn into extremism and terrorism fall into two groups. The one group that concerns us in this discussion is well educated, with degrees or technical/professional qualifications, and is typically targeted by extremist recruiters and organizations circulating on campuses.[2]

Some of these Islamist societies are affiliated with the Jamaat-e-Islami (the "Islamic Group"). They are the Muslim Brotherhood of South Asia. Abul A'la Maududi, an Indian-born journalist, created the organization in British India in 1941 to demand the creation of an Islamic State that would apply Sharia. To him, "the only legitimate state is an Islamic state with the sole aim of applying shari'a."[3] Others are societies led by Hizb ut-Tahrir, the Islamic Liberation Party. Taqiuddin al-Nabhani, a Palestinian religious preacher, created it in Jerusalem in 1953 and called for the reestablishment of the Islamic Caliphate.

All of these societies insist they are nonviolent. They will, one day, accomplish their objectives of creating an Islamic state or a caliphate, but it will happen through peaceful means. *Dawa* is one of their favorite methods. Yet the core of what they are calling for is a theocratic totalitarian ideology, where religious identity is paramount, no separation of state and religion exists, and people are discriminated against based on their religion, denomination, beliefs, and gender.

Back to Leila.

Her teachers loved her. She was an achiever. But then things started to change. Something happened. The university is un-Islamic, she insisted. It supports Israelis. It also runs anti-radicalization programs. She was frustrated and angry as well—at the suffering of her Muslim brothers and sisters in Iraq. Muslims are being attacked, and the West is to be blamed. She considered traveling abroad to join the "cause" but changed her mind. Two years into her university study, she dropped out of her classes and joined al-Qaeda. She tried to assassinate a local politician who supported the invasion of Iraq. Some said she was radicalized online by a charismatic hate preacher.

Omar is a French North African, unemployed and a petty criminal. He grew up in a *banlieue*, one of Paris's neglected suburbs. One of five children, he is in his early twenties; his father left when he was four. His mother is exhausted and overwhelmed. Despite working hard, she is barely able to feed her family, let alone be there for them.

He was not good at school. It would be surprising if he were. Education was not considered important in his neighborhood. And why bother? There's no future for him. So he became a troublemaker, expelled from school for violent behavior. No surprise, he never had a job—just like the others in his neighborhood. He spent his days with a group of young men like him. They drank, wasted their days, and engaged in petty crimes.

In his neighborhood the Salafi mosques controlled the religious scene. He was not involved with them; religion was not his thing. But then he was invited to go to a mosque by a strong charismatic young man, a Salafi. He went first as a courtesy to his friend. One visit followed another, and he started to become a regular visitor. He changed into a new person. You could see the changes visually. He grew a long beard— but, following the Prophet's lead, no mustache, which would imitate the polytheists. He started to wear a short white tunic. You could also see his changed behavior and his strict religious observance. Somehow he liked that order, that structure. He left his group of young petty criminals but kept preaching to them to leave their un-Islamic ways and join the path of God.

He started to control the female members of his family, insisting that they behave differently and dress strictly: "Cover yourself, or I will go to hell because of you." He spared no one—even his mother—from such threats. He said music and TV were tools of the devil and turned them off when family members were watching. In his neighborhood he would spit on women who did not cover themselves, and with his fellow Salafi thugs he would harass any local store that sold alcohol or pork. It was his duty to fight the vice—not only by words but also by deeds. "Jews" were not welcome in the area. He made sure this message was also followed by deeds.

It took a year before he left for Afghanistan. His charismatic friend remained in France. No one noticed his absence, only his mother. His sisters were relieved when he left.

Mehmet is a German teenager with Turkish roots. He lived with his family in a neighborhood in Berlin where most people come from the same rural region in Turkey. The neighborhood had several mosques and youth centers. Some are run by Millî Görüş ("National Vision"), the Turkish version of the Muslim Brotherhood created in 1969 by the engineer and politician Necmettin Erbakan. The Diyanet, the Turkish Directorate for Religious Affairs, controls other mosques.

Mehmet himself was not particularly religious, nor was his family. What they practiced was a form of loose traditional Islam, dutifully celebrating the traditional feasts but leaving the rest of it to personal choice. No one ever tried to force religion down his throat.

At home, the order was patriarchal. Men were at the top of that order, along with senior women—his paternal grandmother was a figure for all to fear. His mother and sisters knew their places, although his younger sisters were not that convinced. All in all, each knew how to play their part. The younger sisters often did what they wanted outside of their neighborhood. Once inside, they performed in the role expected of them. He kept his mouth shut, ignoring what they did elsewhere.

He himself was restless, torn between two worlds. At home, the elders in his family would criticize him for being "too German." "Why are you behaving like a German?" they would ask. "Why shouldn't I?" he would ask himself, puzzled. "Am I not German as well?"

He liked to go out and have a drink with his friends. And yes, he had a girlfriend.

Outside of his neighborhood he was equally unsure about what he was. In his school, his teachers treated him well. Was he really German, he would ask again. He was tired of hearing that question, "Where are you from?" "From here, damn it," he thought. Was he a Muslim? The Turks are called Muslims today. What was he?

Insecure. That is how it felt. Insecure. Looking for an identity.

One day he heard a charismatic preacher. Strong, masculine, charismatic, and confident—oh, that confidence he exuded. "I wish I were like him, so sure of myself and so confident," he heard himself whispering in his head.

That talk was a one-time event; he had just gone along with a friend. But he loved the way that man talked. "Why are you so ashamed of yourself? Be proud of yourself, Muslims. Your society hates you, and you're following it like lackeys?"

So he started to listen more. The more he listened, the stronger he felt. He realized of course that he was not a good Muslim. So he started to immerse himself in religion. He read a lot—and it seemed someone always provided enough information when he needed it. His family noticed the changes. At the beginning they thought that it was some harmless religiosity he was experiencing. Some actually welcomed the change; they thought it would keep him out of trouble.

But then he joined a group of Salafi troublemakers. And then the family started to worry. By the time they thought they should do something, he had left for Syria. Just like that. He called from Syria and told them that he left to fulfill his Islamic duty of supporting oppressed Muslims slaughtered by Bashar al-Assad and the West. His family pleaded with him to return. No success. Neither their pleading nor his mother's tears could sway him. It was too late anyway—he was already *in*. Even if he wanted to, he would not have been allowed to leave. It was a one-way ticket. When he realized what he had gotten himself into, he panicked. But there was no way out. A year later, the family received the news of his death; he was called a martyr.

Lina is no longer Lina. Her name now is Umm Amarah, the Mother of Amarah, the name of a female companion of the Prophet who fought in the early Islamist battlefields, tended to the wounded, and lost two of her sons as "martyrs." She was given the name by her new sisters and brothers.

Born in Austria, she was now settled in Switzerland. When she entered the university to pursue Islamic studies, she was a beautiful wild spirit, with high heels, colored nails, and sprawling dyed hair—red was her favorite color. Her family members were atheists of Christian background, liberal and open-minded. They would do anything for their daughter.

She was fascinated by the world of Islam. She always thought that Islam was portrayed badly in the media. She felt angry and ashamed about that. Her studies only reinforced that belief: what a great, rich civilization! She started to read more about Islam. The more she read, the more she liked it. There was a group in her university, a Muslim students group. She joined and attended their sessions.

She decided to convert. Her parents supported her. When she said she would wear the veil, they almost laughed. They thought it was a fad that would pass, like her other fads.

She wore beautiful colorful veils. She was very critical and thought for herself—an independent spirit. At the university, she was eloquent, intelligent, and also kind—very spiritual in the way she believed in Islam.

She started to dedicate herself to "Islam" and expanded her interests outside of the university, working with a controversial group of Swiss converts. Now she grew more and more withdrawn into herself. Somehow her new social network was like a web that took her away from her surroundings.

She decided to marry, and when she did, she married one of her new group: a second-generation Kosovo Albanian. The colors of her veils changed. No more color. Black. Black became the color. Her smiling shining face started to look gloomy. This wasn't just harsh seriousness; she seemed almost sad, as if she were mourning the vanishing of her smiles and colors. Her veil now covered her forehead and part of her chin.

She was frustrated and angry. Oh, the massacres, the horror endured by these poor Palestinians and now Syrians. Muslims are left unprotected. Someone has to do something to help. Her husband left for Syria. She would have joined him if not for her parents. They alerted the Swiss authorities, who stopped her at the border. She was angry with her parents. They too have long stopped smiling—this is no ordinary fad. Their daughter has been hijacked. Lina is not Lina anymore. She is now Umm Amarah, and when she took that name, her smiles and colors evaporated, as if they had never existed.

Shattered lives and broken families. This is the story of the radicalization—an indoctrination. It leaves these families aching for their beloved lost daughters and sons. They are tormented, asking themselves: Could we have stopped them? What did we do wrong? Are we to blame? Who is to be blamed?

The stories of these four young people can be repeated with different details in the United States, Sweden, Belgium, Denmark, Austria, and Australia as well. The end result of their stories—joining a criminal organization, traveling to join ISIS or al-Qaeda, or committing an act of violence—is often what we focus on. But we often leave in the background the other crucial questions: what happened at the beginning, who radicalized them, what ideology did they transmit, what was the social context of the indoctrination, and who were the actors shaping that context.

Radicalization: A Troubled Term

Scholars disagree on the main factors that lead to radicalization. They agree that radicalization is a *process* of some sort and try to understand what motivates an individual to engage in violent acts, but there is little consensus or clarity about *how* and *when* this takes place.

Gilles Kepel, if you remember, was not exactly a fan of the term "radicalization." Yes, he talked about the "radicalization of Islam," but the term itself he called a "mantra that indicates an absence of analysis."[4] While his disdain of the concept may not be globally shared, many scholars would agree that it has received its share of criticism. Lorenzo Vidino, an expert on jihadi radicalization, argued that the term has become extremely fashionable in the counterterrorism community over the last decade. Its critics, however, see it as an arbitrary concept that lacks a common definition and is very often used to label ideas one does not like.[5]

The history of the term itself helps clarify this point. The term "radical" was first used in the eighteenth century and was often linked to the progressive values of the Enlightenment and the French and American revolutions of that period. It became widespread in the nineteenth century and referred to a political agenda advocating for systematic social and political reform. Over time, it also came to signify support for an extreme section of a party.[6]

In other words, the term "radicalization" changes over time.

Today, because I am leading mixed-gender prayers in an open mosque without covering my hair, I would be called a radical—radical in my aspirations for reform. These aspirations are part of a nascent global reform movement. That is not bad by itself. It is not bad at all for that matter. It is just a position that is not globally shared by many religious Muslims.

"Radical" is a relative term. In the early twentieth century, those who supported the Suffragette movement—which advocated giving women the right to vote—were called radicals. By the same token, what is considered radical in one culture may be considered moderate or even mainstream in another.[7] If you are a woman and dare to walk without a mandatory hair cover in Iran, you will be called promiscuously radical. And you will get arrested for it. Walking with one's hair uncovered in Europe is normal. You certainly do not get arrested for it. By the way, it is not culture that says women must cover their hair or be arrested— what says that is an Islamist ideology. But that is not our subject now.

So if we are to narrow down the definition of "radicalism," two main elements emerge. The first involves advocating sweeping political change, based on a conviction that the status quo is unacceptable. At the same time, a profoundly different alternative appears to be available to the radical. The second, relating to the methods used to achieve that change, can be nonviolent and democratic, or violent and nondemocratic.[8]

Despite the term's shortcomings, it remains useful in describing the dynamics of political violence. For the purpose of this book, I use Charles Allen's definition of radicalization: "the process of adopting an extremist belief system, including the willingness to use, support, or facilitate violence, as a method to effect societal change."[9]

The four young men and women presented earlier went through a two-stage process of radicalization. At the beginning, they gradually adopted an extreme belief system and experienced a cognitive radicalization. At this stage, they adopted ideas that were severely at odds with those of their surroundings, rejected the legitimacy of the existing social order, and sought to replace it with a new structure. At a second stage they underwent a violent radicalization: they were ready to take the additional step of employing violence to advance the views derived from their cognitive radicalism.[10] The readiness to act on these beliefs, especially the willingness to use violence, often comes at the end of that spectrum.

All of them strongly believed that they were fighting for a "just" cause, defending "victims" against an "evil enemy."

Leila thought she was "punishing" the politician she stabbed because of his "politics," which she described as "anti-Muslim." Omar thought he was fighting "vice" in his family and neighborhood; later he decided to join his "fellow brothers" in Afghanistan to fight the infidels who are oppressing the Muslims there. Likewise Mehmet traveled to Syria thinking he could be of help—he would fight for the cause of Islam. And Lina's attempt to leave Switzerland was her form of *hijra*, migration to the land of Islam.

All of them wanted to "help," to "defend." It was a "perceived aggression" they were reacting to—and that perceived aggression and victimhood is the core of the narrative of Islamism in all its forms.

Islamism: A Mission of Conquest

The sense that one is a victim is integral to Islamism. Once individuals are infected with this worldview, they are constantly told that Islam and Muslims are continuously being attacked, humiliated, and undermined by the West, Israel, Zionism, and corrupt local regimes in Muslim and Western countries. Islamism tells them they have a duty to fulfill: a duty to redress this humiliation, these attacks. In fact, in order for the society to go back to peace, harmony, and social justice, Muslims have "to stand up for their faith." Violence, including violence against civilians, is religiously sanctioned and brings the fighter closer to God.[11]

The narrative is based on Islamism: a religious ideology, a mixture of political Islam and a fundamentalist reading of Islam, the Medina reading of Islam. It is a worldview that constructs religion and history and that invents a story of grievances and victimhood.

I think it is time to present a more specific definition of Islamism—one suggested by Mehdi Mozaffari, a professor of Iranian roots who teaches Islamic Studies in Denmark. He says that "Islamism" is a "religious ideology with a holistic interpretation of Islam whose final aim is the conquest of the world by all means."[12]

Mozaffari's definition contains four elements:[13]

- *A religious ideology.* That the term is a combination of *Islam* and *ism* shows us that it is a constructed worldview. *Islam* is a world religion and a civilization with its specific and diverse history; and "*ism*" is a non-Arabic suffix. Hence it is a construction that leans on two pillars: religion and ideology. The ideology is regressive. That is, it is oriented toward the past (*salaf*), toward the Medina model of Islam, as implemented under Prophet Muhammad and the first four caliphs (*Khulafâ al-Râshidûn*).

- *Based on a holistic interpretation of Islam.* Islamists select a set of religious elements and then claim that these and only these represent the "true" Islam. Thus they are seen as holistic, embracing all aspects of Muslims' lives in eternity. The holism is based on the absolute indivisibility of the trinity *din* (religion), *dunya* (life), and *dawla* (government). This indivisibility is supposed to be permanent and eternal. The ultimate goal is to bring this trio into a totalitarian order, not only at the local level but also on a global scale.

- *Conquest of the world.* The Islamist ideology regards the existing world order as both wrong and repressive. It is wrong because it does not correspond to Islamic principles and because Islam as a political power is no longer as predominant as it was in the past. It is repressive because non-Muslims occupy what the Islamists consider to be Muslim territory (e.g., Palestine, Kashmir, Chechnya) and because Muslims live under severe repression from their own anti-Islamic governments. The remedy for this situation relies on two ideal reference points. The first is the "Medina model" of Islam: society during the last decade of Muhammad's life. The second is the classical era of the Caliphate, which extends from the year 632, right after the death of Muhammad the Prophet, until its abolition by Kemal Atatürk in the year 1924.

  To Islamists, restoring the Caliphate is the first step toward Islamizing the world. From their perspective, Islam constitutes a universal religion, whose aim is to rule over the entire world. After all, Allah promised the regency on the earth to His "virtuous servants."

- *By all means.* This is exactly what you're reading: *all means* includes both violent and nonviolent approaches. Islamists use a wide spectrum of means to accomplish their goal of totalitarian domination. They include propagation (*dawa*), activities in civil society, peaceful indoctrination, and political struggle—but also violent methods such as assassination, hostage taking, terrorist and suicide actions, and massacres of civil populations.

  The use of violence depends on the context: "Islamists use extremely violent methods in one part of the world while other Islamists use non-violent methods in another part."[14] Various factors shape the choice of methods. The leadership may make a strategic and deliberate choice, as al-Qaeda did. Or the choice can result from prudent and long-term considerations when a group of Islamists living in a particular situation prefer to follow a relatively quietist and hence pacifist line for a while. The Muslim Brotherhood adopted this line of action for certain periods of time in Egypt and Jordan—and it follows it now in the West. Similarly, in Europe, Hizb ut-Tahrir, the Islamic Liberation Party, is a good example of an Islamist movement that for the time being claims to be nonviolent. Nevertheless, the "quietist attitude of some Islamists is an exception."[15] In general, using violence is integral to their strategy for achieving their ends. It is integral to their own worldview as military jihad is part of their core messages. But choosing when to resort to military jihad depends on being in the "right circumstances."

Whenever they gain power, as is true in any totalitarian regime, they ensure that violence, repression, and instilling fear become the normal order.

Mozaffari's definition clarifies the picture for us: whether violent or nonviolent, immediate or gradual, national or global, Islamism has one ultimate aim: domination. It aims to bring this trio of *din*, *dunya*, and *dawla*, based on a selective Medina Islam, into a theocratic totalitarian order, and to do so not only locally but globally. The scope of their objectives is tailored to the contexts they operate within.

It is a theocratic totalitarian ideology in all its forms, full stop.

And ideology is core to radicalization.

Ideology is Core to Radicalization

Scholars also disagree on the main factors that lead to radicalization.

Some argue that there is neither a single explanation of violent radicalization nor a single profile of radicals in Europe. They offer many sociological factors—including socioeconomic marginalization, lack of education, neighborhood solidarity, and peer pressure—to explain radicalization not only of individuals from Europe's lower social strata but also of members of a well-off, apparently well-integrated Muslim middle class in Europe with no apparent lack of education, job opportunities, or resources to engage in constitutional politics.

From this perspective, violent radicalization "arises out of the par-ticular challenges faced by an increasingly Westernized generation of young Muslims in Europe, who attempt to carve out an identity for themselves."[16] Both Roy and Kepel belong to this school of thought—but they clashed, as I explained in chapter 3, on the role of religious ideology in the radicalization process of youths.

Others focus on the specifics of recruitment in the process of radi-calization. Hence, violent radicalization is more about whom you know and the social networks that transmit extreme ideas. Violent radicaliza-tion takes place within smaller groups, where "bonding, peer pressure, and indoctrination gradually change the individual's view of the world."[17]

In other words, grievances and discontent do not automatically lead to action, or to outright violent actions. Instead, radicalization is a social process that results from interaction with and within a radical group. Through this process an individual is gradually convinced that the per-ceived injustices require that individual to engage personally—and they see that religion sanctions violence.[18]

These approaches and definitions look at specific dimensions of vio-lent radicalization in connection to militant Islamism. They agree that it is a process of some sort and try to understand what motivates an individual to engage in violent acts, but again there is little consensus or clarity about *how* and *when* this takes place. All of them agree that whatever process is taking place, it transmits ideas and a worldview: an ideology.

Acknowledging the divergence of opinions, a group of research-ers constructed a framework for understanding radicalization, based on three distinct elements that motivate individuals to commit terrorist acts.[19] These are:

- the *ideas of the radical narrative* that provide a filter for understand-ing the world;

- the *sociological factors* that compel an individual to embrace this radical narrative; and

- the *psychological factors*, characteristics, pathologies, and triggers that may prompt an individual to use violence in order to promote or consummate this narrative.[20]

These three factors do make up a complete picture, but I want to emphasize the central role that ideology plays in the radicalization process.

Radicalized young men and women are not crazy people. They act from a worldview that tells them they have to defend their religion. While many of them are not well versed in their religion, the radicalization starts with their engagement with a fundamentalist reading of Islam. Again, what they learn is seen through the eye of a needle, an interpretation that tells them there is only one Islam, holistic and uncompromising.

Ideology, with its religious content, behaves like a virus. Once individuals are infected with it, they change radically: an uncle will call for the death of his niece because of her "different" reading of Islam. A young woman will stab a politician as a punishment for his politics, which she considers anti-Muslim. A brother will try to control his mother and sisters, making their lives hellish because they are not leading a "moral Islamic way of life." A fascinating young woman will become so immersed in her belief that the world is persecuting Muslims that she is ready to join the so-called Caliphate in Syria and Iraq.

These are the actions of individuals who became immersed in an ideology to the point that they were brainwashed. And the initial process of immersion in the ideology took a longer period, with peer pressure working as a check on their doubts and hesitations, until it gave them the necessary assurance that what they are now doing—the horror they are causing—is "good" and "necessary" for the utopia they are seeking.

Simply put, these young men and women did not just wake up one morning and decide to use violence or join a criminal organization. No, they were readied and primed for that action. It is a process that occurs incrementally over time. It escalates gradually, as the person is immersed in this worldview, primed for what should occur at the next level. The resort to violence comes after much preparation.[21]

Therefore, ideology not only matters, it is the core matter.

∽

With this background in mind, let us look again at the intellectual fight between Roy and Kepel, mentioned in chapter 3. Are we dealing with an Islamization of radicalization or a radicalization of Islam?

You see, if it is just an Islamization of radicalization, as Roy insists, we will be content to simply look at individuals who are marginalized and have psychological traits that make them vulnerable. We can place the blame on the larger society that marginalized them. Or we can easily say they were radicalized through the Internet. One day they were normal, the second they ceased to be!

But if it is a radicalization of Islam, then we will have to go beyond that narrative of victimhood. Other migrant communities also had terrible colonial experiences, and some have been badly mistreated by their host countries, and yet they are doing well. They have integrated and are not blowing themselves up to express their frustration—and taking others with them. Just think of the Asian communities—Chinese, Japanese, South Koreans, and Vietnamese—in Western democracies.

If the issue really is the radicalization of Islam, then we will be compelled to look at what takes place in Muslim closed communities: the mosques that preach Salafi or Deobandi Islam; the Muslim Brothers, Millî Görüş, or Jamaat-e-Islami societies and councils working with youth and children; and the global Islamist movement that provides them with financial support and aid. We will have to look at the funding provided by foreign governments that facilitate the rise of radical Islam in our societies. We will be forced to look at the social entrances to radicalization: mosques, Quran schools, Muslim student societies, and youth camps, in addition to prisons, sports clubs, and peer groups.

You see, when I see a person of sixteen or seventeen years old committing a terrorist act, my first question is not why he/she did that. It is who radicalized him/her, where, and in what context. The "why" is often related to "an identity crisis," but the "who," "where," and "in what context" are connected to a system and structures that deliberately spread an ideology.

In 2015, young people began leaving the Swiss city of Winterthur to join ISIS. In the beginning, the public discourse was about Internet radicalization. Youth radicalized alone through the Internet. I was not convinced. The numbers and their specific location told a different story. Before long, professional journalists started to ask the obvious question: Is there a radical mosque in the area? No surprise, there was a Salafi mosque, which created a small hub of "community" around it. The mosque had to close in 2017.

Both Roy's theory of the Islamization of radicalization and the theory of the lone terrorist radicalized by the Internet are politically correct. Unfortunately, they do not provide us with coherent answers, only with an illusion of safety.

In other words, we should stop taking the easy way out and start looking at what takes place before those young people decide to blow themselves up. That is, we must look at the whole landscape, the structures, faces, and actors that contribute to the radicalization. We should look closely at the type of ideology these actors propagate, and comprehend it. And I am afraid that entails reading its literature and listening to what its leaders and actors are saying. Would it have been possible to understand Marxism without reading the work and ideas of Karl Marx, Friedrich Engels, Vladimir Lenin, Leon Trotsky, or Mao Zedong?

Once we do, we will be forced to ask very critical questions—necessary questions for a difficult discussion.

Perhaps now is the time to ask the first of these questions: How does integration, or rather the lack thereof, contribute to the radicalization of our youth?

6

Closed Communities:
A Fertile Ground for Radicalization

L IKE IT OR NOT, the lack of integration is part of the problem we are
looking at.

I prefer to use the expression "closed communities" rather than the
common term "parallel societies." The English-speaking expat communities in many European countries can be described as parallel societies,
but no one bothers with them. They work, they do not cause problems, and they subscribe to the same humanist norms as their Western
democracies.

So the term "closed communities" better captures the situation we
are dealing with. Closed communities feature patriarchal power structures and suffocating social control. Those who do not conform to
the imposed social order are intimidated and disciplined. Women are
strongly controlled in closed communities. Their behavior, clothes, and
manners are watched and followed. If a young woman decides to behave
freely and independently—as an adult person, who can decide for herself—she will be called a whore and will be punished in various ways.

Closed societies are religiously or ethnically based groups. They develop certain collective attitudes. They are separated, culturally and/or
socially, and often spatially, from the surrounding larger society.

They have rigid group identities, they often orient themselves to
other reactionary norms, and they have different forms of parallel legal

systems. Sometimes these parallel legal systems are tolerated by the state, as is the case in Great Britain. In other countries, as in Germany, it is a de facto situation: some groups in their closed communities use and enforce norms and codes of conduct, formal or informal.

It is important to emphasize that closed societies do not necessarily lead to radicalization. Closed communities of Hindus exist in both Switzerland and Britain. They have their own patriarchal structures with social problems such as forced marriages, child marriages, and forms of biased caste systems.

But when we talk specifically about Muslim closed communities, we see the added factor of radicalization. Hence, while closed communities lead to social problems, not all of them have to do with Islamism and radicalism.

Muslim closed communities are more likely to experience high rates of radicalization. A high number of fighters joining ISIS come from these ghettoized communities. There are systematic structures that pave the grounds for this radicalization; chief among them is the work of nonviolent Islamism. To deal with that problem, I believe policy makers should dismantle these structures.

Perhaps a concrete example will illustrate my point. In September 2017, I went to Belgium, specifically to Brussels and Antwerp, and met with experts, including a high-ranking police officer, a social worker, and three school and education officials, in addition to an expert working on an anti-radicalization program, now called anti-polarization. Half of my interviewees were North Africans of Islamic faith. The outcome was a sketch of the story of Molenbeek—a sad story of disintegration and radicalism. We have no one but ourselves to blame for that situation.

The Story of Molenbeek in Belgium: They Called Him Their "Hero"

They were celebrating. Youths in the middle of Molenbeek, a neighborhood far removed from the elegant shopping hubs of Brussels. They were dancing and chanting. The police had to intervene to stop it.

It was not a national anniversary day, a football victory, or some sort of feast they were celebrating. No. What they were rejoicing over was the Brussels attacks of March 22, 2016: three coordinated suicide bombings, two at Brussels Airport in Zaventem and one at Maalbeek metro station in central Brussels. In those attacks, 32 civilians were killed and 340 were injured, 60 of them critically.

And these youths were celebrating these atrocities.

"We had to send a police force to the area to put a stop to this. It was a public disorder. People were angry about the news of that celebration,"[1] a high-ranking police officer told me. He asked to remain anonymous.

When you applaud the death of your fellow citizens, rather than mourning and feeling empathy for them, something is wrong.

We are talking about youths from third- and fourth-generation migrant families. They are Belgians by law. You automatically gain Belgian nationality if you are born in Belgium to a parent who is either Belgian or holds another nationality but was born in Belgium and has lived in Belgium for at least five years during the ten years preceding your birth.[2] The kids who were celebrating were between twelve and fourteen.

Their great grandparents would not have celebrated. I bet you they would have been scared of that chanting. They would have been disgusted: they know, better than anyone, that you do not bite the hand that was extended to you with help.

These young people's stories are like those of many of their migrant counterparts in other European cities. In the 1950s, coal mining and various other industries faced a labor shortage. Domestic workers would not apply for these jobs despite efforts to improve the working conditions and salaries. The Belgian authorities were forced to look elsewhere for laborers. Until the end of the 1950s, they recruited from European countries such as Italy, Spain, and Greece. In the 1960s and 1970s, the recruitment expanded to other countries such as Morocco, Turkey, Tunisia, Algeria, and the former Yugoslavia.[3]

Many, grateful to have work, went to Molenbeek-Saint-Jean, generally known as Molenbeek.

Today it is a big district, one of the nineteen communes of Brussels, with around 100,000 inhabitants. It has two distinct parts, covering a total territory of 5.9 square kilometers. The lower part of the commune, including the more historical areas, is made up of working-class neighborhoods; up the hill is a more modern, more residential urban landscape, with plenty of green space. In other words, some parts of the commune are fairly luxurious, with a middle-class population, but other parts are poor and poverty is an issue. Overall, it is the second poorest commune in Belgium: 57 percent of people live in poverty, and in 2015 unemployment was 27 percent among males and 31 percent among females.[4]

The problems are connected to the areas surrounding the historical part of the commune. Not everyone living there is Moroccan. There are Turks and sub-Saharan Africans as well, but the majority come from Morocco, and from a specific ethnic group, the Riffian Berbers or Amazigh, who derive their name from the Rif (countryside) region on the northern edge of Morocco.

In the 1960s, you would not have recognized the Moroccans who live in Molenbeek today. They were practicing Moroccan Maliki Islam, a moderate Sunni tradition often intertwined with Sufi tradition. It was a Meccan tradition of Islam, reflecting their history, tradition, and way of life. Religion was a private matter. People went to the movies, drank alcohol, and listened to music, and women did not cover their hair. Only elderly women wore the traditional jellaba with its beautiful colorful designs. There was social cohesion; each person could have his or her space regardless of their differences, as one interviewee told me.

So what happened?

A mixture of factors turned Molenbeek into the hub of extremism it is today.

It started with a mosque: the Great Mosque of Brussels. The building of the mosque was the outcome of a political decision by Belgium's King Baudouin. In 1967, Belgium's state coffers were empty and the nation needed access to cheap oil, so the king engaged in what any politician would see as negotiating a deal with Saudi Arabia's King Faisal. In exchange for cheap oil, the Saudis could build their mosque. A 99-year lease was issued. The site was the former Oriental Pavilion from the 1880 National Exhibition in Brussels, situated in Cinquantenaire Park. Imams and preachers from the Gulf were allowed to come and work from the mosque. And then the mosque started to become a training center for imams for new mosques.[5]

The Islamic Cultural Center of Belgium, created at the same time, had its seat in the mosque and became a de facto representative of Muslims in Belgium before the formation of the Muslim Executive, a controversial official body representing Muslims that was created after

Belgium recognized Islam in 1974. I will come back to the Muslim Executive later on.[6]

Now, let's connect the dots here.

All the news coverage and policy reports detailing what happened in Belgium and Molenbeek after the Brussels attacks seem to focus on the Salafi indoctrination that was made possible by the creation of the Great Mosque and the missionary work conducted by the Islamic Cultural Center. They ignore the central role that the Muslim Brotherhood played in this indoctrination.

Today it is becoming easier to recognize the dark side of radical Salafi Islam. While this recognition is long overdue, what is more problematic is our ignoring the role of the Muslim Brotherhood in this radicalization—for it too played a central role in spreading extremism in Molenbeek. At the time the mosque and cultural center were founded, the Brotherhood was working hand in hand with the Salafis to spread its line of Islamism as well as Salafism.

Do not forget the history of the global Islamist movement. It is essential for us to see the whole picture. From its very inception, the Muslim Brotherhood found an ally in Saudi Arabia and in conservative Gulf countries. The connection started in 1936, with a historical meeting between Hasan al-Banna and King Abdul Aziz, the founder of modern Saudi Arabia, at the end of the hajj season. The king would not allow the Brotherhood to work in Saudi Arabia, but it was clear that al-Banna considered the kingdom to be "one of the sources of hope for Islam and Muslims," as he wrote in his memoir.[7]

The marriage between the two forms of political Islamism and radical Islam (societal Islamism) started in the late 1950s. After the Muslim Brothers were blamed for a failed assassination attempt against Egyptian President Nasser, some of their members were persecuted. Some landed in Egyptian prisons; others fled to Gulf countries.

In Saudi Arabia they found a welcoming host. It was a match made in heaven. The Saudis had the funds but lacked the educated class required to translate their newfound wealth into geopolitical influence. When Saudi King Faisal came to power in 1964, "spreading Islam" was used as a foreign policy tool to counterbalance the spread of communism and the ideology of pan-Arabism in the region, which threatened the legitimacy of Saudi Arabia's regime and its regional position. Highly educated Muslim Brothers were the ideal candidates to transform Wahhabism into a global ideology. They worked together to spread their two forms of Islamism worldwide. They also recruited the Arab Afghans and sent them to fight the Soviet Union in the late 1970s. The Brotherhood used the bulk of the funding it received to create Islamic centers and mosques and to disseminate publications and organizations worldwide. The outcome of that marriage was the formation of the Muslim World League in 1962, based on Brotherhood brainpower and Saudi financial patronage.[8]

This very Muslim World League, the child of the Salafi–Muslim Brotherhood marriage, created and financed the Grand Mosque and the Islamic Cultural Center of Belgium in Brussels. In other words, functionaries of Saudi Salafi Islam and the Muslim Brotherhood were equally responsible for the spread of extremist Islam in Belgium, and especially in Molenbeek.

Let me go back to the factors that led to the spread of extremism in Molenbeek.

We saw a king in need of money make a deal with Saudi Arabia. He literally invited two forms of Islamism to enter his country, eradicate the moderate form of Moroccan Islam, and replace it with a fundamentalist reading of religion based on Medina Islam.

We saw the systematic work of a global Islamist movement (represented in its outreach arm, the World Muslim League) acting to spread two forms of Islamism by building mosques, training imams, and setting up Islamic centers and bookshops. The latter were dedicated to disseminating the writings and literature of Wahhabi Islam and the Muslim Brothers. Concurrently, connected Islamic bodies and councils started to claim that they were the representatives of Muslims in Belgium and of their demands.

Onto this stage, we now introduce the Belgian system and its polarized politics. Belgium has a confusing federal system: it is a country of six governments and eight parliaments (federal, three regions, three language communities, and the EU). Brussels alone has nineteen different mayors and six separate police departments. Compared to the orderly, well-organized, and neatly functioning Swiss federal system, the Belgian system is a mess. These bodies often do not even communicate with each other, let alone share information. Because Brussels is French by language and Flemish by geography (the city of Brussels is actually the capital of Flanders), it became nobody's first priority in providing services.[9]

Certainly Molenbeek was nobody's first priority. And the system allowed it to be the private fiefdom of its former Socialist mayor Philippe Moureaux, who governed it from 1992 to 2012.

A pattern that has repeated itself in many other Western democracies materialized here: a mayor (or a political party, a prime minister, etc.) starts to court migrant groups out of sheer political calculation. They represent a new pool of voters for his/her party. That mayor is also a staunch defender of a multiculturalism of difference. He institutes a culture of silence; some might call it a culture of indifference. However problematic the situation people perceive, it can be explained by cultural and religious differences: that is the way "they" do things, and "we" cannot criticize them, because that is "their culture," that is "their religion." Certain themes became taboo, and those who dared to touch on them, often leftist and liberal personalities, were defamed and discredited. The accusations of Islamophobia and racism were ready-made labels used to silence serious and legitimate critiques of the Islamists' work and the mayor's politics of difference. The outcome was this: whatever demands the Islamists made were accepted during his tenure without any questions asked.

Even today, this former mayor insists he had nothing to do with what took place in Molenbeek, as if his nineteen years of tenure were of no consequence. His paternalistic discourse—which sees radical Muslim youths as, above all, victims of social and economic exclusion and Islamophobia—does not help at all. Especially as the Muslim youth internalize this frame of reference, which frees them from taking responsibility for their actions.[10] And then what happens? Those "who point to unpleasant truths such as the high incidence of crime among Moroccan youth and violent tendencies in radical Islam are accused of being propagandists of the extreme-right, and are subsequently ignored and ostracized."[11]

A culture of denial has long persisted and still persists.

What does the picture look like today in Molenbeek?

The traditional tolerant form of Moroccan Islam is all but gone. Some in the older generation still subscribe to it, but the younger generations are left hostage to an extremist reading of Islam. Those propagating the two forms of Islamism are telling them that the Islam they are practicing is not the right one. It is a corrupt form of Islam. Have we heard that before?

And the thinking took hold among Muslims in Belgium. Libraries opened in the past few decades disseminated their reading of Islam and the ideology. Technological tools of the day also spread the word: in the 1980s cassettes propagated the writing of Sayyid Qutb and the Salafi and Muslim Brotherhood sheikhs, and today they use the Internet and Islamist satellite TV channels.

Gradually, the concepts of *halal* (religiously permissible) and *haram* (religiously prohibited) were introduced. Muslims previously had no problem eating the food in Belgium, but now they are told that this food is prohibited; it must be halal. Even sweets have to be halal. A whole global industry was built on these two concepts, and guess who profits from it?

Over the past few decades girls and women started to wear headscarves, and later the niqab started to make inroads as well. Some young female students started to become vocal about wearing the headscarf in their schools. Very often they pressured their Muslim female peers to wear it. "Are not you a Muslim? So why are you wearing the clothes of these non-Muslims?" Homogenization becomes easy, especially when the majority of school students in such areas, up to 80 percent, are of migrant backgrounds, mostly Muslims.

Others were pressured by their parents and male siblings: wear the headscarf or else. Sometimes that pressure did not even emanate from their immediate family, but from the social control that spread its mantle over the closed community. Today, you would be hard-pressed to see a woman without a headscarf.

Social control also entailed controlling what others were doing. In the Islamist thinking, a girl should get married at fifteen or sixteen. If she continues to study and does not get married, people in her neighborhood will start to talk. And in these neighborhoods parents *have* to send their children to the Quran schools in the mosques. Every day during the week, from 3:30 to 6 p.m., on Saturdays from 8 a.m. to 3 p.m., and on Sundays from 9 a.m. to 3 p.m. Children do not have real free time: they are either in school or at the mosque. Now, of course, these are the new Muslim religious schools propagating the two forms of Islamism. When social workers try to convince the parents not to send the children to the mosque for these Quran lessons, they shy away from answering—they fear that social control.

Public schools have recognized the problem. Children are entitled to two hours of religion classes every week. All the public schools provide teachers for each of the seven recognized religious groups in the country—Roman Catholic, Protestant, Jewish, Anglican, Islamic, Orthodox Christian, and secular humanist—if enough pupils wish to attend.

Because public school religion teachers are nominated by committees from their religious groups, there is no real supervision over them, or over Muslim or other religious groups for that matter. The Muslim Executive, the controversial official body representing Muslims that was created after Belgium recognized Islam in 1974, supervises these teachers. Muslims in mosques elect the members of the Muslim Executive. Clearly this is a vicious circle.

The government provides financial support for certain officially recognized religious groups. Recognized groups receive subsidies such as payment of clergy salaries, maintenance and equipment for facilities and places of worship, and tax exemptions. This holds true for the Islamic religion.

Yet the relationship between the Muslim Executive and the government was rocky from the start because some were concerned at the growing role of fundamentalism within the body. The conflicts between the Muslim Executive and the state have led to problems distributing the money for mosques and imams. Since 2004, the leadership of the Muslim Executive Council has been overhauled, largely at the urging of government officials who were suspicious of the radical tendencies of the council's former leaders. The government pledged that once a new council and executive were formed, funding to clergy and teachers would begin.

But the problem persists. Belgium houses an estimated 328 mosques, the majority of which are not recognized. Of these, 77 are located in the Brussels region; the Brussels regional government recognizes only eight of them.

Muslim religion teachers mirror the radicalization that shaped Islam in their closed communities and their original home countries and are therefore working in the public schools. Hence, you have teachers from the Salafi, Muslim Brotherhood, and Millî Görüş groups teaching religion to Muslim pupils in public schools.

Questions about reasonable religious accommodations in schools and workplaces became less and less reasonable, especially because of the high proportion of students of Muslim background. Here are a few examples: Muslim pupils and students need to eat halal food in the cafeteria. They need a prayer room in the school. They want to leave classes during the times of prayer throughout the day and on Fridays. They organize ritual foot washings in the bathrooms. For swimming classes, the genders must be segregated and girls must wear a burkini. School trips are frowned upon; some schools had to reduce these trips from several days to just one to ensure girls would participate. Classes should also be gender segregated. Muslim pupils are not allowed to play with non-Muslim pupils on the playground, and vice versa.

And it continues into secondary and vocational schools. Youths studying to become cooks in hotel schools refuse to prepare food that is not halal. Students in vocational schools request exemptions from cooking classes during Ramadan. Youths studying to become caregivers refuse to provide medicines to or bathe elderly people of the opposite sex.

The public transportation organization STIB had to hire mediators because some drivers would not take over a shift after a woman had driven the vehicle. And it had to negotiate because so many drivers were of Muslim background. The same problem is taking place within some other professions, such as garbage collectors.

And anti-Semitism is a serious issue among the youth. When I asked a female social worker with North African roots whether this problem is present in Molenbeek, she looked at me and said, "People call me a Jew, so what do you think?" She does not wear a headscarf and for twenty-one years has been committed to helping the youth in her neighborhood to overcome the alienation caused by racism and by low expectations from their teachers and parents, as well as the active recruitment of Islamists.

Islamists wait for kids in front of their schools, she told me. They give them money and show them an "empathy" that they do not find in their surroundings. She works hard with others to provide the kids with a different viable alternative. Naturally, the Islamists there constantly attack her. And they call her a "Jew" to discredit her.

In light of all the above, is it really difficult to see why Molenbeek has become a breeding ground for terrorists connected to al-Qaeda since the 1990s and more recently for ISIS? Belgium has the highest percentage of foreign fighters in Syrian contingents: 45 percent of them come from Brussels, specifically from Molenbeek and Schaerbeek.[12]

Is it difficult to see why some youths were celebrating—with dancing and chanting—the 2016 Brussels attacks? Or why youth protesters in Molenbeek threw stones and bottles at the police and the press during the arrest of Salah Abdeslam, an accomplice of the 2015 Paris bombers?

They called him their "hero."

7

The White Man's Burden
and the Mainstreaming of Islamism

Y OU HAVE TO GIVE the man credit!
I mean Justin Trudeau, Canada's prime minister. I follow him, and frankly I love his sunny smile, his youthful optimism, his inclusive approach to minorities, and his clear rejection of Donald Trump's populist streak. His heart is certainly on the right side.

So you can imagine my disappointment every time I read about his gestures to Canadian Muslims. I do not mean his kind congratulatory video messages at every Ramadan and Eid (feast). These I like. It is the people he always chooses to work with among Canadian Muslims that make me wonder.

Consider his participation in a charity food distribution during Ramadan on June 16, 2017. He did it with a Muslim charity, Islamic Relief Canada, a Canadian affiliate of Islamic Relief Worldwide. The chair of its board of directors is Dr. Hany El-Banna, the grandson of Hasan al-Banna, the founder of the Muslim Brotherhood. El-Banna is the founder of Islamic Relief Worldwide,[1] which has well-known connections with the Muslim Brotherhood. Its co-founder, Essam El-Haddad, is also a famous figure in the Egyptian Muslim Brotherhood. In 2014 the United Arab Emirates included the charity on the list of organizations it banned for having ties to terrorism (al-Qaeda) and extremism (the Muslim Brotherhood), stating that "many of them have engaged in incitement and the creation of an atmosphere of extremism."[2]

In 2016 the UK-based banking giant HSBC cut its ties with the charity, citing concerns that cash meant for aid could end up with terrorist groups abroad. HSBC is not the only major bank to do so. In 2012 the Swiss bank UBS cut its business relations and stopped all charitable donations for the organization using its accounts. The charity responded with an internal audit that cleared it of any wrongdoing—but note that it never sued HSBC over its allegations.[3]

Affiliates of Islamic Relief also faced scrutiny for supporting militias linked to the Muslim Brotherhood in the war in Syria. For instance, the former imam of Stockholm's mosque, Haytham Rahmeh, long active in Islamic Relief Sweden, was reported to be actively involved in sending weapons and money to extremist fighters in Syria.[4]

So given this cloudy background, why not engage in charity food distribution with another Muslim charity?

∽

This is not a mere coincidence.

Many of our politicians and policy makers work with groups known to have affiliations with Islamist ideology. They are not doing so only out of sheer political opportunism—although many are. It is a pattern, an expression of a paradigm of thinking.

You see its footprints in our daily lives, everywhere.

You see it in the organizers of the Women's March working with CAIR, an organization known to be affiliated with the Brotherhood,[5] as a gesture for the "inclusion of Muslims" in their protest event against Trump. And then you see them using the photo of a woman with a headscarf as a symbol for a minority of women of Islamic faith and solidarity with *Muslim* women.

The headscarf (veil) is a controversial symbol. If you are working in defense of women's rights, you would know that. Some consider it a religious symbol; others see it as a tool of patriarchal control and oppression; and still others see it as symbolizing the march of political Islam. Why do women wear the headscarf? Some do so because they truly believe it to be part of their faith. But others, many others, are forced to wear it. So why choose a controversial symbol—considered a tool of oppression for many women in different parts of the world—as a symbol of a rich and diverse religion like Islam?[6]

You see this thinking as EU policy makers work closely with a well-known Islamist organization, the Federation of Islamic Organisations in Europe (FIOE), and its youth arm, the Forum of European Muslim Youth and Student Organisations. FIOE is described by the *Online Muslim Brothers Encyclopedia*, published in Arabic, as "the European wing of the global Muslim Brothers movement."[7] This political affiliation was simply absent from the English website of the FIOE (currently offline). Instead, it defines itself as an independent organization formed to cater to the religious, social, and cultural interests of Muslims in Europe.[8] No surprise: the EU invites FIOE members to participate in EU work as the "authentic Muslims" representing the *Muslim minority* in Europe and their *needs*.

You see it in the absurd suggestion that Austria's president, Alexander Van der Bellen, made on a TV show: "If it goes on like this…in the face of mounting Islamophobia, the day will come when we must ask all women, all, to wear a headscarf—to show solidarity with those women who do it for religious reasons."[9] He was expressing his opinion about Muslim women wearing the headscarf and the type of hostility they are facing. I understand that it is important to take a stand against this type of racism, but that is not the way to do it: to ask *all* other women to wear the headscarf. Would he have made the same suggestion about those "Muslim women" who do not want to wear the headscarf but are forced to? That would never occur to him.

We also see the paradigm's footprints in the constant attempts by intellectuals, academics, and politicians, liberal and leftist alike, to dilute, relativize, and curtail core human rights in Western democracies in the name of respect for religion. We see it in the attempts to restrict freedom of expression, opinion, and the press in Europe and North America—just recall the controversies over the Muhammad cartoons.

We see it in the 2014 refusal by the UK National Union of Students (NUS) to condemn ISIS atrocities for fear that doing so would be construed as "Islamophobic." A student motion called on the NUS to "condemn the IS and support the Kurdish forces fighting against it," while also expressing "no confidence or trust in the US military intervention." Members led by Black Students Officer Malia Bouattia, who became president of the NUS later in 2016, rejected it. It was reported that Bouattia spoke against the motion: "We recognise that condemnation of

ISIS appears to have become a justification for war and blatant Islamophobia [*sic*]. This rhetoric exacerbates the issue at hand and in essence is a further attack on those we aim to defend."[10]

Seriously? It is Islamophobic to criticize the targeting of minorities and the enslaving of women? Please read the text of the motion—in the link provided in the endnote above—to understand why this argument twisted the facts in the name of a sick identity politics.

The Essentialist Paradigm: The Muslim You Only See

All the actions above are examples of an essentialist worldview shaped by identity politics. Muslims are not individuals with nationalities, people with a diverse range of thinking, traditions, cultures, and worldviews. No. All that stands out in this view is the religious identity—a view that is shaped by what, in another book, I called the "essentialist paradigm": a way of thinking that reduces people of different nationalities to their religious identity, treating them as one homogeneous group, and in the process essentializing their cultures and religion.[11]

Four features characterize the essentialist paradigm:

One feature of this paradigm is the way it views multiculturalism and substitutes for it a de facto *monoculturalism*. It cannot understand multiculturalism as an approach that treats people equally regardless of their origin, color, race, religion, or gender, or that understands they are equal in rights and responsibilities. No. Instead, it is based on a politics of difference: dividing people along cultural, religious, and ethnic lines, and designing polices that enshrine these "differences," setting the people apart, and placing them in parallel enclaves.

Another feature is connected with the first: Because of its focus on what sets people apart, the essentialist paradigm does not treat members of society as individuals with equal rights. Instead, rights are attached to groups and become *group rights*. The group has the rights, not the individuals within it, and this view insists that each group has a collective identity and culture, an essential identity and culture, that does not change and should not be changed, and that this identity should be protected and perpetuated even if doing so violates the rights of individuals within the group.

This leads to violations of human rights, especially for women, children, and individuals of different ideological and sexual orientations, rights that are swiftly downplayed. This brings us to *cultural relativism*, the third feature that shapes the essentialist worldview. It argues that human rights are culturally determined. Hence, the essentialists would insist that we only think that people are suffering when we see their rights being violated, but that in fact they are not, because they understand rights and justice "differently" from us. So a child being forced into marriage at age ten is not really suffering? When her husband insists on having sex with her, it is not the rape of a child? A girl undergoing the mutilation of her sexual organ is not feeling pain? And the health consequences of that mutilation are not real?

This whole picture is very much haunted by the fourth feature: the *white man's/woman's burden*, which is formed from a strong sense of shame and guilt over the Western colonial and imperial past and a paternalistic desire to protect minorities or people from former colonies. It is a mindset that perceives the other, whether a member of a minority group or a citizen of a Third World country, as the oppressed, and that views human rights as the tools imposed by the Western oppressor.

Most troubling, it sees those who are fighting for universal human rights in their own societies as not being authentic representatives of their own countries, and in the process it ignores or justifies dire violations of human rights committed in the name of a group's rights or cultural and religious rights.

～

The essentialist paradigm, with its profound sense of shame, has paved the way for the identity politics that is so widespread today, especially in the United States and Canada. It has shaped the way that policy makers in Western democracies treat the migrants from Muslim-majority countries. When the essentialists look at Muslims, all that stands out for them is the *religious identity*. That is all they see.

The following example from Switzerland highlights what I mean by the essentialist prism: the lens through which we only see the "Muslim" in any person with national roots in a Muslim-majority country.

Kacem El Ghazzali, the young Moroccan intellectual I mentioned in chapter 3, had to flee from his home country to Switzerland because he blogged about his beliefs as an atheist and his critique of Islam. In an interview with a Swiss national newspaper, he recounted an experience he had with a leftist group in Zurich, one that provides language courses for refugees.

In one session of the language class, he explained that he was an atheist. After the end of the class, two refugees with Algerian roots approached him and said he was not welcome in the class. They said they considered what he said a personal attack against them, and they could not sit in the same class with a godless person. He immediately went to the school office and made a complaint; he hoped that what took place would be discussed in the class and that the teacher would make the point that such behavior is not accepted in Switzerland. But, he said, the teachers did not consider this necessary from their perspective.

El Ghazzali then said this:

> I think that many honest Swiss citizens engaged in the refugee sector are afraid of criticizing Islam. They are afraid to be labeled Islamophobic and racist. Therefore, the school has shied away from a debate with my classmates about their intolerant attitude. I can understand that a bit. But integration cannot work this way. Since then, I have not gone to this school anymore. The behavior of my classmates was a clear threat to me.[12]

The young Moroccan thinker was criticizing a pattern that others have observed. But this is not what I would like you to focus on, despite its importance to our discussion.

Instead, consider how a well-known politician reacted to El Ghazzali's comments on Facebook. Jacqueline Fehr, a Zurich government councillor and a member of the Social Democratic Party, obviously pissed off, wrote on her Facebook page: "Is this all it takes to be considered an expert: just be a Muslim criticizing Islam? Why can't journalists check the accuracy of the allegations presented?"[13]

Now I can and do understand that she was trying to defend the leftist group that is working so hard to support refugees. I would have done the same. El Ghazzali was also considerate in his critique, given their efforts to support him. But what raised his eyebrows—and mine—is how she described him: a *Muslim*! The young man just said that he was an atheist, a Moroccan atheist. But all she could see in him was a religious identity he does not even subscribe to: "a Muslim criticizing Islam."

His reaction to her post was simple and right to the point: "Why are you calling me a Muslim?"[14] He added that Fehr perceived him as a "Muslim" in an ethnic sense, which was "typical of the regressive leftists, right-wing populists, and Islamists. For them, a Muslim-born man always remains a Muslim, even if he becomes an atheist."[15]

I realize the parallel I am drawing here may be harsh, but it is like an anti-Semite who looks at a person of Jewish heritage and can only see the Jewishness in that person, nothing else. The *anti-Semite* will feel hate for the *Jew*; the *essentialist* will feel an urge to protect that *Muslim*. They are two faces of the same coin: a racist prism used to approach a complex multifaceted human being.

The essentialist prism is very patronizing. It rarely treats the person as an equal. The essentialist gains a sense of superiority through the way he/she is "supporting"—but in reality condescending to—this "Muslim."

That is why El Ghazzali hit a raw nerve with his direct language. You see, he does not talk or behave like a "Muslim refugee" should talk: ever thankful and grateful for the support he is getting. He was criticizing a culture of silence, and doing so in a civil manner. In effect he was saying: "You are not listening to what I am telling you. You think you can tell me what to discuss, how to be and think, but I am telling you, I am my own person. I am your equal."

Fehr apologized after the issue was splashed across the newspapers, and I respect her for being ready to apologize so promptly. But the perception of this Moroccan atheist is the core of the essentialist paradigm's prism.

Now, if it were only a perception that did not have consequences, I would not have bothered you with it. The problem is it does have consequences—and they are dire. It leads to integration policies based on identity politics that undermine that very integration. Do not forget the Molenbeek case. This perception strengthens the Islamists' control over a diverse group of migrants. It lets people ignore real issues connected to gender equality in the name of cultural sensitivity. And it very often obstructs important policies that should be adopted.

Simply put, essentialists develop a reflex that avoids speaking about problems and addressing them for fear of either being labeled an "Islamophobe" or aligning oneself in one way or another with the far right.

And who has that helped? You guessed it: that approach has led to the rise and popularity of the far right. The far-right forces exploit these problems; they use them as a pretext to air their racist views, without ever seeking real solutions. Yet their message resonates with a wider public: people who are not racist but are simply fed up with mainstream politicians who downplay the significance of real problems with integration.

The essentialist prism has another dire consequence: it designates Islamists as the authentic speakers for "Muslims," their "gatekeepers," so to speak. Just like the essentialists, Islamists insist that migrants of different nationalities, religious orientations, and traditions should be treated as one homogeneous group. They present their own Islamist demands as those of the "Muslim minority," they maintain that they should be given special treatment, and they insist on their "right to difference," which usually translates into violations of human rights. The outcome has been straightforward: they mainstream Islamism through their systematic work on educational projects for children and youth, control the discourse of "Muslim demands," and keep "Muslim" communities separated in closed enclaves.

Four Essentialist Types:
The Intellectual, the Religious Believer, the Leftist, and the Politician

Essentialists come in several varieties. The types I see are the intellectuals, the religious believers, the leftists, and the politicians.

We see the *essentialist intellectuals* in our academic circles. A product of the postcolonial and postmodern paradigms, they can be leftists or liberals. Identity prisms shape them. This type would subscribe to the idea of group rights and hence would insist on treating Muslims as "different," entitled to "special treatment" and consequently to "special laws."

Introducing Islamic law in the Western legal system is one common demand made by this type of intellectual. The impact that Islamic law has on women's rights? That is brushed aside under the banner of "choice": Muslim women can choose which law they want—like groceries in a supermarket. The social pressure that would constrain that "choice"? Also downplayed. And the fact that introducing Sharia law is a core demand of Islamists? No, that does not seem to be a concern for these intellectuals.

In fact they would treat Islamism as a kind of activism: Islamic activism. The totalitarian racist content of the Islamist ideology does not seem to concern these intellectuals; they discard it as part of the "right to difference." Besides, they are sure Islamists will moderate their positions once they learn about the give-and-take of politics. To them, Islam is a political religion, so it should be treated differently anyway.

Many of those intellectuals work in our universities and are financed by monies from the Gulf. That money does not buy their positions on intellectual and political matters. No need for that; they already honestly believe in the ideas they promote. Some of you reading these lines may have already identified some of the more famous ones.

The *essentialist religious believer* is a Western person of faith who does not like the way secularism is encroaching in our societies. These believers see faith as retreating and the role of the church or other religions as under attack or shrinking. They feel uncomfortable in a context where being a person of faith is looked at with ridicule if not rejection; from their perspective, secularization in society has surely gone too far. The presence of what they call the "Muslims" provides a golden opportunity to bring religion back into the public sphere in Western democracies. Supporting the demands of the "Muslims" becomes a way to keep the institutions of their faith relevant in a secularized society. In reality, essentialist religious believers are supporting the demands of Islamists.

One well-known example of an essentialist religious person is Rowan Williams, the former Archbishop of Canterbury, who in a now famous speech in 2008 suggested "integrating elements and mechanisms of Islamic law into British Common Law."[16] Reading his lecture carefully as I wrote my book *Women and Shari'a Law*, I became convinced that what he was actually protesting was the secular encroachment into religious space, using the issue of Islamic law as a stealthy, sophisticated way to do so. I am not alone in this opinion. Bernard Jackson, a world-renowned expert on Jewish law, has suggested that in giving his lecture, Williams's primary interest was in building "a religious coalition, led by the Church of England (as the 'established'

Church)," that would "favour...exemption from secular law on grounds of religious conscience."[17] From this perspective, I found his speech utterly irresponsible.

The third type, the *essentialist leftist*, has yet to metabolize the collapse of the Soviet Union. These people still believe in certain aspects of communism, but today they prefer to call it socialism. They oppose both capitalism and globalization. They are anti many things. That is their position, their opinion. I am not judging here—although I do not hesitate to call communism a totalitarian ideology.

In fact, the problem with essentialist leftists is the way they perceive Islamists. They see them as *allies* against a common enemy: *the capitalist West*. You know the saying "the enemy of my enemy is my friend"? Well, that is how they think.

Because Islamists have presented Muslims as an oppressed group, the essentialist leftists tend to see them as the new exploited proletariat. Here we can see a distorted parallel to Lenin's view of imperialism. Later leftists who take up that view believe that the key divisions are now among nations rather than among classes within states. In the Islamist concept, imperialism means that Muslims are oppressed by external attacks and foreign conspiracies.[18] In the worldview of the essentialist leftist, that means they deserve support in the face of that oppression. So they end up working together, supporting each other.

Finally, the *essentialist politician* can be an opportunist, a believer in the politics of difference, or both. Such politicians know that Islamists can deliver votes—because they are well organized and succeed in mobilizing people. So they work with them because, after all, these are the "authentic" voices of their communities. They are certainly the loudest.

Philippe Moureaux, the Socialist mayor of Molenbeek from 1992 to 2012, is a good example of the *essentialist politician*: he acted out of sheer opportunism but also out of conviction that the "Muslims" are "different," that they need "special treatment" and should be "protected." In the end, he was simply catering to Islamist demands. The result? The neighborhood became a ghetto.

All four types of essentialists have been shaping our policies toward the diverse migrants from countries with Muslim majorities.

The outcome has been a slow erosion of hard-won rights. Gender equality is being compromised within closed communities; freedom of expression is being attacked and curtailed in the name of respect; lines separating religion from state are being blurred as religion seeks to encroach on the education and labor sectors. A group of Islamists are allowed to dictate a policy of exceptions that ultimately leads to the reality of Muslim segregation. The outcome has endangered social cohesion. Popular frustration is coming to a boil: people express anger at the way they see one group treated "differently," given a "free ride," exploiting the "social welfare system," and eroding the major achievement of Western society, namely, the liberal and universal norms and values that protect the dignity and rights of the individual.

~

So I repeat what I said at the beginning of this chapter: all this is no coincidence. Many of our politicians and policy makers work with groups known to be affiliated with Islamist ideology. They are not doing so out of sheer political opportunism—although many are. It is a pattern, an expression of a paradigm of thinking.

And it is more easily done with organizations affiliated with political Islamism than with societal fundamentalist Islamism. Today, it is possible to recognize the dark side of the radical Salafi Islam (or the Deobandi). Today, many politicians are willing to admit that these forms of Islam are extremist by nature and can lead to radicalization.

Jacqueline Fehr, the Zurich government councillor of the Social Democratic Party, whom I mentioned earlier, was quite matter of fact in discussing her reaction to the El Ghazzali interview: "To put it quite plainly, we have a problem with extremism in the dress of Salafism and not a problem with Muslims. The media should also take this into account."[19]

Her accurate assessment does not seem to resonate in Antwerp, where children are sometimes taught in public schools by Salafi teachers, and in Molenbeek, where children are required to go to Quran schools attached to mosques—some of them undoubtedly Salafi.

That said, it is more difficult to make the same judgment about that soft-core smiling Muslim Brotherhood (or its other versions). The first type does not hide its intention; it speaks it, because it believes it, and it is direct and forthcoming with its totalitarian worldview, yet it falls far short of the ISIS style of implementation. The second, smiling type is all about building bridges, creating dialogue between cultures and civilizations, and persistently working with children and youth. It is slippery, like a fish you cannot hold in your hand; it keeps sliding out from between your fingers just when you think you have finally caught it.

The Muslim Brotherhood is like a leviathan with two heads: One smiles, embraces, and speaks a language Western democracies understand. The other is uninhibited, vicious, and only speaks its own language to those who will listen from the "community," preaching a discourse of victimhood and separation, and sowing hatred through the political exploitation of selective chapters of Medina Islam. And in its own closed community, it does not tolerate dissent or deviation.

Because this second type is so hard to pin down, it has been able to make major inroads into the political and party systems of Western democracies. In countries where the political elite embraces essentialist worldviews, they have made the task much easier for political Islamists.

The Swedish case can illustrate this point.

Sweden: Speak Truth to Power?

"Did they smoke something before they read this?"[20] That was Magnus Norell's reaction.

Norell is a Swedish expert on terrorism and political violence, and his remark refers to a report he co-authored, *The Muslim Brotherhood in Sweden*, commissioned by the Swedish Civil Contingencies Agency (MSB). The MSB is Sweden's national intelligence agency, responsible for issues involved with civil protection, public safety, emergency management, and civil defense. It is organized under the Ministry of Defense.[21]

The MSB commissioned Norell and professors Aje Carlbom and Pierre Durrani to conduct a feasibility study. They were to look into the influence of the Muslim Brotherhood in Sweden and to present proposals for future studies and research in the area. The outcome was a thirty-page report with six suggestions for future research.

The argument was straightforward. The authors clearly stated that Islamism is not a distinct type of Muslim faith; rather, it is a political ideology that uses religion to gain legitimacy. They argued that since the 1970s the Muslim Brotherhood has infiltrated Swedish society and its political parties through several organizations and individuals. They maintained that the Muslim Brotherhood succeeded in establishing a completely dominant position in the so-called Muslim civil society sponsored by the Swedish state, and that millions of kroners from Swedish taxpayers have been funneled into these efforts. They argued that the Muslim Brotherhood is building a parallel societal structure and closed enclaves that promote its political agenda. And they warned that these developments represent a long-term challenge to the country's social cohesion and create problems for Swedish society's ability to conduct an effective integration policy.[22]

This is the core of the paper's argument. What obviously hit a nerve was another conclusion of the report. It stated that the structure of values espoused by the country's political elite has provided an ideological opportunity for the Swedish Muslim Brotherhood to promote its own agenda and political project. The political elite has insisted that society should offer minorities cultural and religious rights "in order to be able to preserve or perhaps 'develop' their specific lifestyles." Even if the values espoused by these lifestyles present serious problems, critiquing them has become close to impossible politically.[23]

The political agenda of the Muslim Brotherhood was promoted in Sweden under the banner of minority group rights, multiculturalism, and the politics of difference. A Muslim far-right religious group was allowed to homogenize a diverse community, claiming to speak for it.

It took exactly four days for a backlash against the paper and its authors to be published. Twenty-two Swedish researchers specializing in religious studies signed a letter entitled "Substandard Research in Government Report," which was posted on a blog. The letter stated that the authors of the report made several claims about the Muslim Brotherhood in Sweden for which there was no empirical evidence. It called "problematic" the way the report portrayed the Muslim Brotherhood as an essentially anti-democratic, violent, and society-destructive organization. It said the report named people or organizations that publicly denied any connection with the Muslim Brotherhood. Finally, the letter claimed that the report concluded that Swedish Islam is a homogeneous phenomenon, but that conclusion contradicts existing research that highlights Muslim diversity and inter-Muslim competition in Sweden.[24]

Hence Norell's response: "Did they smoke something before they read it?"[25]

When I asked him to explain what he meant by that response, he laughed and said, "I really did think they might have smoked something. But it is more likely they felt that we were trespassing on their territory" with this report on the Muslim Brotherhood in Sweden.[26]

But Norell was not surprised by that reaction. He said it came from a group of researchers with strong connections to the side of Sweden's political spectrum affiliated with the Muslim Brotherhood: the Social Democratic Party, the Green Party, and the former Communist Party. He said that he would have welcomed any study those researchers conducted about the Muslim Brotherhood in Sweden, but so far there was none. The MSB alluded to this fact in its defense of the report—after all, that is why they commissioned this feasibility study. More such studies are needed because Sweden clearly needs to understand what influence this Islamist network is having on Swedish society and its impact on the country's security.[27]

That fact tells you something about Sweden, Norell insisted. It is not necessarily a lack of interest that led to the dearth of research on the Muslim Brotherhood in Sweden. "It is fear," he said.

He is not exaggerating. A culture of silence is prevalent in Sweden. Those who challenge the way things are being done lose their jobs and political positions and/or become labeled as Islamophobic and racist. Now the interesting part here is that those who are seriously criticizing the status quo in Sweden come from the left side of the political spectrum. So they are not your usual "racists" or "Islamophobes." In fact, they are anything but racists. They are merely concerned about the rise of a political group that is hijacking democratic values and norms to further its far-right religious political agenda. But today it is becoming easy to use the "Islamophobe" label to discredit any critique.

Magnus Norell is a member of the Social Democratic Party—a leftist to the core.

∼

If you think I am misrepresenting the situation, consider the case of the sociologist Göran Adamson, who lost his position as an assistant professor at Malmö University because of a book he published in 2014 criticizing multiculturalism.

Adamson is an accomplished scholar. He earned his PhD from the London School of Economics with a dissertation about right-wing populism in Europe, using the Austrian Freedom Party as a case study. Why are these parties so successful, he asked. And why do people vote for them? He found that only part of their success could be traced to "racism"; a bigger factor is populism, based on critiques of the elite. He found that many voters felt less like insiders than outsiders, so the rhetoric of these parties appeals to their sense of alienation.[28]

Like Norell, Adamson describes himself as a leftist. But as he emphasizes in the English translation of his book, he belongs to the old left, not the new multicultural left. His old left, he insists, advocates for an interesting combination of values:

> meritocracy instead of group rights, majority and democracy instead of adoration of minorities, equality between men and women instead of patriarchy, the rule of law instead of 'minority legislation', science instead of belief, debate instead of censorship, modernity and the bliss of forgetting instead of an obsession with historical injustice.[29]

What really hit a chord, as he critiqued the type of multiculturalism implemented in Sweden, was his ability to show how conservative and racist the roots of the concept were:

> Multiculturalism is a conservative idea, which is seen as progressive. Multiculturalism and diversity are about background, ethnicity, belonging, spokespersons and roots. Those who talk about roots talk about an idyll of the past, a historical Eldorado in contrast to universal suffrage, technological progress, and everything else that belongs to modern society. A conservative ideology does not become more radical just because it is being cherished by journalists, politicians, and academics who say they are.[30]

If that sounds abstract, let me clarify his idea. Remember the expression "separate but equal"? Does that ring a bell? It used to be the core of the racial segregation system in the United States and the apartheid system in South Africa. It divided people into groups based on their race and color, separated them, and then claimed that these groups of people were equal despite their separation. In the United States this idea of legal separation was sanctioned in 1896 by a Supreme Court decision that held that separate but equal facilities did not violate the Fourteenth Amendment of the U.S. Constitution, which applies to citizenship.[31]

To the outside world this kind of system was racist to the core. You can call these groups equal as much as you want, but they remain different and hence should not mingle or marry. And from the outset it was very clear which group was superior.

Now the multiculturalism of group rights does the same thing, but with good intentions. As I put it elsewhere,

> it tends to divide people into boxes: of origin, culture, religion, and, ultimately, gender. It sets them apart, and places them into parallel legal enclaves. Each enclave is governed by a different set of rules: rules that may or may not subscribe to the same notions of law and justice dominant in the larger society.[32]

Do you see what Adamson means? Multiculturalism and "separate but equal" are two faces of the same coin. The type of nationalism advocated by far-right groups, which cannot get enough of their own cultures, is similar to the type of diversity politics espoused by the multiculturalists, with one exception: they are enthusiastically advocating the cultures of "others." It is no wonder, as Adamson says, that the "only Swedish political party talking about roots with an enthusiasm like that of advocates of diversity is... [the] Sweden Democrats," the far-right populist party.[33]

Now you may agree or disagree with his opinions, but for these opinions to get him fired from his teaching position at the university is simply outrageous. The university said that his firing was part of a downsizing of its academic staff. But Academic Rights Watch, an independent organization that monitors academic freedom in Sweden, criticized the firing in a very clear and unambiguous way. In a statement, it emphasized Adamson's excellent teaching and academic record during his ten years at the university, and it maintained that his case was about the right of an academic to write and publish controversial views without being punished for them. Interestingly, the statement reminded its readers that the very group of university insiders behind Adamson's dismissal had tried to do the same with another famous academic.[34] In 2003, Aje Carlbom wrote his PhD dissertation on the same subject, but he focused on its effects on the representation of Muslims in Sweden.

Based on three years living in the Rosengård area, researching the relations between native Swedes and immigrant Muslims, his analysis indicated that Islamist groups were allowed to become the sole speakers for the "Muslim minority" and hence misrepresented their "size" and "demands."[35] Carlbom is one of the co-authors of the *Muslim Brotherhood in Sweden* report.

Given this background, Magnus Norell may have a point in asserting that the real message of these researchers, who are affiliated with the same political side that advocates for Swedish policies of monoculturalism, was not so much about the quality of the research. Rather, it was a warning that fits a particular pattern: "Do not do this. Do not continue doing this. This is going to hurt you. If you continue to dig and look at the Muslim Brotherhood–affiliated organizations, we will come after you."[36]

∽

It should be emphasized that what the report said about the strategy of the Muslim Brotherhood in Western democracies is public knowledge. Starting in the middle of the twentieth century, the Muslim Brotherhood's affiliated organizations have been working systematically to influence the diverse Muslim communities in Western democracies and the political systems of those countries. That strategy has been studied thoroughly, and the literature on the topic is considerable.

For instance, Alison Pargeter, a British scholar of the Muslim Brotherhood, referred to this strategy in a quite matter of fact way in her book on the group. She said that the Brotherhood began to have a presence in Europe in the 1950s and 1960s through students coming to Europe to study and through figures such as the Egyptian Said Ramadan, who sought to spread *dawa*. They became more politicized over the decades, especially in the 1980s, when the International Tanzeem, the Muslim Brotherhood's international organization in the West, was at its peak and Europe became its financial and media center. As a result:

> The Brotherhood built up a network of mosques and Islamic centres, often with money from backers in the Gulf, and was able to spread its *dawa* among Islamic communities. By the end of the 1990s the Ikhwan [the Arabic name of the Muslim Brotherhood] had in many countries been able to establish itself as the primary Islamic organisation, quietly dominating religious institutions across the continent.[37]

There is no secret about that, and the Muslim Brotherhood leadership itself acknowledges it. One of its leaders told Pargeter in an interview: "Wherever Muslim Brothers go they establish institutions. They don't like to work individually."[38]

The strategy was also publicly discussed in 2001, following the 9/11 terrorist attacks, after Swiss police discovered a document when they raided the house of an influential Muslim Brotherhood leader, Youssef Nada, and his associates. The raid was connected to his function as the head of Al Taqwa Bank, which is based in the Bahamas, Switzerland, and Lichtenstein. Founded in 1988 with significant support from the Muslim Brotherhood, and with Brotherhood members on its board of directors, the bank was considered a front for the Brotherhood's financial empire and was accused of supporting terrorism. Two of the bank's directors were supporting the Islamic Centre in Milan, Italy. American authorities identified it as the principal base of Osama bin Laden's networks in Europe. They also accused it of having clear connections to terrorist groups: Hamas, Algeria's Armed Islamic Group, and Egypt's Gamaa Islamiyya. The charges were later dropped due to lack of evidence, but the Bahamas office linked to the Italian center was forced to close.[39]

Nada is an Egyptian businessman who helped arrange financing for the Munich mosque—considered the first beachhead of radical Islamism in the West—and facilitated the setting up of the Muslim Brotherhood in the United States.[40] He never disputed the existence of the document, although he said the title used in the media and in the book by the Swiss investigative journalist Sylvain Besson was wrong. He said the document was not a strategy, only a research paper designed to show how to spread Islam worldwide—and what, he asked, was wrong with that?[41]

The document,[42] dated December 1, 1982, offers guidelines on how to gradually promote the interests of Islamists on a worldwide scale. It lists twelve points of action with practical measures for implementing each point. It calls for the group to "know the terrain [context] and adopt a scientific methodology for its planning and execution" and to "reconcile international engagement with flexibility at a local level."[43]

It calls on its followers to keep the movement from being involved in "major confrontations, which could encourage its adversaries to retaliate, condemning it fatally." It says they must "coordinate the efforts of all those who struggle for Islam in every country and establish quality contact between them, whether they be individuals or groups."[44]

Point five specifically calls for "channeling the thought, education and work to finally establish an Islamic power on earth." This can be done by influencing "the local and world centers of power in the service of Islam." The recommended procedure is "to prepare a scientific study on the possibility of establishing the reign of God throughout the world according to established priorities."[45]

Point nine calls for constructing "a permanent force for the Islamic *dawa* and support movements engaged in jihad in the Muslim world." Here it suggests building "bridges between movements engaged in jihad in the Muslim world and Muslim minorities in the West."[46]

Point eleven makes the Palestinian cause a core issue and calls for its support by "political means and jihad." It suggests the need "to do studies on the Jews, enemies of Muslims," and to "nourish the sentiment of rancor in regard to the Jews and refuse all coexistence."[47]

Besson, an award-winning Swiss investigative journalist, was the first to publish the content of the document and describe its significance in his 2005 book *La conquête de l'Occident: Le projet secret des Islamistes.* The similarities to the popular front techniques the Soviets used in the 1930s were not lost on him—nor on his reviewer. Point seven, for instance, calls for "working with non-Muslim groups on areas of common interest such as Palestine and anti-colonialism."[48]

One of the few undercover agents who had access to the document after its discovery told Besson: "This is a totalitarian ideology of infiltration that represents, in the end, the greatest danger to European societies.... This plan is important because it has been partially placed into service, with some success."[49] Besson himself does not consider the document merely theoretical but rather a "practical guide."[50]

Pargeter downplays the importance of these guidelines, calling it a "fairly mundane wish list."[51] Lorenzo Vidino, the respected expert on the Muslim Brotherhood in the West whom I mentioned in chapter 5, sees the document as the movement's "approach to cultural domination of Western Islam."[52] Neither one denies its existence.

Whether it is a wish list or a strategy, one thing is clear to anyone researching this group in its various geographical contexts: this is exactly what the movement has been doing for the past few decades. In

Vidino's words, it has been the *"modus operandi* of the Muslim Brotherhood in the West."[53] No secret about it.

~

So, I repeat: much research has been conducted, and published, on the strategy the Muslim Brotherhood uses in the West. It is absurd for the twenty-two Swedish researchers to act as if Norell and his colleagues made some kind of "allegation." More absurd is their attempt to disassociate the Islamist organizations mentioned in the report from their connections with the Muslim Brotherhood, insisting in a naïve manner that defies reason that these organizations "publicly denied any connection with the Muslim Brotherhood."[54]

The main organization mentioned in the report, the Islamic Association in Sweden, states quite clearly on its website that it is a member of the Federation of Islamic Organisations in Europe (FIOE).[55] If you remember what I said earlier in this chapter, the FIOE was described by the *Online Muslim Brothers Encyclopedia*, published in Arabic, as "the European wing of the global Muslim Brothers movement."[56] That too is no secret.

Moreover, this connection to the Muslim Brotherhood, now downplayed by the organization's leaders, was openly discussed and acknowledged in 2010 by none other than the current chairman of this very Islamic Association in Sweden. Mahmoud Aldebe is a well-known Swedish Islamist leader who, in addition to his role as a chairman, was previously the vice chairman of the Muslim Council of Sweden. In 2010 he wrote an article in Arabic about the history of the Muslim Brotherhood and Swedish elections. Here is what he said:

> The Muslim Brotherhood started in Sweden through the Islamic Association in Sweden and its different institutions, especially the Stockholm mosque, when it called for political participation in 1986. This took place during the time of the virtuous brother Ahmed Ghanem, who is one of the prominent founders of the Muslim Brotherhood's mission in Sweden.[57]

As far as he is concerned, there is nothing to hide here. The organization and its institutions *are* the Swedish Muslim Brotherhood. Full stop.

Aldebe, who is controversial for several reasons, including his call

to apply Sharia law in Sweden, explains in his article that the association's decision to be politically active in Sweden faced opposition from
the main Muslim Brotherhood and other Islamist groups. The association had to enlist the support of the Lebanese Sheikh Faisal Maulaw,
a well-known Muslim Brotherhood leader, to resolve the conflict.[58]
In 1997, Maulaw worked with Sheikh Yusuf al-Qaradawi, the Muslim
Brotherhood's spiritual leader, to create the European Council for Fatwa
and Research (ECFR), a religious arm of the Muslim Brotherhood in the
West.[59] He helped draft a document that considered political participation an obligation for Muslims. Then the objections subsided.

It is a success story by any measure.

Here you have a group promoting an Islamist religious far-right
agenda. Its ideology calls for the creation of an Islamist state ruled by
Sharia law with no separation between state and religion. It insists on
the supremacy of Muslim believers and hence on a hierarchy of citizenship, at the top of which stand male Sunni Muslims. It segregates
men and women, requires women to cover their heads, and treats them
as minors in need of guardians. It endorses a discourse of victimhood,
fosters hatred against the West and its liberal values, and promotes
intolerance against non-Muslims and non-Sunni Muslims. In the 1980s
it was considered fringe among those migrants of Islamic heritage, and
yet it was turned into the gatekeeper and mouthpiece of the so-called
Swedish "Muslim minority."

Depending on whom you ask, the number of Muslims who live in
Sweden varies. In February 2017, the official website of the Government
Offices of Sweden stated that the "Muslim faith communities" have ap-
proximately 140,000 members, which is about 1.5 percent of Sweden's
population.[60]

The scholar Aje Carlbom, whom I mentioned earlier, says that while
the numbers vary, they are frequently estimated at about 200,000 to
300,000. The majority are migrants who moved to Sweden since the
1960s and live in the three largest cities: Stockholm, Gothenburg, and
Malmö. Their social situation is similar to those in other parts of Europe.
Unemployment is rampant. Segregation, both ethnic and religious, is
a daily reality. And they feel discriminated against. These migrants of
Islamic heritage are diverse. Many come from the Middle East: Egypt,
Iran, Iraq, Lebanon, Palestine, and Turkey. Others come from North

Africa, Algeria, and Tunisia, and still others from Somalia. Bosnians are also part of the demographic picture of Swedish Islam.[61]

And yet, the Islamist umbrella organization Swedish Muslim Council (SMC, Sveriges muslimska råd), whose members are affiliated with the Muslim Brotherhood and include the Islamic Association in Sweden, is considered today the most powerful Islamist movement in Sweden. It has an influential consultative role in matters dealing with immigration and Islam in Sweden.[62] Whenever the government wants advice on the "Muslims," it turns to those affiliated with the Muslim Brotherhood.

Most importantly, as the report on the Muslim Brotherhood in Sweden affirmed, they have infiltrated the political system. How did this happen?

Listen to how Aldebe described it:

> With the blessing and facilitation of the Social Democratic Party and the Christian Democrats within the party, a political committee was formed of prominent leaders in the group. These included, in addition to myself, Ahmed Ghanem, Mostafa Kharraki, Shaykh Haitham,... and Chakib Ben Makhlouf. As a result, dozens of cadres were trained in political affairs. In 1995 the Islamic Political Bloc was created, and it had a strong presence on the political scene. In 1998 the bloc reached the decision-making centers of the Socialist Party and launched a large national campaign in Sweden to urge people to participate in politics, and in return the Socialists made many promises to facilitate the integration of Muslims and to nominate a number of them to party lists.[63]

Remember the *essentialist religious believer* type? The one who does not like the encroachment of secularism in society, who sees faith retreating and the role of the church or other religions under attack or shrinking? The one who feels uncomfortable in a context where being a person of faith is looked at with ridicule if not suspicion? The one who sees in the presence of the "Muslims" a golden opportunity to bring religion back into the public sphere in Western democracies? Well, this essentialist type was central to the success of the Islamists in Sweden. It was the blessing of these people, to use Aldebe's words, that paved the way for the Islamists to become dominant in Sweden's political system.

It started with a crisis of a political nature. The Social Democratic Party (SAP) was losing a large chunk of its constituency. In 1990 the party abolished its policy that made it compulsory for blue-collar workers to join the party. For decades, members of trade unions had been automatically registered as members of the SAP. The decision to end that system led to a great loss for SAP: from around 1,137,042 members in the 1980s, its membership dropped to 284,192 in 1990.[64]

The party had had an unbroken run in office from 1932 to 1976 (except for a three-month interregnum in 1936), returned to power in 1982, and then lost power in the 1991 election. Clearly this was a crisis.

To return to power, it had to seek new constituencies and pools of voters. And which group was considered a likely new pool? You guessed it: the so-called "Muslims." Just as the British Labour Party had done, SAP used communal intermediaries to get that vote. Instead of dealing with these Muslims as Swedish citizens, the strategy was to use gatekeepers to appeal to them through their religious identity and get their votes en masse. But these gatekeepers were not even elected.

Now let's look at the role the Christian bloc played within the SAP.

Unlike most socialist parties on the continent, in the early 1900s the Swedish SAP articulated a moderate position toward religion and the church in Sweden, after a period of anti-clerical and anti-religion hostility toward the end of the nineteenth century. In the 1930s it incorporated religion into its party apparatus by establishing a religious Christian bloc within the party: the Christian Social Democrats. The bloc was ecumenical, open to SAP members of all Christian denominations, and had the effect of depoliticizing religion within the party.[65] This was the group that worked with the Islamists.

In 1994, the Sweden Muslim Council (SMR) wrote to all political parties in Sweden asking them to be part of a dialogue on how Swedish Muslims could be more integrated and active in political work. Two parties responded: the SAP and the Green Party. The SAP Minister of Integration at the time asked the Christian Social Democrats to carry out that dialogue on behalf of the party, as they "understood religion."[66]

The Christian Social Democrats obliged and engaged in a dialogue with the SMR, one that was dominated by the Muslim Brotherhood. It continued until 1999, when they produced a document with the title *Participation, Identity, and Integration*, describing the stages of that dialogue and a strategy to incorporate the "Muslims" into the party's structure and its election lists. Islamists inside and outside Sweden were invited to participate in all these dialogue sessions. These were allowed to define what the "Muslims wanted" and to shape the party's policy measures regarding the "Muslim minority." But the most important measures were those that would integrate the "Muslims" selected by the SMR into the party structure.

The outcome was a strategy suggested in 1999. The joint working group of the two Brotherhoods set up concrete objectives and pledged to actively promote "Muslims" for positions on boards and committees. In addition, by the 2002 term, it promised, Muslims would be elected representatives on fifteen municipal plenary lists and five county lists, and on parliamentary lists in at least five counties. It also vowed that by then SAP would have 2,000 Muslim members, of whom 300 would have received an undergraduate education in political science.[67]

∽

A Swedish journalist, who is a member of the SAP, gave me a copy of that document. It was written in Swedish, of course. I asked a good friend, a brilliant linguist, to translate it for me. Danish of Iraqi origins, he speaks nine languages, including Swedish. His translation was verified independently. When he sent me the translated text, he wrote this sentence at the top: "Wow, how naïve the Swedes were at the time!"

That word naïve sums up the actions of this group of Christian Social Democrats. They did engage in this dialogue with good intentions. If you had asked them at the time what they thought they were doing, they would have said, "We were engaging with the Muslim civil society organizations, and it led to much stronger involvement by Swedish Muslims in political work." That is in fact what a former president of the Christian Social Democrats told me in an email correspondence.[68] Of course that was not how the Swedish Muslim Brotherhood saw it.

Listen to how Aldebe describes this dialogue and its outcome:

> In the nineties, the Jamaa [another Arabic word for the Muslim Brotherhood] presented its best leaders for a dialogue with Swedish parties to emphasize that the Islamic heritage and the peaceful missionary methods the Muslim Brotherhood is using in Sweden are worthy of respect. And indeed the Social Democratic Party, through the Christian Democrats, opened the doors for the Muslim Brotherhood's work through the political bloc.[69]

The Muslim Brotherhood ensured that its leaders were engaged in this dialogue. And those leaders included Haytham Rahmeh, the former imam of Stockholm's mosque, who, as I mentioned at the beginning of this chapter, was "discovered" to be involved in sending weapons and money to extremist fighters in Syria.[70]

For the Muslim Brotherhood, the dialogue meant that the path was opened to their group and their demands. They do not represent the Muslims. Their demands represent only themselves and their political ideology. But that was not how the Christian Social Democrats saw it. From their perspective, they were engaging with a minority faith group—the Muslims—and while they recognized that the dialogue was politically motivated, they honestly thought it could also help with the integration of these Muslims.

Next question: Did that dialogue lead to improved integration policies?

The Christian Brotherhood Movement declared its party's commitment to "intensify the work on current policy issues...specifically [those] pointed out by the Sweden Muslim Council." What were those issues?

- Integration, through deliberations with the Integration Board and the responsible minister
- Employment issues, with the responsible politicians and then with LO, the Swedish Trade Union Confederation, and SAF, the Employers Union
- Day care centers and schools
- Agreements on workplaces regarding Friday prayers
- Legislation, or agreement, regarding Muslim holidays
- Imam education, with the Swedish National Agency for Higher Education and the Ministry of Education
- Halal issues [slaughter] with the Agriculture Minister, the Agriculture Committee, and the Swedish Agriculture Agency[71]

Put simply, the party decided to shape its integration policies in a way that allowed the Muslim Brotherhood to de facto monopolize the measures meant to "integrate the Muslims." This put the Muslim Brotherhood in a position to propagate and institutionalize its ideology and reading of Islam through several venues, including the education of imams.

Education, as one would expect, was on the agenda, and the Swedish Muslim Council was a major force demanding separate facilities for Islamic education.

Aje Carlbom, in his thesis, described in detail the ramifications of these demands. The SMC considered the relationship between Muslim children and the Swedish public schools to be a "most serious problem." It argued that since Muslim families in Sweden live as a minority group among a majority of Swedes, Muslim children would be "affected in the development of their personality and religious belonging."[72] To come to terms with this "problem," the SMC argued for two kinds of social separation, one strong and one weak. The strong model sought a complete break with Swedish institutions. It envisioned the establishment of a public sphere, organized along Islamic lines, that would exist in parallel with other institutions in Swedish society. Here, the SMC held that the solution of the Muslim identity problem was to build a separate system of schools, day care centers, and religious institutions to be run by religiously educated individuals.

The weak model sought to integrate the SMC's reading of Islam with the already established Swedish public sphere by Islamizing literature and religious education, and generally by offering greater opportunities for Muslim pupils to preserve and develop a religious lifestyle.[73]

Which model was chosen? No surprise: the independent Islamic schools. The model used for this purpose was the system of *Friskola*, or charter schools, i.e., publicly funded independent schools. Following a change in the law in the 1990s, parents and their children could choose among tuition-free schools, whether municipal or private.[74] Some of these schools are shaped by a political Islamist ethos, and others follow a curriculum imported from Saudi Arabia.[75]

The outcome of this policy was not integration but segregation. Carlbom explains:

> It is not only during school hours that Muslim children (in Islamic private schools) are prevented from having contact with Swedish children. During the other hours of the day, Muslim children tend to socialize with children from their own ethnic group. During fieldwork

in Rosengård, for example, our son attended a class in a school where several of the pupils were Arabic-speaking. They were about six or seven years of age, and were born in Sweden, but they did not understand the Swedish language well enough to carry on an everyday conversation about the weather.

Once these types of Islamic institutions, demanded by the Islamists, are established in urban neighborhoods where many Muslims reside, ethnic segregation becomes more than a question of people having their private lives in one area and public lives in another. The entire situation becomes what Carlbom calls "ethnified": the public and private lives of immigrants merge in one space.[76]

Starting in the late 1990s, the system of independent schools, and Islamic ones in particular, came under great scrutiny. The system itself was criticized because it fostered social and ethnic segregation. In addition, the Islamic schools were criticized for their poor quality of education and for promoting norms and values that are inherently discriminatory, especially in relation to gender roles, women's rights, and segregation between the sexes. Another critique focused more on the role these schools played in radicalizing youth. It was feared that these schools might develop into a natural recruiting base for "future bombers."[77]

Magnus Norell doesn't think the party really understood what it was doing. That said, the 1999 agreement has allowed the Sweden Muslim Council and other like-minded groups to monopolize educational issues on Islam within the party. They turned "Islam" into something the party—and by extension the whole political field—needed in order to integrate the "Muslims." The Islamist idea of "one" Islam as defined by SMR and similar organizations was uncritically accepted. Equally, the idea that Muslims constitute one homogeneous group was believed without question. It was introduced and used throughout the party and, by default, in the other major political parties.[78]

Of course people within the party disagreed about this dialogue. But those who questioned the dialogue format and the participation of this particular Islamist group were successfully silenced. A former politician, a close observer of this dialogue who asked to remain anonymous, told me this:

> I have friends of Islamic faith, and some are very pious. But these participants were of a different sort. I did not know what they were at the time, I did not know the word Islamist; but it was clear they were extremists. And they were allowed to be part of that dialogue over its five-year span. They would tell us what a "Muslim" is. It is not that they were pious. They wanted to change the system and society.[79]

A culture of silence took hold. Anyone who would critique the status quo, the actions of these Islamist groups, the lack of transparency in their educational organizations, or the consequences of the policies of group rights would be labeled as racist and Islamophobic.

"Islamophobe" has become the Islamists' favorite weapon to intimidate critics and stop questions about their political project.

"They are very polite and generous, but as soon as you ask questions, they are not very polite anymore," said Johan Westerholm, another leftist journalist who was labeled a racist because he questioned the political agenda of the Muslim Brotherhood in Sweden.[80]

This other face of the smiling Muslim Brotherhood came to light ten years ago when the former politician just mentioned above witnessed how they behaved in the closed communities they controlled. A system of tight control prevented dissenting views from being aired, and community activities and meetings were closely watched. If anyone from the community dared to organize community-level meetings without the Muslim Brotherhood's leadership, they were prevented from doing so. This is how the former politician described one incident:

> We had to call the police because they interrupted a community-level meeting and stopped it. Concerned women, who wanted to discuss problems in their community, organized the meeting. But the Muslim Brotherhood's activists came in, interrupted the talks, and put a stop to it. Unless their imams led these meetings, no meetings were allowed to take place.... And the same men I met in these areas, I also met in the corridors of conferences, [and in] the party. So they have two faces, one very kind and very nice, and the other, you cannot believe it, very harsh.[81]

This politician raised the issue in the political party and demanded action to stop this undemocratic behavior. But the concerns and demands were all discarded and hushed up, and eventually the person was accused of being Islamophobic, threatened, and faced with a vicious campaign that necessitated police protection and hiding. Colleagues in the party who were sympathetic to this person's concerns were afraid to voice their support for fear of also being branded Islamophobic. Ultimately, the only way out of this seasoned politician's ordeal was to leave politics altogether.

Many social democrats who still think of themselves as social democrats stopped voting for the Social Democratic Party. They cannot fathom how the party can endorse Islamists.

Given all of this background, what Norell and his colleagues described in their paper was simply the reality. The critique of the twenty-two Swedish essentialist intellectuals was not only absurd; it bordered on intellectual dishonesty. The man certainly had a point: "Did they smoke something before they read it?"

The Battle for Values and Norms in Europe and North America

T HERE IS A PATTERN, a structure, and a system. You must have realized that by now.

The pattern starts with a religious message, mainstreamed by mosques, hate preachers, Quranic schools, and civil society organizations working with children and youth. These are the structures erected by generous financial support flowing from governments, private donors, and transnational charity and civil society organizations. The religious message is in the Medina form of Islam, a fundamentalist reading of Islam. Through these structures it is mainstreamed systematically via an educational strategy into a politicized form of religion: an ideology that leads to indoctrination and that shatters social cohesion wherever it metastasizes, in Muslim-majority societies as well as in Western democracies.

A stern angry politicized form of Islam is displacing and eradicating local forms of Meccan Islam, and with it a history, a tolerant tradition, and a rich civilization.

Taizz is a city in the highlands of southwestern Yemen, near the port city of Mocha on the Red Sea. There, in the 1970s, young women would wear their traditional colorful dress, called a *zana*, and underneath it a pair of trousers. The dress would generously highlight the contours of their bodies, and they would stand up proudly: nothing to be ashamed of. This is their traditional dress, beautiful and colorful. Their heads would be covered but also in the traditional way. Their hair would be partly visible and of course their faces. It was a way of dressing that reflected their history and local tradition. People there used to listen to music and celebrate their traditional feasts with dances, and they went enthusiastically to the new movie theaters that were built at the time. Though sectarian differences did exist in Yemen, people experienced a level of tolerance unheard of today. Yemenis would pray in any mosque without asking whether it was a Zaydi (a Shiite form of Islam) or a Sunni mosque. The god they believed in at the time was not so choosy or picky. He or she was a smiling god.

The generations that were born since the mid-1980s do not know that. Today, if a girl does not cover herself in black from head to toe, she is a fallen girl. Today, if she goes to the movies, she will be considered promiscuous: an easy woman, a fair target for any man. Music and dance are considered evil. People do listen, of course; they follow the devious music programs offered by the satellite channels, but the guilt they feel is like torture. These generations are told that in the afterlife, god will pour melted iron into their ears because they listened to music. Imagine that fear. Imagine the guilt. Music and dancing were intrinsic features of Islamic civilization even in the main holy cities of Medina and Mecca. Muslims used to go on pilgrimages in caravans accompanied by dancing and singing men and women. But all of this rich history is lost on these recent generations.[1]

Pray together in a mosque of a different sect? Are you kidding? God will not accept such a prayer. In fact, praying with the "wrong imam" can sometimes lead to more than a frowning god. For example, in India in 2009 the Barelwi mufti, the highest Sufi Barelwi expounder of Islamic law in India, issued a fatwa decreeing that 200 of his followers should marry their wives again because they had participated in a funeral prayer led by a Deobandi imam. The fatwa stated that since they do not regard the Deobandis as being sufficiently Muslim, all those who said their *namaz* (prayers) under that imam ceased to be Muslims.[2]

There was a time when such an outrageous religious edict would be received with laughter and ridicule in Indian Muslim communities and in Yemen. But not today, I am afraid. Sectarian differences are now deeply ingrained, and the radicalization caused by Sunni fundamentalist readings of Islam has led to an equal radicalization of some other forms of Islam.

The footprints of this pattern, with their structures and system, are also discernible in Western democracies. Children born in closed communities after the 9/11 terrorist attacks never really knew the joyful traditional forms of Meccan Islam in their countries of origin. They seem to believe that there is only one form of Islam, one that should govern every aspect of life—and anything else is corrupt and deviant. They may not follow it, but they know that if they do decide to follow the right path of religion, it is their only way toward salvation. They do not know the history of their religion and its diversity or the richness of their civilization. They also seem to internalize the victimhood narrative of the Islamist discourse, strongly adhering to the notion that Islam is indeed under attack, so they tend to fall back into their community— into a self-imposed isolation. Young girls are told to cover themselves in the name of religion, both boys and girls are told not to imitate the *kuffar* (unbelievers), and preachers of hate mainstream segregation and hatred in the name of preserving "identity."

What allowed this form of Islam to become mainstreamed was the politics of survival used by leaders in Muslim-majority countries: "Legitimize my regime, and I will let you spread your message in mosques, schools, and the media."

In Western democracies, it was the essentialist paradigm, laden with its white man's burden and politics of difference that opened the gate for the Medina form of Islam and Islamist ideology: "Welcome 'Muslims,' we respect you and your difference!" Except that the "Muslims" were not really paying attention; they were busy making new lives in their new host countries. But the Islamists, with their resources and organizational structures, were more than happy to jump on the bandwagon and play the game of difference. Indeed, the road to hell is paved with good intentions.

What happened in other parts of the world is not the focus of this book. My concern here is what is taking shape in Western democracies. You must have noticed that. What is at stake here is precisely the hard-won liberal, secular, and universal norms and values that protect the dignity and rights of the individual in our societies. Something is changing in our societies; many realize that, and they react in different ways. Some are unable to articulate it, others hesitate to point it out for fear of being labeled racist, and still others focus on it while steaming with anger. But none of those reactions will do. Silence is a recipe for long-term conflict. It erodes social cohesion, trust, and solidarity, and it paves the way for far-right racism. The core of the issue here is the struggle to preserve universal humanist norms and values. Do not forget how long it took to achieve gender equality. Yes, we are still working on it, but what we have achieved so far is worth preserving. Do not forget why freedom of expression and the separation of religion and state were instituted. Their absence leads to tyranny, abuse of power, the hegemony of religious institutions, and religious conflict.

And yet, instead of firmly defending these values and norms, we watch silently, in agony, while these norms and values are jeopardized, gradually eroded, and diluted. We do not seem to have the strength, the conviction, or the belief that these are norms and values worth fighting for.

"This is what we stand for." How about that for a clear position? It makes you feel uncomfortable. I can sense that. But that kind of stance is what we need today. What is the problem in defending values and norms that were developed to protect the dignity and rights of the human being in our societies? Why should we apologize for doing so? If you have lived, as I did, in countries that do not guarantee these rights, if you experienced the humiliation, violation, and fear that are attached to their absence, you will know why they should be preserved and fought for. Many young men and women are doing just that in Muslim-majority countries: fighting for these rights and paying a heavy price with their liberty, safety, and lives.

And the rest of us? We stand here, haunted by self-doubt, rubbing our palms, sweating, fearful of "imposing our values on the other." We almost seem to be apologizing for having values. One would think you were trying to impose malaise and harm on another human being. If they are only *your* values, why do you think there is a universal struggle for them in many parts of the world?

We stand afraid. So haunted by our essentialist prism and our white man's burden that we are allowing a far-right religious group to erode a heritage of liberal, secular values, norms, and human rights in the name of religious freedom and the protection of religious feelings!

We are losing ground.

In the following sections I will draw you several pictures of what is taking shape in our societies. Islamists understand mainstream Western politicians and intellectuals better than you think. They play on their fears, burdens, self-doubts, and essentialist prism, and of course their self-interests. Those who do not fall for this game are immediately called Islamophobes—a term used to gauge and silence their critics. And it works: they have succeeded in pushing through changes that reflect their religious far-right agenda. Do not blame the "Muslims" for this; the "Muslims" are a construct, created by both the essentialists and the Islamists. Blame those who willingly played themselves for fools.

The Silence of Islamophobia: Shut Your Mouth or Else

I smiled when reading the tweet that Sam Harris alluded to in the *Atlantic*:

> Islamophobia. A word created by fascists, used by cowards, to manipulate morons.[3]

Harsh words, I know, but they do not waste any time in pointing our attention to the core of it: manipulation.

Islamophobia is a term used to stop any discussion on Islam and Islamism, to silence people, and to defame anyone who is critical. While I say that, I do not dispute the existence of anti-Muslim racism. In other words, I distinguish between the *right to criticize* any religion or political ideology that misuses religion, and *racism* toward people because of their religious beliefs. The first should be supported without question, and the second should be condemned forcefully. Many people still do not see that distinction.

For the sake of accuracy, let me state that fascists did not create the term. Some say that it was first used in a 1997 report by the Runnymede Trust, a left-leaning British think tank, with the title *Islamophobia: A Challenge for Us All*. The term was defined as a kind of "hostility toward Islam and Muslims"[4] or a "shorthand way of referring to dread or hatred of Islam—and, therefore, to fear or dislike of all or most Muslims."[5] The editor of that report, Robin Richardson, disputes the "accusation" and insists the report merely borrowed a term that was already in use.

He says that the first known use in print of the word was in French:

islamophobie. It appeared in a book by Alain Quellien, published in Paris in 1910, with the title *La Politique Musulmane dans l'Afrique Occidentale Française.* The author was criticizing the ways that French colonial administrators viewed the cultures of the countries now known as Benin, Burkina Faso, Côte d'Ivoire, Guinea, Mali, Mauritania, Niger, and Senegal.[6]

Edward Said was the first to use the word in English in 1985. He referred to it rather casually, condemning those who criticized his book *Orientalism* for their failure to see a connection "between Islamophobia and anti-Semitism" and to understand that "hostility to Islam in the modern Christian West has historically gone hand in hand" with anti-Semitism and "has stemmed from the same source and been nourished at the same stream."[7]

In the UK, the first known use of the word in print occurred in a book review by Tariq Modood, a British-Pakistani scholar—today a professor of sociology, politics, and public policy at the University of Bristol—in the British newspaper the *Independent* on December 16, 1991. Modood did not define the term but simply used it in his critique of Salman Rushdie's *Satanic Verses.* He wrote of the view that the novel was "a deliberate, mercenary act of Islamophobia" but also stated his own view: "while Islamophobia is certainly at work, the real sickness is militant irreverence."[8]

It should come as no surprise that Said and Modood were the first to use the expression in English. The first was instrumental in creating the framework for the postcolonial paradigm in academia. Well-known postcolonial scholars could be described as having essentialist worldviews of Muslims. The second was crucial in propagating the concept of "equality through pluralism": that rights should be given to Muslims because of their "difference."[9]

So no, it was not fascists who invented the concept, but well-respected intellectuals, who helped produce a paradigm that opened the door to Islamists. I won't use the word cowards for those who use the expression. That does not describe them at all. Instead, they are members of a far-right religious group with a political agenda.

Of course, others use the term too, including well-meaning individuals who are seriously worried about anti-Muslim racism. I do not include them in this discussion. In fact, I applaud their alarm. I only wish they would see how the expression has been manipulated to promote an extremist political project and, as a consequence, has undermined a cherished right, the freedom of expression. They should preserve that right just as they are trying to preserve the dignity and rights of those facing racism.

Hence comes the manipulation. The expression has been used systematically to stifle any critique of an Islamist political behavior, agenda, project, or fundamentalist reading of religion. The former Swedish Social Democrat politician mentioned in chapter 7 only criticized the undemocratic actions of groups affiliated with the Muslim Brotherhood, who stopped any community meetings they had not organized. But a gender dimension was also operating there. Who organized those meetings? Women who were concerned about the developments taking place in their own communities. It is very often women and girls who are the first to suffer within closed communities.[10]

But the Brotherhood-affiliated members would stop any discussion before it even started. They would come and disrupt the meetings: "Either we organize these meetings, or no meeting will take place." That was the message sent by their actions. But how did the Social Democratic Party react? They could have looked at this problem and its implications and acknowledged that there is diversity within Muslim communities and that no group has the right to monopolize community work. Instead, the blame was put squarely on the former politician, whom the Brothers could conveniently accuse of being Islamophobic. And the fools, the ignorant leaders of the Social Democratic Party, followed their lead and condemned this politician.

Within the party, those who disagreed kept silent. They were afraid of being defamed like their colleague. Their silence made them accomplices in spreading a culture of fear: keep quiet, or we will make an example of you.

"I am tired of being called the racist," said Johan Westerholm, the Swedish journalist I mentioned in chapter 7. He is being labeled a racist and an Islamophobe for insisting on knowing how taxpayers' money is being used by educational organizations affiliated with the Swedish Muslim Brothers. Certainly the Brothers are not acting outside the law? Or are they? So why label him an Islamophobe when he is actually demanding transparency from civil society organizations affiliated with a political group?

"Now people [in Sweden] are getting fed up at being called racists, and the real racist neo-Nazis are raising their voices," he continued, his voice laden with worry. The real racists are now starting to make inroads into public discourses. What made their comeback possible? The silence of the well-meaning mainstream.

It is interesting to consider who writes the many reports splashing accusations of Islamophobia against intellectuals, experts, or think tanks. Those authors are often affiliated with the Muslim Brothers or other Islamist groups. But no surprise, those being defamed are often critical of the Brothers in their work and publications. Very often, the Islamophobic Islamist industry uses the strategy of mixing the eggs: good eggs with bad. That is, in their reports they criticize well-known racists, who should be criticized, but then they bring in the names of the personalities who are the real targets of their defamation campaign. These are intellectuals and scholars researching the Brothers or other like-minded Islamists. One writer recently did just that to me. He had nothing to say about me other than this: "[She] argues that Islam has to be fundamentally reformed. What does she mean by that?"[11]

Well, I mean exactly what the words say: my Islamic religion needs to be fundamentally reformed. Where is the problem in airing such an opinion?

⁓

I think you might be inclined to agree with my argument that it is legitimate to criticize the conduct, politics, and ideology of Islamist movements. So let me move to another important dimension in this discussion: Is it legitimate to criticize the Islamic religion or its symbols?

Some of my students are inclined to say no. "We should respect Muslim religion and their sensitivity," they would argue. From my perspective, I think it is important to criticize religions and their symbols, if only for the simple reason that they need to be checked and tamed. How are we supposed to reform a religion if we are faced with defamation, imprisonment, or death? How do we stop the abuse of power when we are told that religious figures, teachings, and symbols are not to be touched? How do we introduce social reforms when we are told that religions are sacred and are not to be criticized? Do not forget the young Mauritanian man who was imprisoned for demanding an end to slavery in his country. His critique of the Islamic religious history that legitimizes this practice in his country landed him in prison and almost cost him his life.

And, I dare ask, why should one religion be above investigation? Islam is just like any other religion in Western democracies and thus should be treated as such. Get used to it.

"Islam is not a race, ethnicity, or nationality: It's a set of ideas," Sam Harris said in an interview in the *Atlantic*. "Criticism of these ideas should never be confused with an animus toward people. And yet it is. I'm convinced that this is often done consciously, strategically, and quite cynically as a means of shutting down conversation [on] important topics."[12]

I agree with him.

It should be possible to address and discuss problems of integration and gender equality, as well as issues related to fundamentalism and extremism within migrant communities, without being defamed as an Islamophobe. That should be possible, right?

It should also be possible to criticize and make fun of the Islamic religion and its symbols.

In 2014 *Charlie Hebdo*, the leftist satirical magazine, was not just targeting the Prophet of Islam with its cartoons; it was targeting all sacred figures of all religions. And it was pushing that point deliberately because a culture of fear was consistently trying to stop satire from doing its job in Western democracies—which is to poke fun at powerful institutions.

Do you remember the twelve cartoons that the Danish *Jyllands-Posten* newspaper published in 2005? Do you know why they decided to publish them? The culture editor, Flemming Rose, explained that it was in fact "in response to several incidents of self-censorship in Europe caused by widening fears and feelings of intimidation in dealing with issues related to Islam." Do you remember what played a major role in that self-censorship? In 2004 an Islamist assassinated the Dutch filmmaker Theo van Gogh over *Submission*, the film he made with Ayaan Hirsi Ali. When Rose learned that a Danish author writing a book on

Muhammad was having problems finding illustrators, Rose contacted forty illustrators and asked them to draw cartoons on the subject. He was curious to see what their responses would be. Only twelve cartoonists responded, and their cartoons were published.[13]

The *Jyllands-Posten* cartoons were mostly harmless; only two depicted Muhammad negatively. One drew him with a bomb-shaped turban and another as an assassin. Some of the *Charlie Hebdo* cartoons were tasteless and offensive. Whether I like them or find them distasteful, the magazine and newspaper have every right to publish them. *Freedom of expression includes the right to offend.* There is no room here for cultural relativism. When people are killed for exercising their right to expression and satire, it is the killers who should be condemned, not the artists and journalists. It is those who are spilling blood, not those drawing with their pens, who should be condemned.

Please note that in all the high-profile cases of freedom of expression, Islamists played an important role, inflating these issues until they took on the proportions of a "clash of civilizations." It is in their interest to do so: it fits into their narrative of victimhood and of the alleged ongoing conspiracy to destroy Islam.

Their role has been documented, starting with the Salman Rushdie affair. Competing groups of Islamist organizations, including Jamaat-e-Islami, the Deobandi movement, and the Muslim Brotherhood, worked hand in hand with Saudi Arabia in orchestrating the demonstrations and the public burning of the book. And Islamist Iran entered the picture by stealing the show when Khomeini issued his famous fatwa.[14]

In the case of the Danish cartoons, three extremist imams created what they called the Committee for the Defense of the Honor of the Prophet and then orchestrated the international campaign. It was no coincidence that the *Jyllands-Posten* had exposed two of them before the cartoons were published. Nor was it a coincidence that the Muslim Brotherhood fanned the flames, with their spiritual leader, Yusuf al-Qaradawi, using his weekly program on Al Jazeera to incite public opinion against Denmark. And, no surprise, the Saudi-owned websites were the first to run articles with headlines such as "Who Will Hurry to the Defense of the Prophet Muhammad?"[15]

In interviews and in a booklet they presented, the three imams deliberately distorted information by showing cartoons that were never published, and they repeated several blatant untruths about the oppression of Muslims in Denmark. They claimed Muslims do not have the legal right to build mosques and that the Danish government was planning to censor the Quran.[16] They were spreading lies, and their strategy fit the actions of Islamists on a mission to create a clash of civilizations.

It is a strategy, well orchestrated and connected to a global Islamist ideology, and it mirrors the tyrannical oppression of freedoms of expression, thought, conscience, and religion within Islamist countries.

So it is imperative to go beyond a localized focus on events and look at the bigger picture: the global context.

Do you remember what happened after the *Charlie Hebdo* massacre? On January 7, 2015, one day after the attack, Saudi Arabia released a statement through its official news agency condemning the massacre, calling it a "cowardly terrorist act...incompatible with Islam." Then, on January 11, the Saudis sent their ambassador to Paris to join more than three million people, including fifty world leaders, marching in solidarity with *Charlie Hebdo* and in defense of freedom of expression.[17]

Yet two days after the massacre, this very same government pulled the Saudi blogger Raif Badawi out of his jail cell in Jeddah, brought him to a square in front of the Al-Jaffali Mosque, and administered the first phase—fifty lashes—of a public flogging. Badawi was guilty, as his indictment put it, of "insulting Islam" and "producing what would disturb public order, religious values, and morals."[18]

The discrepancy could not have been more astonishing.

Here is where we must connect the dots. Those who killed the journalists in Paris were followers of *violent* Islamist extremism. Those who flogged Raif are followers of a *fundamentalist* Islamist extremism. The first group kills in the name of God; the second violates in the name of God.

And yet, while we have no problem at all condemning Saudi Arabia for flogging Raif Badawi, some of us will hesitate to show the same support for the journalists in Paris. You hear people whispering, "Of course we do not condone the killing, but these journalists should have been more sensitive to the religious feelings of Muslims."

Whom are we accommodating here? Muslims or Islamists? The "Muslims" will protest peacefully, but the Islamists will kill those who express views they do not agree with. So whom are you accommodating here? The appeasement and self-censorship only support the Islamists' fear campaign, terrorizing journalists and artists with a single aim: to silence their voices.

There is no room here for cultural relativism. Without freedom of expression, there is no freedom at all. And this freedom should be protected. Think of all the authoritarian and theocratic states around the world: the one thing they have in common, in addition to their human rights violations, is the absence of freedom of expression. Safeguarding freedom of expression is not a luxury. It has a crucial function for any functioning democracy.

Authoritarian governments require that absence: it enables them to exercise unlimited power without opposition and to justify their violations of citizens without opposition. That absence leaves religious institutions free to spread a kind of religious terror that aims to silence critical thinking and demands for accountability.

The choice is clear here, and it does not involve censorship in the name of religion or culture. It requires an unequivocal defense and support of the exercise of freedom of expression. Rather than succumbing to the persistent attempts to circumvent this cherished freedom, we should insist that this is a norm that we are happy to share with the world. It protects against tyranny, corruption, and the excesses of religions. The problem does not lie in the exercise of freedom of expression but rather among those who are curtailing it in the name of religion and culture.[19]

They Start with the Woman First

When she started working at the school in 2001, she did not think the headscarf was an issue. Karin Heremans was headmistress of the Royal Atheneum in Antwerp, Belgium. But by 2009 she made headlines for her decision to ban all headscarves in this very school.

Some of you may be rolling your eyes now. The headscarf again. Can't we just move on? No, we can't. Please indulge me for a moment.

There is something very odd about the issue of the "headscarf" and the "Muslim woman." What is odd about it has to do with its effects on us when we try to discuss it. Yes, there *are* issues to be discussed: it tends to get under our skin, it makes us angry and nervous, and sometimes we end up behaving irrationally. In fact we often try to stop the discussion before it even starts.

I use the pronouns "we" and "us" a lot. And this can be confusing. By "we," do I mean people of the human race, of Muslim-majority countries, or of Western democracies?

The first is my favorite "we"; I use the other two within their contexts. I belong to all three categories, and that makes me a bridge. But when it comes to the "headscarf" and the "Muslim woman," I mean the "we" that is all of us.

We get emotional when we talk about this "piece of cloth" and the "right" of a "Muslim woman" to wear it. Some well-meaning Western women are actually engaging in campaigns to wear headscarves as a sign of solidarity with the "Muslim woman." They sincerely believe that their actions will help the "civil rights" of the Muslim woman. If you are one of these women, I ask you to recognize that the issue is not as simple as you are made to believe. There is an element of choice in the matter, of course, but the issue also has social, power, ideological, and political dimensions. When you look at the issue from all of these dimensions, it becomes clear that it requires action, and those actions certainly do not involve silly campaigns of wearing headscarves. Do I need to remind you who is organizing these campaigns?

Allow me therefore to use Karin Heremans, and her school in Antwerp, as a starting point for this discussion. Hear me out first and don't throw this book at me yet. Heremans is everything you would wish for in a headmistress: energetic, optimistic, dedicated to her students, and a humanist to the core. I met her over dinner in Antwerp during my most recent visit to Belgium in September 2017.[20]

"The decision was necessary," she told me. "It was not a decision against the Muslims or the headscarf. It was a decision against manipulation in the school. I had to protect my students."

And it was a very difficult decision for her. Necessary, and yet as painful as it was difficult.

The school, the Royal Atheneum, has a distinctive history. It was the first state school in Flanders, founded by Napoleon two hundred years ago, and has evolved along with the demographics of the city. As a bastion of freethinking, it has a long tradition of shaking Flanders up a bit. Still, it is known for sending lots of pupils to university. When she started her work, ten days before the 9/11 terrorist attacks, she told an *Economist* journalist, "I spoke to the teachers and they said, oh, the quality is gone, there are so many foreigners." At the time, there were students of forty-five nationalities in the school, and 46 percent were Muslim. Other students were Catholic, Protestant, Greek Orthodox, and Jewish.[21]

She had a rough start at the school. The 9/11 terrorist attacks led to a clash of cultures. A government call for one minute of silence was met with mixed feelings. Students complained: "Nobody held a minute of silence when our family members were killed in Yugoslavia or in Afghanistan." She responded by going around to the classrooms where she proposed a second minute of silence for all victims of war and violence. That went over well.

She knew there was much to do at the school. Together with her team she launched an intercultural religious dialogue, and the religious teachers of different faiths had to do joint projects. Projects about issues that matter to adolescents—like sexuality, elections, living together— were important for that dialogue. Heremans could see it was time to humanize the school. Four themes were launched, one per year for four years: time, choice, space, and humanity.

When it came to choice, the school organized a fashion show with girls wearing scarves or not. "One girl wore half a scarf to show her uncertainty. We wanted girls to decide," she explained.[22]

So what changed then?

A demographic shift, along with the work of a group of Islamist students, changed the situation. In 2001, the student body was 46 percent Muslims; by 2008 that percentage had risen to 80 percent. Two factors can explain this spike. On the one hand, the number of Muslims in Antwerp increased. On the other hand, schools changed their policies on headscarves. They changed their headscarf rules quietly, one by one, and by 2008 only three schools in the city allowed scarves. The Royal Atheneum was one of them.

"At the beginning, I didn't see a problem, we'd do a dialogue among Muslims. But then, because we were one of the only schools to allow scarves, we attracted a very conservative group, who identified very much with the veil."[23]

At the time, Heremans explained to me, she did not know about the Islamist affiliation of this student group. In 2015 she realized they were members of the Sharia for Belgium group, a radical Salafist organization that called for Belgium to convert itself into an Islamist state. In February 2015 the Belgian judiciary designated them a terrorist organization.[24]

Something changed in the school, and the headscarf was central. Things that had been possible before started to be impossible: girls could no longer go on school trips unless they were accompanied by their brothers, and swimming classes became an issue. Bizarre demands were made to separate the boys and girls into different classes. Girls started to wear the veil—one after another. Peer pressure was central to this development. When asked, the girls said they did not feel very comfortable without a veil. Other girls would wear the veil at school, but teachers saw them outside the school without veils. There was a sense that the girls wearing the veil were trying to show they were more pious.[25] In the school year 2007–8, fifteen girls of this Islamist group came to school wearing long robes and gloves, with only their faces showing. The scarves became longer and longer. In 2003, the discussion was still about whether or not the girls should wear the veil. By 2008, the discussion was about how to wear the scarf. Not whether.[26]

Heremans had to change her position on the headscarf. Earlier she had insisted that each girl had the right to wear a veil, to preserve equality. But the heavy oppressive atmosphere over the schoolyard made it clear to her that the choice had been compromised by social and peer pressure—manipulated by a group of savvy young Islamists.

"It was only because of the infiltration of extremists in my school that I had to ban the scarf...because there was no freedom any more. And it is strange: when we took away that symbol, freedom returned. Before that, girls would no longer dance; they did not want to go Paris, or to swim. I took the symbol away, and all that disappeared."[27]

Five girls came to her after the ban was lifted. They thanked her. "We feel freer...you've no idea the pressure we were under."[28]

On September 11, 2009, the Flemish education council followed suit and passed a rule banning the veil across the 700 secular state schools it runs in Flemish-speaking Belgium. Karin Heremans felt supported.

～

Like it or not, the headscarf is political. It is the core of the Islamist political project. With it, they mark their presence.

If you think I am exaggerating, listen to Essam el-Erian. He was the Egyptian vice chairman of the Freedom and Justice Party, the Egyptian political party of the Muslim Brotherhood, as well as a former member of the Guidance Bureau of the Muslim Brotherhood. He was in fact gloating about the Brotherhood's success in spreading the headscarf in Egypt without force. In a recorded talk, he explained:

> When I entered medical school in 1970, there was only one veiled student, and we [the Muslim Brotherhood group] realized that it was necessary to control this situation. So we decided to launch our missionary work, so women would choose the veil for themselves. We started to distribute booklets, statements, and the book *To Every Girl Who Believes in God*, written by the Syrian [Islamist] preacher Mohammed Said al-Bouti. Given the fact that the veil was not used at the time, we took action to remedy the situation [by providing a supply] and made a deal with certain factories, which enabled us to distribute the veil to the students at the university at production cost. Five years later, a third of the female college students were wearing the veil.[29]

When they launch their missionary work, this is how they start. They start with the woman first, controlling her behavior and getting her to cover her body. And they play on her religious feelings, guilt, and fear.

"If you do not cover up, you will be disobeying God, displeasing him," they say, "and you do love God, do you not?" And: "You also will be responsible for the sins committed by men who are seduced by your beauty. These poor men cannot control their desires, and you are constantly seducing them with your hair and body." And: "You will burn in hell if you do not cover up. Hell is filled with women held from their hair, for their sins."

Tell me, please, how is choice being exercised here? Where is choice when young girls and women are constantly told they will burn in hell if they do not cover themselves? This reminds me of a young woman phoning in to Maajid Nawaz, a British activist, radio host, and author of the book *Radical: My Journey out of Islamist Extremism*, on his British talk show on LBC in September 2017. He criticized British schools that allow girls as young as five to wear the headscarf. The young woman condemned him for that, saying she is proud of her headscarf, which she has worn voluntarily since she was seven. When he pressed her to tell him why she is wearing it, she answered that if she took it off, God would punish her by burning her in hell.[30] The irony in what she said was lost on her.

Would she wear it if she were told that God would love her with her hair uncovered and that she would not burn in hell? I am inclined to say no, she wouldn't. And, you know what? God has nothing to do with this. The Quran never mentioned a headscarf. In fact, the Quran never introduced a dress code.

The way women dressed in the seventh century, at the time of Muhammad, the Prophet of Islam, reflected the traditions during that historical period. The verses used to justify covering women were in fact an injunction that asked *free* Muslim women to cover their breasts so that they could be distinguished from *slave* Muslim women. At that time Muslim women, both slave and free, walked in public with their breasts uncovered. During a time when Muhammad had not yet become very powerful, his so-called enemies started to harass his female followers. When he complained, they would reply, "We thought they were slave women." So the Prophet found a solution: ask free Muslim women to cover their breasts. Hence those verses in the Quran.[31]

What people seem to forget today is that for centuries, Muslim women who were slaves would be sold in the market with their breasts bare and would walk in the streets that way. They would pray with their breasts bare. You can find video clips on YouTube showing Saudi slave markets from the 1960s with slave women standing bare-breasted.[32] You can see it in photos and paintings taken in the early twentieth century in Turkey, Egypt, and elsewhere: slave women with their masters. If Muhammad issued an injunction from this custom for all women who are Muslims, why make an exception for slave women? Why would the second caliph, Omar ibn al-Khatab (579–644), the one best known for his rigorous enforcement of religious rules, punish any slave Muslim woman who tried to cover her breasts like a free woman?[33]

I am not inventing this history. It is recorded history in the Islamic tradition and religious books.

The fact that in the 1970s you could hardly find a woman wearing the headscarf anywhere in Egypt, except in rural areas, tells you something about the social change that took place in many Muslim-majority countries—a change mainstreamed by the Islamist ideology of Hasan al-Banna.

Al-Banna first articulated his position on the veil in a tract called *The Muslim Woman*. The original date of this tract is not known, but two points are certain: it was written in the early decades of the twentieth century, and he was in fact reacting to the encroachment of modernity, as more women started to take off the traditional veil. It was also a reaction to Atatürk's vision of a national and secular state. Kemal Atatürk was a young military leader, the first president of modern-day Turkey, and he abolished the Ottoman Caliphate in 1924. To him the answer to the problems of his nation was clear: build a nation-state, modernize it through a comprehensive program of reforms, and adopt secularism as the cornerstone of that state. Central to his vision was the role of the women, who were encouraged to take off the veil and participate actively in society. They were assisted by a new family law imported from Switzerland; conservative as it may have been, it was nonetheless a welcome departure from the Islamic provisions of the Ottoman family law.[34]

Al-Banna answered with his own vision of an Islamist state, one that would ultimately lead to the creation of the Caliphate. To match that ideology he needed a dress code: the veil that covers the woman and leaves her hands and face visible. It was the symbol for a political project, one that sought to create a puritanical society based on a fundamentalist view of gender roles.[35]

Three principles stand at the core of al-Banna's view on women:

1. Men and women have different rights because of their biological differences. It is determined by their biological nature. Accordingly, women should only be taught what suits a woman's natural function and duty. She should be taught "what suits her task and function that God has created her for: to take care of her house and raise children."[36]

2. Segregation between the sexes is a must because men and women cannot be trusted to be alone. They cannot control their sexual

desires and will always be tempted sexually. Hence al-Banna sees "a true risk" in any "mixing between sexes" and insists on separation "between the two of them unless they marry."[37]

3. Wearing the veil is a duty and mandatory. In fact, al-Banna insists that "Islam forbids a woman to reveal her body; be alone with someone; to imitate a man"; it encourages her to "pray at her home" and orders her to "wear the veil."[38]

Of course, it is al-Banna who insists on according different rights to women because of their biological differences, and on segregation between the sexes and veiling for women. God has nothing to do with any of that.

Do you see why, wherever this ideology starts to spread, the veil appears in tandem? The veil is core to its teaching, just as segregation between the sexes is central to its vision of a fundamentalist society. This explains why segregation between the sexes and avoidance of contact between males and females in schools and workplaces start to become integral demands of the Islamists, as they claim to speak for *all* Muslims in Western democracies.

The veil is a symbol. It is the symbol of political Islam. But some of the women who are wearing it today truly believe they are following God's orders. They think that when they wear it, they become "good Muslims." Some of my female relatives in Egypt wore miniskirts in the 1970s but turned to the veil in the 1990s—and think they did so of their own free will. Today a reverse wave is taking place in Egypt, as young women are rebelling and taking off their veils. But, for doing so, many of them endure psychological and physical punishments, defamation, and threats.

In Western democracies the picture is also complicated. In Europe, some young immigrants from Muslim-majority countries turn to the veil as a means of asserting their identity—but it becomes an identity of seclusion. In fact, I know of young women who were so enraged by the Danish caricatures of Muhammad that they began to wear the headscarf. Their decision was not a matter of religion. It was a way of expressing their anger and defiance.

But many others are forced to wear it. Those who insist on not wearing it face both physical and physiological sanctions from their family and community. This pressure and punishment stems from several sources: patriarchal structures, religion, and efforts to control woman's sexuality. I deal with many such cases in my contact with educational authorities here in Switzerland. In certain parts of the UK, some women's rights activists have to wear the headscarf in order to get access to the women trapped in their closed communities. That tells you something about the suffocating social control in place there.

Most importantly, wherever the numbers of Muslim students reach a critical mass in either a school or a neighborhood, peer pressure and group dynamics gain a certain level of clout and force girls and young teenagers to wear the veil. Some will tell you that it was their free choice. But when they try to take it off, they learn that free choice only applies to choosing to wear the headscarf. No free choice the other way around.

Karin Heremans had a point when she said that in her school, there was no freedom any more. What she was facing was extremism infiltrating the school. In the five years between 2003 and 2008, the discussion changed from *whether* girls should wear the veil to *how* they should wear it. The word *whether* had vanished.[39] When she says that these girls needed a safe space, we should listen carefully. Banning the veil in her school was the way to provide that safe space.

When Rules Are Applied Selectively and the Vanishing Social Cohesion

"How would you have reacted if it were Swiss Christian fundamentalist youths making such demands?" I asked the Swiss journalist. He looked at me surprised. It was clear he was thinking about the answer, however obvious it was for the two of us: "Of course I would have criticized it and made an issue of it." But the same reaction does not seem obvious when it concerns a Muslim fundamentalist group.

It was early in the summer of 2016, and we were on the train. He was covering a story, and my role was to comment on the subject as an expert. We had finished our work and were heading back to Bern, and the discussion took us to an issue being hotly debated in Switzerland at the time. Two young teenagers of Syrian origin, brothers aged fourteen and fifteen, refused to shake the hand of their female teacher. Their argument was essentially religious: they are following the commands of their religion not to touch a person of a different sex.

In Swiss schools it is customary for the class teacher to shake each student's hand when they come to class in the morning and when they leave at the end of the day. This custom transmits the message to the students that they are taken seriously as individuals and fosters mutual respect.

The female teacher didn't buy that argument. The school's administration came to a compromise: the two teenagers would refrain from shaking the hands of all teachers, male and female. That way, no discrimination based on sex would take place. At least that was the argument. The compromise made some teachers uncomfortable.

The story quickly became public. Beatrix Grüter, a retired teacher and politician in her seventies, criticized the school's decision on a well-known TV debate program, *Arena*, in a program dedicated to the topic "Fear of Islam." She was expressing the anger and frustration among a circle of women teachers she knows; she said they feel that this compromise discriminates against them.[40]

The debate that ensued drew international attention, and the school had to seek legal advice from the educational authorities in the canton. The latter came to a decision: pupils should shake the hands of their teachers regardless of their gender, and normal disciplinary measures can be applied in case of a deadlock. The importance of integrating the children outweighs religious freedom. That said, the canton's decision fell short of introducing a general rule and left it to each school to apply the measure.[41]

Reactions were mixed. Some supported the decision wholeheartedly: tolerance has limits, the same rules should apply to all children, and there is no room here for exceptions. Others shook their heads in disbelief. And they were frustrated: maybe this was just a matter of teenage rebellion, two kids pushing the limits. Why the big fuss, some said: it's just a handshake. Are we going to force people to shake hands against their will? And others argued: can a person not be religious in our society?

I understood that reaction, but I wasn't convinced. So I wrote an op-ed in the national weekly newspaper *NZZ am Sonntag* with the title "Declining the Handshake Is Just the Beginning."[42] Do not just focus on the handshake, I said. Look at the bigger picture: the handshake within its general context.

The first question I asked when I heard the story was this: Where did these young teenagers get their reading of Islam? It didn't just fall from the sky, did it? There must be some social religious context that taught them this reading of Islam. They were insisting that their religion tells them not to shake hands with a female. Now if you pay even the slightest attention, you will realize that in Arab and Muslim-majority countries, people *do* shake the hands of people of the other sex. The highest religious figures in these countries shake the hands of women. So do presidents, kings, and sheikhs. On our TV programs you see men and women shaking hands. In other words, the majority of people there—except those from very rural areas—shake the hands of those of the other sex.

The only reading of Islam that sexualizes any contact between the two sexes is the fundamentalist reading—represented in Salafi Islam—and political Islamism, in its two forms, Sunni and Shiite. It is this reading of Islam that frowns upon the handshake.

So it was obvious that a fundamentalist form of Islam was at work here. It did not take long before it was confirmed that the boys' father was an imam in a mosque known for its financial connection to Saudi Arabia and its history of extremism. The two boys were regular visitors to the mosque. And they were being mentored by a fringe radical Salafi group of Swiss converts.[43]

We fail to see the bigger picture if we ignore the broader pattern. The pattern starts with pupils declining to shake hands with their teachers. Then they refuse to participate in music and art classes, and then classes on sex education and evolutionary theory. Then they demand separate rooms for prayers in schools.[44]

Please note that the demands regarding music, drama, and drawing in fact represent the most fundamentalist reading of Islam; these subjects are taught in many Arab and Muslim-majority states. Please also note that prayer rooms have no place in a school; that is not the public mandate of a school.

Many other demands include a gender dimension that reflects this Islamist ideology and fundamentalist reading of Islam. Aside from not shaking hands, parents insist that at ages four, five and six, their daughters must wear the headscarf, and they refuse to let them participate in swimming classes and school trips. This social control over the girls in the school starts early on and continues into forced marriages at a later stage. Girls are often married off before they realize that they have rights in their new Western society.

Those two boys also have four sisters. Two disappeared after a while, and the rumor was they were sent back to Syria. The two younger girls would wear the veil when they left their house to go to school. The moment they escaped the watchful eyes of their family members, they took them off, in the street. Later, one of them fled to a shelter for women.[45]

Once the politics of difference starts, a certain dynamic is set in motion, leading to segregation, human rights violations of women and children within closed communities, and the erosion of social trust and solidarity. A monocultural society is created.

I saw this pattern of fundamentalism in the UK, where I researched the Muslim Sharia Councils. It began more than fifty years ago, when Islamist groups successfully campaigned for exceptional treatment for Muslim students in public schools: a religious curriculum shaped by a fundamentalist reading of Islam was introduced. Religious taboos were enacted, necessitating the need for halal food and Islamic financing, girls were permitted to wear headscarves, and prayer rooms were erected for Muslims. The pattern went hand in hand with a gradual ghettoization of some Muslim communities and a spread of Quranic schools attached to mosques that taught a fundamentalist reading of Islam.[46]

Fifty years ago, British teachers, just like Swiss teachers today, were overwhelmed. They were not prepared to distinguish between culture, religion, and a fundamentalist reading of Islam. They had trouble explaining why they wanted to say "no," so they didn't dare oppose the changes. They felt left alone—by their superiors and most importantly by their politicians, who turned to Islamists for advice on "Muslims' needs."

Today, a recent study revealed, Islamic schools—some funded by the government—instruct girls as young as four to wear the veil as part of the official uniform policy. In fact, some even demand they wear the burka when they walk out of school each day.[47]

Some British Muslims are seriously worried about the gender segregation, and with it the discrimination, taking place in the schools.

But they are not simply hushed up. No, they are punished politically. Amina Lone, a Manchester Labour councillor, was sacked and deselected by her party after she campaigned against the segregation and veiling of children in the schools, along with extremism and sexism in her community. She is a reminder of the high price that courageous British activists of Islamic heritage are paying for speaking truth to power.[48] Those who rock the boat and insist on articulating problems they see in their own communities are not tolerated. In Lone's case, there was a need to "teach her a lesson," and the lesson was sacking her, she told me in an interview.[49] It reminded me of the former Swedish politician I mentioned earlier.

Today, in some closed Muslim communities in the UK, core messages of fundamentalism have become mainstreamed. A 2016 survey commissioned by Channel 4 suggests that while a large majority of British Muslims feel a strong sense of belonging to Britain (86 percent), a chasm develops between those Muslims who were surveyed and the wider population on attitudes toward gender equality, homosexuality, and the freedom of expression. It also reveals significant differences in attitudes toward violence and terrorism.

For example, only 34 percent of those surveyed said they would inform the police if they thought someone they knew was getting involved with people who support terrorism in Syria. Only 32 percent would condemn those who take part in violence against people mocking the Prophet. On more personal issues, 23 percent support the introduction of Sharia law, 31 percent think it is acceptable for a man to have more than one wife, and 39 percent agree that "wives should always obey their husbands." And 52 percent do not believe that homosexuality should be legal in Britain.[50]

Fundamentalism goes hand in hand with segregation, which is a significant issue in the UK. In 2016, an independent government report by Dame Louse Casey made headlines by stating the obvious, something that is public knowledge: minorities are segregated.

The report said that as diversity has increased in the United Kingdom, another dynamic has become clear. People from minority groups have become both more dispersed and in some cases more concentrated and segregated. And people of Pakistani and Bangladeshi ethnicity tend to live in more residentially segregated communities compared to other ethnic minority groups. In many areas, these concentrations are growing at the ward level.[51]

Segregation is compounded by the pattern of marriages taking place. The report states that high levels of transnational marriage may have undermined the rates of integration in some communities. In other words, marriage partners, both men and women, are imported from outside the country: people who are not familiar with UK traditions and the way of life. As native-born people marry foreign-born partners, they create the phenomenon of "first generation in every generation," in which children in each new generation grow up with one foreign-born parent. This seems particularly prevalent in South Asian communities. The writers of the report "were told on one visit to a northern town that all except one of the Asian Councillors had married a wife from Pakistan. And in a cohort study at the Bradford Royal Infirmary, 80% of babies of Pakistani ethnicity in the area had at least one parent born outside the UK."[52]

If you are reading these lines in Germany, you may be reminded of Necla Kelek's book *Die fremde Braut*, which focused on the "first generation in every generation problem" within the Turkish minority. Please also remember how she was attacked at the time and accused of blowing the issue out of proportion.[53]

Back to the UK and the Casey report. It tells us that the demographic structure of schools mirrors the segregation described above: more than 50 percent of ethnic minority students are in schools where ethnic minorities are the majority. This school segregation was highest among students from Pakistani and Bangladeshi ethnic backgrounds, compared to other ethnic groups. Taken together, the report tells us, this high concentration of ethnic minority children in residential areas and in schools increases the likelihood that they will grow up without meeting or better understanding people from different backgrounds.[54]

Where will this segregation lead? Likely to monoculturalism, fear, mistrust, and lack of social cohesion. No surprise that a 2015 survey found that more than 55 percent of the general public agreed that "there was a fundamental clash between Islam and the values of British society." On the other hand, 46 percent of British Muslims felt that "being a Muslim in Britain was difficult due to prejudice against Islam." In addition, the polling indicated a growing sense of grievance among sections of the Muslim population, and a stronger sense of identification with the "plight" of the *ummah*, the global Muslim community.[55]

Segregated British Muslim communities have a parallel legal system. I researched this issue and wrote about it in my 2016 book, *Women and Shari'a Law: The Impact of Legal Pluralism in the UK*. When I came back from my field research in 2013, I had to stop working on the book for three months just to get some distance from what I had seen and learned. I needed space to comprehend what I had learned, to try to look at it objectively.

Those using fieldwork in their research on difficult issues or in conflict areas know what I have experienced. It is called secondary trauma stress: the distressing psychological effects of listening to another person's first-hand traumatic experiences. I saw a situation I had seen elsewhere but never thought I would see in living color in London or Birmingham: women treated as inferior, restricted and socially controlled, and subject to violence, forced marriage, and child marriage.

While this type of patriarchal structure and treatment of women does exist in other traditions and cultures, the problem in the UK is further complicated because a mainstreamed fundamentalist reading of Islam is legitimizing it. Salafi and Deobandi strands of Islamic fundamentalism treat women as a source of evil and as having less value and intellect than their male counterparts. Violence and forced marriage are religiously sanctioned: a husband may beat his wife as a disciplinary measure if she disobeys, and the combination of male guardianship and no minimum age for marriage means that girls can be forced to marry.

On top of this, the UK legal system allows the application of Islamic law in family affairs. Though I focused on the separate Muslim legal system, the Muslims are not the only ones there who resort to their own religious laws; Jews and Hindus also use their own laws.

I define Sharia by the way it is being implemented in Islamic states and within Muslim family law. I see it as a set of laws selected from the corpus of jurists' legal opinions developed over the course of Islamic history, especially between the seventh and tenth centuries. Looking at Sharia from this perspective, we can see its problematic nature. What we are in fact looking at is its actual implementation and hence its obvious limitations and how it contravenes *modern* concepts of human rights. What matters is how it is being interpreted and used today.

In the worldview of this classical Islamic law, a woman is part of a hierarchical social structure dominated by the man at the top. As a legal person, the woman is controlled before her marriage by her male guardian and after marriage by her husband. The rules regarding marriageable age and guardianship make child marriages and forced marriages possible, and rules on divorce and maintenance rights discriminate against the wife.

The Islamic law implemented in Sharia councils and Muslim arbitration tribunals in the UK contravenes concepts of gender equality and human rights with impunity. I have written far more on this, but for the moment suffice to say that the *kafaa* principle in this law gives a father the right to annul the marriage of his daughter if she married against his wishes. *Kafaa* states that the bride and groom should be equal in status. And make no mistake, this is no theoretical example. It is a rule accepted and practiced by some of these courts, as I learned in interviews with their sheikhs.[56]

Let me go back to my original point. I said before that segregated British Muslim communities have a parallel legal system. I am sure it is no surprise that applying Islamic law to Muslim communities is a core demand of the Islamist movements in their two forms, societal and political. Wherever they work and metastasize, they demand the application of Sharia. Regardless of the country, whether Muslim-majority or Western democracy, the application of Sharia is their rallying point. In a Muslim-majority country, they would insist on applying corporal punishment (cutting off hands, stoning, etc.), along with Islamizing the financial system and introducing an Islamic way of governance. In Western democracies, in addition to their demands in the school system, they focus on applying Islamic law in family affairs and forms of Islamic arbitration and finances in areas where Muslims are concentrated.[57] In areas where Muslims are the majority, Islamists would start patrolling the neighborhood, demanding compliance with "an Islamic way of life."

It should also come as no surprise that members of the two types of Islamism, societal and political, often control the main British Sharia courts. It is no coincidence that the first Islamic Sharia Council, created in Leyton in 1982, was founded by several organizations that are known to be affiliated with political and societal Islamism: Jamaat-e-Islami (UK

Islamic Mission), the Muslim Brotherhood (Muslim Welfare House), and global Wahhabi Islam (Muslim World League).[58]

〜

Do you understand me now when I say that there is a pattern, a structure, and a system?

In the British case, the pattern started with specific South Asian Islamist fundamentalist movements working since the 1950s within South Asian communities to separate "Muslims" from the outside world and create a supreme Islamic identity. They did so through their mosques, Quran schools, bookshops, and missionary work. This in turn set the stage for a strategy promoted by supporters of political Islam to present themselves as the sole speakers for the Muslim community, and then portray their own *Islamist* demands in schools and workplaces and in family affairs as the demands of *all Muslims and Islam*. The British authorities' compliance with these demands did not lead to more integration. Instead, it fostered extremism, segregation, monoculturalism, and a lack of social cohesion. The Casey report exists to showcase the magnitude of that segregation.

Some of you might say, well, that might be true, but Britain is a special case. How about Belgium then? What happened there? Is the pattern different there? And Sweden? Are the structures different there? All of these are different states, with different relations between state and church. And yet the pattern, the structure, and the system were and are the same. It starts with a religious message, spreads through structures, based on a systematic approach to education and politics, and ends up with segregation and extremism.

Which brings me back to the question I started this section with. This time it is directed to you: How would you have reacted if it were Swiss Christian fundamentalist youths making such demands? I dare say you would not have been ready to compromise. This is pure fundamentalism. Full stop.

Somehow I cannot help but remember what Richard Dawkins said: "They are very happy about me bad-mouthing Christianity, but when it comes to Islam, the rules of the game change."[59] It is the same essentialist pattern at play here. We criticize "our religion" or react strongly to "our fundamentalists," but when it concerns "Muslim fundamentalism" we tend to think, "Oh, well, that is the way Muslims are."

The handshake rejection was an expression of a fundamentalist reading of religion. It should be dealt with in the same way that we deal with any religious fundamentalist demands. Religious freedom is sacred; some of its manifestations are not. If these manifestations lead to social conflict, division, and violations of human rights, they should be circumvented. Religion should be confined to its private sphere; the moment it encroaches into the public space, it starts to sow anger, hatred, and conflict. And in schools where the majority are of a certain religious faith, when that critical mass is reached, the dynamics of oppression and social control will come into play. Do not forget what happened in Molenbeek and Antwerp.

Schools should be a safe space for their pupils, not a hotbed of religious conflict. They should be provided with the necessary support and training to recognize the patterns, tools, and binding guidelines for a code of behavior that applies to all.

In schools, students should be united in their humanity, not their religion.

Conclusion

T HERE'S A PINK ELEPHANT in the room.

We all see the elephant. Standing right there in the middle of the room: huge, outrageous, bright pink. But we are afraid to say it: there is a pink elephant in the room. Instead we insist that the room is empty.

Empty is easy. Empty is reassuring. Empty is not complex. Empty is just empty.

The fact is, we are dealing with nothing other than a *radicalization of Islam*. That is the elephant in the room. And that is the core of the problem. And it is a problem that concerns us all, around the world. I do not think I am exaggerating when I say that it is the global challenge of the twenty-first century.

We can spend all we want—hundreds of millions—on anti-terrorism programs. But unless we acknowledge this simple fact in our policy measures, we may as well shred those millions and throw them into a river. They are wasted.

Throughout this book I have repeatedly emphasized that what matters is ideology. I have also emphasized that this ideology—mainstreamed through a systematic process and spread through structures flush with resources—is based on a radicalized politicized form of Islam.

Those facts complicate the situation. Do they not?

Some countries in the Middle East and North Africa are coming to terms with this fact. The Islam they have mainstreamed for so long is not only fundamentalist and radicalized, but it is also wreaking chaos in their midst. It has changed their societies, and now they have to live with the consequences. The ghosts they unleashed are haunting them now. The challenge is to tame the monster they released.

Here, in Western democracies, we are also charged with a daunting task.

Not only do we need to fight criminal organizations such as ISIS and al-Qaeda. We must also deal with the nonviolent form of Islamism: the ideology and its fundamentalist reading of Islam. And that in turns requires that we look more closely at what takes place within our closed communities.

Again, these facts complicate the matter.

Security measures are the easy part. But alone, they are futile. They do not solve the problem. They do not tackle its roots or structures.

What are needed are more painful measures.

We need to dismantle the structures and the system that spread this ideology and its radicalized form of Islam.

We need integration policies that actually lead to integration—not segregation.

We need clarity about relationships between states and religions.

We need a policy that deals with migrants of Islamic faith as citizens, not as a religious group.

We need to confront our well-meaning essentialist reflexes.

The threat has to be stopped. A paradigm shift is indispensable.

So, where do we start?

We start by learning from the mistakes of other countries. The policy mistakes made in Britain, Belgium, and Sweden should be our guide as to *what not to do*. One cannot combat an ideology and fundamentalism by working with the very groups that promote that ideology and reading of a religion. Can you put out a fire by pouring on more oil? Not very effective—surely you agree.

I hope by now you have realized that Islamist groups know you better than you think. They know how to play on your guilt, fear, insecurity, and desire to do the right thing.

So do the right thing. Please.

Working with Islamists is certainly not the right thing. You will be working with a far-right religious group that espouses a totalitarian ideology concealed in a religious cloak.

If you heard a Christian fundamentalist group calling for segregation and a stratified society, along with hatred and violations of fundamental human rights, would you hesitate to criticize it—even for a moment?

Would you hesitate for a moment to condemn your country's fascist or racist far-right groups?

If your answer is no, I suggest that you extend the same courtesy to the Muslim religious far-right groups. They represent the same values.

Fight them as you fight your own fundamentalists, fascists, and racist groups.

Be consistent.

When we want to make a difference, first we must strive to hold our policy makers accountable.

In a democracy we cannot stop a Muslim Brotherhood group from organizing itself.

They know how to exploit Western democratic rules and manipulate the loopholes. They are masters at it.

But we can have an effect. We can insist that our politicians and policy makers stop working with such groups. No funding. No mainstreaming. Hold them accountable for these policy mistakes.

And especially important: we can make sure that such groups do not work with children. Would we trust a non-Muslim fundamentalist or totalitarian group (neo-Nazi, fascist, racist, etc.) to have control over a kindergarten or Boy Scout troop, or to develop policies on youth education?

We can do something else too: insist on accountability and transparency, along with systematic periodic auditing and supervision of their programs. Please make sure to vet those who are doing that auditing and supervision. Given what I noticed in some auditing conducted in the UK, such vetting is crucial.

Easy solutions are not possible here.

The task is daunting and frightening because we will have to walk a tightrope. We have to be careful not to erode our cherished values and norms that protect the freedom of religion. These are hard-won achievements, and we should defend them and not dilute them. But it would certainly be naïve not to acknowledge that mosques and religious teaching can be either part of the solution or part of the problem.

We have to take concrete measures that help establish a localized form of mosques and religious teachings that preach love rather than hatred.

I daresay, however, that the struggle to reform the theology of Islam is an internal task that should be done by Muslims themselves. Just as in Muslim-majority countries, here in Western democracies we see a nascent movement rising, working persistently on this task. Hope is what I see in the developments and actions taking place worldwide.

I see hope in the men and women standing bravely against this extremism in their own societies, risking their jobs, freedom, and lives.[1] I see it in the work of intellectuals and thinkers, old and young, who are providing an alternative reading of their religion and/or insisting that human rights are universal. They know that these rights are not optional, and they demand respect in each society regardless of religion.

I see hope in the rise, since 2004, of inclusive mosques on different continents, including Europe and the Americas. These inclusive spaces welcome all people, men and women and all genders, in their diversity of beliefs, sects, opinions, and sexual orientations—thus challenging the status quo. One prominent example is the Ibn Rushd-Goethe Mosque, established in Berlin in June 2017.

I see it in the "Stop Extremism" initiative, also launched this year by European citizens of Islamic heritage to combat both far-right and Islamist extremisms. I see it in the foundation in October 2017 of AIM, the Alliance of Inclusive Muslims, an umbrella organization that brings together global movements promoting the work of progressive Muslims whatever their nationality, race, or sect. And I see it in the women's movements within Muslim-majority countries, groups that are challenging the patriarchal orders and archaic religious interpretations in their societies, now demanding their equality and rights. The Saudi women's movement is one inspiring example.

Hope and optimism: this is what I feel when observing these developments.

That does not mean that our policy makers should relax and depend on such developments. Remember how long it took here in Europe to tame Christianity and force it into the private sphere?

And this also does not mean that we should aspire to uniformity or try to impose one form of religion. No, that is not wise, and it will backfire. Just like all religions, Islam has its different traditions and orientations—liberal, esoteric, conservative, and orthodox—and this diversity should be respected. But no room or toleration should be given to a politicized and radicalized form of Islam that preaches hatred, segregation, and exclusion. You cannot tell me that we should tolerate for a second a form of religion and an ideology that tell our children to hate "others" because of their "difference." That hatred paves the ground for the jihad and the killing that would follow.

This is what makes the issue very difficult. Fundamentalism is a problem in all religions, but in Islam this fundamentalism is spreading quickly and is intrinsically connected to violence. Wherever it spreads it sows division and shatters social cohesion. To stop this form of radicalized religion, we need policy measures that end the importation of its ideology and religious teachings into our societies.

We need laws that insist on transparency, that end the external financial and logistical support of mosques and religious societies. When money flows from the transnational Islamist movements, that money builds mosques and supplies imams and religious literature and materials. It provides copies of the Quran in whatever language is needed. The Quran remains the same, but the interpretations that come with it reflect the fundamentalist politicized message of the funders. This has to stop.

In March 2015 Austria introduced an Islam Law, which regulates the state's relations with recognized Muslim religious communities. It guarantees Muslims freedom of religion, while demanding transparency and a stop to the flow of foreign financing to mosques. It also secures scientific education for young clerical academics through a theological program at the University of Vienna. Recognized Muslim communities must adhere to specific conditions, such as upholding the norms and values of the Austrian constitution.[2] Such measures are positive and badly needed. But they require vigilance in avoiding the loopholes of the Austrian law.

Heiko Heinisch, an Austrian historian who has extensively researched Austrian Islam, explained to me that the wording of the Islam Law only prohibits the foreign financing of the "usual activities" of a religious society.[3] However, it is nevertheless possible for foreign money through existing societies in Austria to finance the building of a mosque because this is not part of the usual activities.[4]

Also, it would be wise to make sure that the Muslim societies recognized are thoroughly vetted, lest we end up designating Islamists as the gatekeepers for "Muslims."

In addition, please keep in mind that the law did not lead to better monitoring of the religious teachings provided by Muslim societies. It took research by a professor of Islamic faith—Ednan Aslan—to raise the alarm bells and introduce a new law on religious kindergartens. Nor did the law stop state and municipalities of working with Islamist groups.

We should follow the best practices available, but make sure to avoid these loopholes.

Hence, a law regulating the flow of money to mosques and religious institutions is needed but in itself is not enough. It is a necessary first step.

Another necessary measure is well-designed theological programs to train and graduate imams and teachers who are qualified to preach and teach a peaceful spiritual form of religion. Such programs should be designed by groups of multidisciplinary experts who are capable of generating a theology based on the rich religious traditions of Islam but who do not shy away from providing these imams with a critical comparative approach to their religion and other religions.

Do not repeat the mistakes of Britain, where imams are trained in highly conservative literalist Deobandi seminaries. They do meet the British government's demand for English-speaking imams, but they fail to support the humanist values of equality, tolerance, liberty, and religious pluralism.[5]

And please plan well so you do not create a vacuum that will immediately be filled by Islamist groups and their structures.

Likewise, all forms of religious education that target children should be monitored and supervised, whether in schools or in mosques. I know that statement may make you uncomfortable. But I am afraid it is necessary. Just as we insist on educational policies and curriculum guidelines that instill our norms and values in our school systems, it should be possible to expect the same from any religious curriculum—and not only that of Muslims. It is legitimate to require supervision. Would you allow a far-right, or far-left, group to build kindergartens to teach children their ideas? Apply the same rules to all far-right groups, religious and nationalist alike.

We certainly do not want a Muslim Brotherhood curriculum. Or do we? Remember how it systematically uses carefully selected Quranic verses, Sunna sayings, and events from Islamic history to instill its ideology? It is masterfully designed to indoctrinate children. Remember how it glorifies killing infidels? Or what the curriculum tells instructors to convey to the children about the Jews? Here's a reminder: "Jews are the enemies of God. The Muslim knows that the Jews are characterized by all evil, for they are cowards and traitors, and cannot be trusted."[6]

This requirement—that all forms of religious education should be monitored and supervised, in schools or in mosques—is necessary. The results of studies on Muslim religious teachings for children in Europe are disturbing.

For example, Ednan Aslan, the professor of Islamic studies at the Institute of Islamic Studies at Vienna University whom I mentioned above, studied a selected sample of Muslim kindergartens in Vienna. He raised alarming questions about the limits of religious accommodation, especially when they involve politicized religious teaching tailored to indoctrinate children and separate them from the larger society.

The study alluded to the presence of religious kindergartens that encourage unconditional openness to other cultures and religions. But it revealed at the same time the existence of substantial numbers of religious kindergartens that foster programmatic political and societal Islamism, with isolationist features.[7] Was it surprising that the Islamophobia industry tried to defame him and the study? He was not at all surprised, he told me.[8]

And yet, thanks to his study, a new stricter kindergarten law has been approved in Vienna and took effect. The law focuses on pedagogical concepts and transparency.[9]

This brings me to the issue of integration. This type of ideology and radicalized form of religion feeds on segregation, victimhood, and the clash of civilizations. And now it is time to consider your role as citizens of your respective countries—and here I mean citizens of all faiths and persuasions.

What happens when you avoid addressing the problems that you clearly see and prefer the comfort of silence, when you think it is safe not to say anything? Let me tell you this: if you do not lead others in seeing these issues in all their nuance, you pave the way for the real far-right racists, the ones who would gladly eradicate people who are Muslim or Jewish, who come from African countries, or who are simply foreigners. Your silence and inaction will only backfire as religious conflict and strife are exacerbated and fostered.

Most importantly, if you think that the measures I am suggesting will cost a lot, allow me to quote Sylvie Durrer, director of the Swiss Federal Office for the Equality of Women and Men (EBG). She tells any policy maker who will listen that it will be far more expensive *not* to invest in policy measures addressing different forms of violence against women: "Inaction is more costly," she will say.[10]

By the same token it will cost us more in Western democracies if we let things get further out of control. Inaction will cost us all far more.

Which brings me back to the type of integration policies we need here. What we need is *active citizenship* based on reciprocity.

"You are a member of this society, we cherish and value you as an individual. And just as you have rights, you also have responsibilities. Respecting the humanist values and norms of society is one of those responsibilities." This should be the core of these policies.

"Tolerance is a one-way process. Reciprocity is two ways, and it exists in all religions," Karin Heremans, headmistress of the Royal Atheneum in Antwerp, told me.[11]

"Previously we were aiming for *active pluralism*—now the aim is *active citizenship*," Elias Hemelsoet, a Belgian educational policy advisor at the Flanders Community Education, told me.[12] In the schools, this is what brings these kids together and what is promoted now.

Rather than tolerance, reciprocity is now being fostered. Just as you take, you should give. Treat people the way you want to be treated. People in all cultures know this concept. Its baseline is straightforward:

learn how to live together. Be a responsible citizen. Youth should be citizens and should respect and accept each other regardless of their religion, beliefs, gender, or sexual orientation.

This is imperative if we are to face the rising tide of polarization we are experiencing today.

You see, if some segment of society is treated differently, social cohesion is the first thing to suffer. If people think the system is not just, that will erode the social trust and solidarity that are the basis of our system. Hence, there must be clear rules of the game, based on common humanist values and norms, and these should be applied to everyone, no exceptions. Full stop.

When the authorities in Flanders experienced such polarization and conflict, they simply had to introduce neutrality as an active concept in their school system. Neutrality creates a safe space for children and youth in schools, a space that protects them against pressures, whether peer pressure, social pressure, or religious pressure.

The aim of neutrality is to defuse polarization. One approach to this was introducing a measure that prohibited religious symbols in the schools. No one, except teachers of religion, is allowed to wear religious symbols, including the veil. Mandatory courses on active citizenship from childhood to adulthood are being introduced.[13]

Neutrality has another name. It is also called secularism, the separation of state and religion. Historically, secularism was necessary in Western democracies to protect against the tyranny of religions and to end religious wars. I hope by now you recognize that we need this separation again today more than anything else.

We need a secular state, neutral to people of all religions, faiths, and persuasions. And it should actively ensure that the public space remains secular: free from religious encroachment. It has to apply the same law for all its citizens; that law must be secular and civil, and must adhere to universal principles of human rights. Only in this way will it protect *all* of its citizens. If you start to apply different laws to different groups, you end up with a mess, one that is unjust, discriminatory, and racist to the core.

All of these measures are necessary to deal with the challenges we are facing.

They are designed to protect all members of society, to safeguard our cherished humanist liberal norms and values, and to confront the Islamist challenge. The challenge can be defeated, but only if all of us, citizens of our respective countries, work together and lead the way in this polarized discourse on "Islam" and "Muslims."

Do not ignore the pink elephant in the room. It won't disappear if you just ignore it. Stop being afraid. Stop hesitating. Break the silence. It is time to stand firm in our humanity.

Notes

Foreword: Islamism, Ideology, and Lessons to Learn

1. Saad bin Tafla al-Ajami, "We Are All 'ISIS'!" [in Arabic], *An-Nahar*, August 7, 2014, https://goo.gl/mCusZF.

1. Introduction

1. "Tausende Muslime wollen gegen Terror demonstrieren," *Zeit Online*, June 9, 2017, http://www.zeit.de/gesellschaft/zeitgeschehen/2017-06/oeln-demo-muslime-islam-istischer-terror-nicht-mit-uns; "Wer wir sind?," Türkische Islamische Union, http://www.ditib.de/default.php?id=5; Tim Beyer, "Was zählt, ist doch die Botschaft," *Zeit Online*, June 17, 2017, http://www.zeit.de/gesellschaft/zeitgeschehen/2017-06/koelner-frie-densmarsch-muslime-demonstration-terror-islamismus.

2. "Ditib will nicht an Friedensmarsch teilnehmen," *Zeit Online*, June 15, 2017, http://www.zeit.de/gesellschaft/zeitgeschehen/2017-06/anti-terror-demo-ditip-koeln.

3. Institute for Economics and Peace, *Global Terrorism Index 2017: Measuring and Understanding the Impact of Terrorism*, November 2017, pp. 10–14, https://drive.google.com/file/d/1SfpFJB8EVuoDPJ2yJjDOoiIR1yKzsXkf/view.

4. See Institute for Economics and Peace, *Global Terrorism Index 2020: Measuring and Understanding the Impact of Terrorism*, November 2020, https://www.visionof-humanity.org/wp-content/uploads/2020/11/GTI-2020-web-1.pdf.

5. "'Burned to the Ground': Boko Haram Razes at Least 16 Nigerian Villages," *Al Jazeera America*, January 8, 2015, http://america.aljazeera.com/articles/2015/1/8/nigeria-bokoharamattack.html; Mausi Segun, "Dispatches: What Really Happened in Baga, Nigeria?," Human Rights Watch, January 14, 2015, https://www.hrw.org/news/2015/01/14/dispatches-what-really-happened-baga-nigeria; Adam Nossiter, "Satellite Images Show Ruin Left by Boko Haram, Groups Say," *New York Times*, January 15, 2015, https://www.nytimes.com/2015/01/16/world/africa/boko-haram-rampage-in-nigeria-is-shown-in-satellite-images-groups-say.html.

6. "Al-Azhar Professor Suad Saleh: In a Legitimate War, Muslims Can Capture Slave Girls and Have Sex with Them," *MEMRI*, September 12, 2014, video clip no. 5252, 2:48, https://www.memri.org/tv/al-azhar-professor-suad-saleh-legitimate-war-muslims-can-capture-slavegirls-and-have-sex-them.

7. "Saudi Sheikh: Slavery of Women—as War Loots—Is Allowed and Whoever Denies This Is an Atheist" [in Arabic], *Albawaba.com*, June 30, 2015, https://goo.gl/Nn2Tp; Ahmed Al Musaind, "The Plight of the Yazidi Women Brings Slavery to the Forefront, and Jurists Consider It Now Evil and Obscene" [in Arabic], *Al Hayat*, August 22, 2014, https://goo.gl/hcyrpH.

8. Brian Whitaker, "Saudi Textbooks 'Demonise West,'" *Guardian*, July 13, 2004, https://www.theguardian.com/world/2004/jul/14/saudiarabia.schoolsworldwide.

9. Mohammad Al-Terkait, "Scholar Saleh Al-Fawzan Responds to Those Who Says Islam Does Not Condone Slavery," SoundCloud audio, 3:37, https://soundcloud.com/mohammad-al-terkait/3dx8rayhzio3.

10. Elham Manea, *Women and Shari'a Law: The Impact of Legal Pluralism in the UK* (London: I. B. Tauris, 2016), pp. 11–34.

11. Ibid.

12. Domenico Montanaro, "Six Times Obama Called on Muslim Communities to Do More about Extremism," *National Public Radio*, December 7, 2015, http://www.npr.org/2015/12/07/458797632/6-times-obama-called-on-muslim-communities-to-do-more-about-extremism.

13. Kate Samuelson, "Read Prime Minister Theresa May's Full Speech on the London Bridge Attack," *Time*, June 4, 2017, http://time.com/4804640/london-attack-theresa-may-speech-transcript-full/.

14. Ibid.

15. David D. Kirkpatrick, "Britain Debates Saudis' Ties to Extremism, with May in an Uneasy Spot," *New York Times*, July 5, 2017, https://www.nytimes.com/2017/07/05/world/europe/saudi-arabia-islamist-extremism-terrorism-britain-theresa-may.html; Bethan McKernan, "Terror Funding Report: Calls Grow for Release of 'Sensitive' Home Office Document 'Pointing Finger at Saudi Arabia,'" *Independent*, June 5, 2017, http://www.independent.co.uk/News/uk/terror-funding-report-home-office-saudi-arabia-jihadis-attacks-suppress-tory-uk-release-sensitive-a7773146.html.

2. Radicalized at Sixteen

1. Michael Cohen, "Peace in the Post-Cold War World," *Atlantic*, December 15, 2011, https://www.theatlantic.com/international/archive/2011/12/peace-in-the-post-cold-war-world/249863/.

2. U.S. Department of State, "Reagan Doctrine, 1985," U.S. Department of State Archive, https://2001-2009.state.gov/r/pa/ho/time/rd/17741.htm; Charles Krauthammer, "The Reagan Doctrine," *Time*, June 24, 2001, http://content.time.com/time/magazine/article/0,9171,141478,00.html.

3. Alan Taylor, "The Soviet War in Afghanistan, 1979–1989," *Atlantic*, August 4, 2014, https://www.theatlantic.com/photo/2014/08/the-soviet-war-in-afghanistan-1979-1989/100786/; Bill Keller, "Last Soviet Soldiers Leave Afghanistan," *New York Times*, February 16, 1989, http://partners.nytimes.com/library/world/africa/021689afghan-laden.html; "The Life and Death of Osama bin Laden," *Washington Post*, May 2, 2011, http://www.washingtonpost.com/wp-srv/special/world/timeline-life-of-osama-bin-laden/;

Robert Fisk, "Anti-Soviet Warrior Puts His Army on the Road to Peace," *Independent*, December 6, 1993, http://www.independent.co.uk/news/world/anti-soviet-warrior-puts-his-army-on-the-road-to-peace-the-saudi-businessman-who-recruited-mujahe-din-1465715.html.

4. Charles Mohr, "Europeans Link Terror to Arabs but Disagree on Soviets," *New York Times*, June 23, 1981, http://www.nytimes.com/1981/06/23/world/europeans-link-terror-to-arabs-but-disagree-on-soviets.html; Nick Lockwood, "How the Soviet Union Transformed Terrorism," *Atlantic*, December 23, 2011, https://www.theatlantic.com/international/archive/2011/12/how-the-soviet-union-transformed-terrorism/250433/.

5. David K. Shipler, "Israel Completes Pullout, Leaving Sinai to Egypt," *New York Times*, April 26, 1982, http://www.nytimes.com/1982/04/26/world/israeli-completes-pullout-leaving-sinai-to-egypt.html; Russell A. Stone et al., "Israel: War in Lebanon," *Encyclopaedia Britannica*, July 26, 2017, https://www.britannica.com/place/Israel/War-in-Lebanon.

6. A shorter version of this radicalization story was first published in Elham Manea, "Tackling Militant Islamism Means Also Confronting Its Non-violent Forms," *Europe's World*, May 5, 2015, http://europesworld.org/2015/05/05/tackling-militant-islamism-means-also-confronting-non-violent-forms/#.WYMNIdOGMWo.

7. Author interview with Raufa Hassan, professor of sociology at Sanaʿa University, Sanaʿa, October 13, 2006; Elham Manea, *The Arab State and Women's Rights: The Trap of Authoritarian Governance* (London: Routledge, 2011), p. 109. For more information about the political history of Yemen, see Elham Manea, *Regional Politics of the Gulf* (London: Saqi Books, 2005), pp. 32–55; Abd al-Wahab Al Rowhani, *Yemen: The Specificity of Governance and Unity* [in Arabic], PhD Thesis, (Amman: Dar Zahran Publications, 2010), pp. 347–48.

8. Elham Manea, *Echo of Pain* [in Arabic] (Beirut: Dar Al Saqi, 2005).

9. Hasan al-Banna, *The Five Tracts of Hasan Al-Banna (1906–1949)*, trans. and annot. Charles Wendell (Berkeley: Univ. of California Press 1978), p. 97.

10. Muslim Brothers, "The Muslim Brothers and the Jews (1)" [in Arabic], *Islamonline*, August 2, 2008, https://www.ikhwanonline.com/article/39305.

11. Ahmed Abo Elmagd, lawyer and former member of the Muslim Brothers, interview by author, February 12, 2012; Moomen Sallam, editor-in-chief of *Civil Egypt* and former member of the Muslim Brothers, interview by author, Skype, June 23, 2017; Rabab Kamal, radio journalist and former member of the Muslim Brothers, interview by author, Skype, June 31, 2017.

12. Daniel Fuchs, "Das erste Islam-Museum der Schweiz: Was taugt die neue Ausstellung?," *AZ Nordwestschweiz*, July 13, 2016, https://www.aargauerzeitung.ch/kultur/buch-buehne-kunst/das-erste-islam-museum-der-schweiz-was-taugt-die-neue-ausstellung-130422068.

3. Is Islam the Problem?

1. International Conference on Free Expression and Conscience, "Blasphemy, Islamophobia, Free Expression Panel," London, July 22–24, 2017, YouTube video, 1:30:55, https://www.youtube.com/watch?v=seJkIGV8urc.

2. "Richard Dawkins' Berkeley Event Cancelled for 'Islamophobia,'" *BBC News*, July 24, 2017, http://www.bbc.com/news/world-us-canada-40710165; Frank Bruni, "These Campus Inquisitions Must Stop," *New York Times*, June 3, 2017, https://www.

nytimes.com/2017/06/03/opinion/sunday/bruni-campus-inquisitions-evergreen-state.html.

3. Aftab Ali, "Muslim Students from Goldsmiths University Islamic Society 'Heckle and Aggressively Interrupt' Maryam Namazie Talk," *Independent*, December 4, 2015, http://www.independent.co.uk/student/news/muslim-students-from-goldsmiths-university-s-islamic-society-heckle-and-aggressively-interrupt-a6760306.html.

4. Ibid.

5. "Muslim Imams March against Terrorism in Europe," *Deutsche Welle*, July 8, 2017, https://www.dw.com/en/muslim-imams-march-against-terrorism-in-europe/a-39608229.

6. "Anti-terrorist 'March' of Muslim Imams Comes to Berlin," *Deutsche Welle*, July 9, 2017, http://www.dw.com/en/anti-terrorist-march-of-muslim-imams-comes-to-berlin/a-39617364.

7. Ibid.

8. "Muslim Imams March against Terrorism in Europe."

9. Ali Alrabieei (@DrAliAlrabieei), Twitter, August 11, 2017, https://twitter.com/DrAliAlrabieei/status/896117261777240064.

10. Rabab Kamal, Egyptian radio journalist, writer, and civil rights advocate, Skype interview by author, July 31, 2017.

11. "An Open Letter to Dr. Ibrahim Awad Albadry, known as Abu Bakr al-Baghdadi," English version, July 4, 2014, pp. 1, 9–10, http://www.lettertobaghdadi.com/14/english-v14.pdf.

12. "Five Years Prison for an Egyptian for Blasphemy," *Alhurra*, February 26, 2017, https://www.alhurra.com/a/egypt-abdalla-nassr/349611.html; Facebook page of Sheikh Mohammad Abdullah Nasr, https://goo.gl/tfk1xk.

13. "An Open Letter to Dr. Ibrahim Awad Albadry," English version, p. 1.

14. Ibid., p. 11.

15. Yazidis are regarded by Muslims as devil worshippers, which led to a continuous horror of persecution in different periods. "An Open Letter to Dr. Ibrahim Awad Albad," Arabic version, July 4, 2014, p. 16, http://www.lettertobaghdadi.com/ar/.

16. "An Open Letter to Dr. Ibrahim Awad Albad," English version, pp. 1, 6–11.

17. Ibid., p. 6.

18. Ibid., p. 1.

19. Ibid., p. 7.

20. Manal Omar, "Islam Is a Religion of Peace," *Foreign Policy*, November 9, 2015, https://foreignpolicy.com/2015/11/09/islam-is-a-religion-of-peace-manal-omar-debate-islamic-state/.

21. Ibid.

22. See Manea, *Women and Shari'a Law*, pp. 54–61; Manea, *The Arab State and Women's Rights*, pp. 42–43, 52–55.

23. Elham Manea, *Regional Politics in the Gulf: Saudi Arabia, Oman, Yemen* (London: Saqi Books, 2005), pp. 26–28; Alastair Crooke, "You Can't Understand ISIS If You Don't Know the History of Wahhabism in Saudi Arabia," *Huffington Post*, August 27, 2014, http://www.huffingtonpost.com/alastair-crooke/isis-wahhabism-saudi-arabia_b_5717157.html.

24. "Urgent Action: Religious Minority Members Forcibly Evicted," Amnesty International, February 11, 2016, https://www.amnesty.org/download/Documents/ASA2134092016ENGLISH.pdf; "Indonesia: Ahmadiyah Community Threatened Religious

Minority on Bangka Island Ordered to 'Return to Islam' or Be Expelled," Human Rights Watch, January 16, 2016, https://www.hrw.org/news/2016/01/16/indonesia-ahmadiyah-community-threatened.

25. Ashfaq Yusufzai, "Taliban Attacks Show No Mercy for Children in Pakistan," *Pakistan Forward*, June 20, 2017, http://pakistan.asia-news.com/en_GB/articles/cnmi_pf/features/2017/06/20/feature-01.

26. Jerry A. Coyne, "If ISIS Is Not Islamic, then the Inquisition Was Not Catholic: There Is No Such Thing as 'True' Religion," *New Republic*, September 13, 2014, https://newrepublic.com/article/119433/if-isis-not-islamic-then-inquisition-was-not-catholic.

27. Ibid.

28. Sam Harris, "The Reality of Islam," author's blog, February 8, 2006, https://www.samharris.org/blog/item/the-reality-of-islam.

29. Ibid.

30. Sam Harris, "A Few Thoughts on the Muslim Ban," author's blog, January 29, 2017, https://www.samharris.org/blog/item/a-few-thoughts-on-the-muslim-ban.

31. Sam Harris and Maajid Nawaz, *Islam and the Future of Tolerance: A Dialogue* (Cambridge, MA: Harvard Univ. Press, 2015).

32. Sarah Knapton, "Richard Dawkins: Religious Education Is Crucial for British Schoolchildren," *Telegraph*, June 11, 2017, http://www.telegraph.co.uk/science/2017/06/11/richard-dawkins-religious-education-crucial-british-schoolchildren/.

33. Karima Bennoune, *Your Fatwa Does Not Apply Here: Untold Stories from the Fight against Muslim Fundamentalism* (New York: Norton, 2013), p. 3.

34. Eoghan Macquire, "The Abolitionist Fighting to Free Mauritania's Slaves," *CNN*, June 21, 2017, http://edition.cnn.com/2017/06/21/africa/mauritania-slavery-biram-dah-abeid/index.html; "Mauritania," Global Slavery Index website, https://www.globalslaveryindex.org/country/mauritania/.

35. Mohammad Cheikh Ould Mkhaitir, "Religion, Religiosity, and the Craftsmen" [in Arabic], *Modern Discussion*, December 28, 2014, http://www.ahewar.org/debat/show.art.asp?aid=447867.

36. Elham Manea, "Who Is Afraid of Mauritanian Mohamed Cheikh? It Is about Slavery, Not the Prophet," *Huffington Post*, August 23, 2015, http://www.huffingtonpost.com/elham-manea/who-is-afraid-of-mauritanian-mohamed_b_8026724.html; "Mohammed Shaikh Ould Mohammed Ould Mkhaitir: Mauritania," Freedom Now website, http://www.freedom-now.org/campaign/mohamed-ould-cheikh-ould-mkhaitir/.

37. For more details on this Saudi foreign policy, see Manea, *Regional Politics of the Gulf*, pp. 34, 123–29.

38. SouthAsiaNews, "Hillary Clinton speaks out about US links with Taliban," April 28, 2009, YouTube video, 1:34, https://www.youtube.com/watch?v=X2CEofyz4ys.

39. Bennoune, *Your Fatwa Does Not Apply Here*, p. 18.

40. Saad bin Tafla al-Ajami, "We Are All 'ISIS'!" [in Arabic], *al Sharq*, August 7, 2014; reprinted in *An-Nahar* newspaper, Beirut, August 7, 2014, https://goo.gl/mCusZF.

41. Turki Al Hamad (@TurkiHAlhamad1), Twitter, June 29, 2017, https://twitter.com/TurkiHAlhamad1/status/880496436214992896.

42. Aziz Alqenaei, Kuwaiti intellectual, Skype interview by author, August 9, 2017.

43. Elham Manea, "We Respect Our Holy Texts, but They Are Human Made Text" [in Arabic], *Modern Discussion*, February 8, 2012, http://www.ahewar.org/debat/show.art.asp?aid=294512.

44. Ayaan Hirsi Ali, "Islam Is a Religion of Violence," *Foreign Policy*, November 9, 2015, https://foreignpolicy.com/2015/11/09/islam-is-a-religion-of-violence-ayaan-hirsi-ali-debate-islamic-state/.

45. Elham Manea, *Ich will nicht mehr schweigen: Der Islam, der Westen und die Menschenrechte* (Freiburg: Herder Verlag, 2009), p. 67.

46. Ibid., p. 154.

47. Interview with Kacem El Ghazzali, secular Moroccan blogger, August 19, 2017.

48. This dispute was first presented in an article by the author; see Elham Manea, "Defining the Phenomenon of Jihadist Radicalisation: Drivers and Catalysts—Local and Global," in *The Challenge of Jihadist Radicalisation in Europe and Beyond* (Brussels: European Policy Centre and European Foundation for Democracy, 2017), pp. 23–34.

49. Anja Dalgaard-Nielsen, "Violent Radicalization in Europe: What We Know and What We Do Not Know," *Studies in Conflict & Terrorism* 33, no. 9 (2010): 799; Adam Nossiter, "'That Ignoramus': Two French Scholars of Radical Islam Turn Bitter Rivals," *New York Times*, July 12, 2016, https://www.nytimes.com/2016/07/13/world/europe/france-radical-islam.html. Examples of their books are: Gilles Kepel, *Terror in Frankreich* (Munich: Verlag Antje Kunstmann, 2016); Kepel, *Allah in the West: Islamic Movements in America and Europe* (Cambridge: Polity Press, 1997); Olivier Roy, *Globalized Islam: The Search for an New Ummah* (New York: Columbia Univ. Press, 2004).

50. Dalgaard-Nielsen, "Violent Radicalization in Europe," p. 799.

51. Olivier Roy, "Le djihadisme est une révolte générationnelle et nihiliste," *Le Monde*, November 24, 2015, http://www.lemonde.fr/idees/article/2015/11/24/le-djihadisme-une-revolte-generationnelle-et-nihiliste_4815992_3232.html; cited in Robert Zaretsky, "Radicalized Islam, or Islamicized Radicalism?," *Chronicle of Higher Education Review*, May 26, 2016.

52. Gilles Kepel, "'Radicalisations' et 'islamophobie': le roi est nu," *Libération*, March 14, 2016, http://www.liberation.fr/debats/2016/03/14/radicalisations-et-islamophobie-le-roi-est-nu_1439535.

53. Zaretsky, "Radicalized Islam"; Kepel, "'Radicalisations' et 'islamophobie.'"

54. Zaretsky, "Radicalized Islam"; Kepel, "'Radicalisations' et 'islamophobie.'"

55. Nossiter, "'That Ignoramus.'"

56. Zaretsky, "Radicalized Islam."

4. Forms of Nonviolent Islamism

1. Chapter 4, verse 3, says: "And if you fear that you will not deal justly with the orphan girls, then marry those that please you of [other] women, two or three or four. But if you fear that you will not be just, then [marry only] one or those your right hand possesses (slaves). That is more suitable that you may not incline [to injustice]. Quran, surah *Al Nisaa* 4, verse 3. Chapter 23, verses 5–6, reads: "and they who guard their private parts, except from their wives or those their right hands possess (slaves), for indeed, they will not be blamed."

2. Research field visit, South Africa, summer 2015.

3. Manea, *Women and Shari'a Law*, p. 145; Field visit, UK, 2013; Roel Meijer, ed., *Global Salafism: Islam's New Religious Movement* (London: Hurst & Company, 2009), p. 126; Oliver Roy, *Islamic Radicalism in Afghanistan and Pakistan*, UNHCR Emergency and Security Service WRITENET paper no. 06/2001 (Paris: CNRS, January 2002), http://www.refworld.org/pdfid/3c6a3f7d2.pdf; Kalim Bahadur, *The Jama'at-i-Islami of*

Pakistan: Political Thought and Political Action (New Delhi: Chetana Publications, 1977), p. 4; Gilles Kepel, *Allah in the West: Islamic Movements in America and Europe* (Cambridge: Polity Press, 1997), pp. 90–91.

4. The Tablighi Jama'at, often referred to as Tabligh. This group formed in 1927, under the influence of the Muslim scholar Muhammad Ilyas. This fundamentalist movement pushes the desire for autonomy to the extreme and defines the community on the basis of strict religious observance. It propagates as widely as possible, but especially among the uneducated. Thus, it is a rigorous Islam cut from the literalism of religious scholars and purged of Sufi practices. Kepel, *Allah in the West*, pp. 91–92.

5. Ghaffar Hussain, interview with author, St. Albans, England, August 6, 2013; quoted in Manea, *Women and Shari'a Law*, p. 144.

6. Manea, *Women and Shari'a Law*, pp. 146–47. See also Innes Bowen, *Medina in Birmingham, Najaf in Brent: Inside British Islam* (London: Hurst & Company, 2014), p. 27. For the WikiLeaks cable, see "Confidential cable written by Richard LeBaron, deputy chief of the US embassy in London. Passed by WikiLeaks to the *Daily Telegraph* and published by the *Telegraph* on 3 February 2011," http://www.telegraph.co.uk/news/wikileaks-files/london-wikileaks/8304926/EUR-SENIOR-ADVISOR-PANDITH-AND-SP-ADVISOR-COHENS-VISIT-TO-THE-UK-OCTOBER-9-14-2007.html.

7. Manea, *Women and Shari'a Law*; Bowen, *Medina in Birmingham, Najaf in Brent*.

8. The statement says: "[W]hen ulama say that they are supportive of peaceful co-existence with all the people of South Africa, this is often misunderstood and the ulama are accused of being accommodating and anti-jihad. What the ulama are saying is that they do not give up their right to help the *ummah* [the whole community of Muslims worldwide bound together by ties of religion] wherever the need may be. This may include the need to exercise the right to bear arms in struggles against the oppression of the ummah. The caricature of the ulama that some sketch conveniently miss[es] out on the nuances of the ulama statement. We all know that as Muslims we have to make efforts to realise our dreams of implementing a system of governance and a political way of being as envisioned in the pure shari'ah. We have to hold that vision high and dear. It is an accepted fact that the layman and ulama alike will never be satisfied with the predominant ungodly system. Nevertheless, we realise that getting there is not achieved through a shallow reading of our own situation, or a rhetoric of hate that belies the true Din. There can be no doubt that the Ulama of South Africa have been, and continue to be supportive of Jihad. This support is not only a duty they have as Muslims, but one they shoulder as *warathatul ambiy*ah—the inheritors of the Prophets." *Umm Abdillah*, Radio Islam, June 2, 2015, https://www.radioislam.org.za/j3/index.php/latest-news/opinion-and-analysis/15660-answering-the-isis-propagandists-in-our-midst-part-1-fake-deobandi-muhajids-and-anti-jihad-south-african-ulama.html.

9. Manea, *Women and Shari'a Law*, pp. 147–48; Anya Hart Dyke, *Mosques Made in Britain* (London: Quilliam Foundation, 2009), pp. 5, 15–16; Change Institute, *Pakistani Muslim Community in England: Understanding Muslim Ethnic Communities*, March 2009, p. 39.

10. Manea, *Women and Shari'a Law*, p. 153.

11. Michael Crawford, *Ibn Abd al-Wahhab* (London: One World Publications, 2014), pp. 21–27.

12. Ibid.; Manea, *Regional Politics of the Gulf*, pp. 20–22, 73–74; Madawi Al-Rasheed, *A History of Saudi Arabia* (Cambridge: Cambridge Univ. Press, 2002), p. 16.

13. Muhammad Ibn Saalih Al-'Uthaymeen, *Explanation of the Three Fundamental*

Principles of Mohammaed ibn Abd al-Wahhab [in Arabic] (Alexandria: Dar al Madina, 2001), pp. 39–43; Mohammad Ibn Abd Al Wahhab, *Kitab At-Tawid: The Book of Monotheism* [in Arabic] (Egypt: Library of Ibad Al Rahman, 2008); Crawford, *Ibn Abd al-Wahhab*, pp. 47–72.

14. Crawford, *Ibn Abd al-Wahhab*.

15. For more detail see Saalih Al-'Uthaymeen, *Explanation of the Three Fundamental Principles*, pp. 25–27.

16. Crawford, *Ibn Abd al-Wahhab*.

17. Quoted in ibid., p. 69.

18. For more information, see Quintan Wiktorowicz, "Anatomy of the Salafi Movement," *Studies in Conflict & Terrorism* 29, no. 3 (2006): 207–39.

19. Ibid.

20. For more information on Salifism and the principle of *al-wala' wa-l-bara*, see Benham T. Said and Hazim Fouad, eds., *Salafismus: Auf der suche nach der wahren Islam* (Freiburg: Herder Verlag, 2014), pp. 64–74.

21. The video of the interview and its transcript can be found on Haitham al-Haddad's blog, *The Islamic Far-Right in Britain*, under the heading "Islamic Supremacy," http://tifrib.com/haitham-al-haddad/; quoted in Manea, *Women and Shari'a Law*, pp. 154–56.

22. Ibid.

23. Ahmed Abo Elmagd, human rights lawyer, interview with the author, Cairo, February 12, 2012.

24. Ahmed Abo Elmagd, follow-up interview, Skype, August 24, 2017.

25. UK Government, *Muslim Brotherhood Review: Main Findings*, December 17, 2015, https://www.gov.uk/government/uploads/system/uploads/attachment_data/file/486948/53163_Muslim_Brotherhood_Review_-_PRINT.pdf.

26. Munir al-Ghadban, *The Kinetic Approach of the Prophet's Biography* [in Arabic], vol. 1, 6th ed. (Jordan: Dar al-Manar, 1990), p. 4.

27. Ibid., p. 16.

28. Ibid.

29. *Al Rashad on Raising Sons* [in Arabic], pt. 2, *Al Manara*, p. 10.

30. Ibid., pt. 1, *Al Manara*, p. 9.

31. Ibid., pt. 4, p. 22.

32. Moomen Sallam, interview with author; "A Conspiracy Hatched against the Youth" [in Arabic], YouTube video, 3:35, June 9, 2013, https://www.youtube.com/watch?v=pg5Uhobqqg4; Islamic Nasheeds Lyrics, "A conspiracy is going on for the youth to be exposed to hug the bayonets," Facebook, July 8, 2013, https://www.facebook.com/Islamic.n.l/posts/677888602228393/.

33. Elham Manea, "Be Ambassadors for Islam," *Swissinfo*, September 20, 2004, https://goo.gl/tsZV1b.

34. Rabab Kamal, interview with author.

35. Moomen Sallam, interview with author.

36. Ahmed Abo Elmagd, interview with author, Cairo.

37. Abo Elmagd, interview with author, Skype.

38. Abo Elmagd, interview with author, Cairo.

39. Al-Banna, *The Five Tracts of Hasan Al-Banna*, p. 78.

40. Abu Elmagd, interview with author, Skype.

41. "Katiba," *Ikhwan Wiki*, https://goo.gl/pr7xe2.

42. Al-Banna, *The Five Tracts of Hasan Al-Banna*, p. 18. For more information see Barry Rubin, ed., *Political Islam I* (London: Routledge, 2007), pp. 1–44.

43. Munir al-Ghadban, *The Kinetic Approach of the Prophet's Biography*, pp. 72–73.

44. Sheik Yousuf al-Qaradhawi, "Islam's 'Conquest of Rome' Will Save Europe from Its Subjugation to Materialism and Promiscuity" [in Arabic], Qatar TV, July 28, 2007. A video clip, translated and posted by MEMRI TV, the Middle East Media Research Institute, is available at http://www.memritv.org/clip/en/1592.htm.

5. How Nonviolent Islamism Changes Behavior and Communities

1. The term was introduced by Amartya Sen, the Indian economist and Nobel Prize winner. See Amartya Sen, *Identity and Violence: The Illusion of Destiny* (London: W. W. Norton, 2006). For a short summary of his concept, see Sen, "The Uses and Abuses of Multiculturalism," *New Republic*, February 27, 2006, pp. 25–30.

2. John Gieve, Home Secretary, *Draft Report on Young Muslims and Extremism* (London: UK Foreign and Commonwealth Office/Home Office, 2004), p. 5.

3. Manea, *Women and Shari'a Law*, p. 161.

4. Manea, "Defining the Phenomenon of Jihadist Radicalisation," p. 27.

5. Lorenzo Vidino, "Jihadist Radicalization in Switzerland," Center for Security Studies (CSS), ETH Zurich, November 2013, p. 11.

6. Alex P. Schmid, "Radicalisation, De-Radicalisation, Counter-Radicalisation: A Conceptual Discussion and Literature Review," International Centre for Counter-Terrorism, The Hauge, ICCT Research Paper, March 2013, p. 6.

7. Vidino, "Jihadist Radicalization in Switzerland."

8. Schmid, "Radicalisation, De-Radicalisation, Counter-Radicalisation," p. 8.

9. This definition by Charles E. Allen brings in many of the elements used by most scholars. See Vidino, "Jihadist Radicalization in Switzerland," pp. 11–12.

10. Ibid.

11. Anja Dalgaard-Nielsen, "Violent Radicalization in Europe: What We Know and What We Do Not Know," *Studies in Conflict & Terrorism* 33, no. 9 (2010): 798.

12. Mehdi Mozaffari, "What Is Islamism? History and Definition of a Concept," *Totalitarian Movements and Political Religions* 8, no. 1 (2007): 21.

13. Ibid., pp. 21–24.

14. Ibid., p. 24.

15. Ibid.

16. Dalgaard-Nielsen, "Violent Radicalization in Europe," p. 800.

17. Ibid., p. 801.

18. Ibid., p. 803.

19. Randy Borum, "Radicalization into Violent Extremism II: A Review of Conceptual Models and Empirical Research," *Journal of Strategic Security* 4, no. 4 (2011): 43–44.

20. Ibid.

21. Ibid., pp. 44–45.

6. Closed Communities: A Fertile Ground for Radicalization

1. Author interview with police officer, September 20, 2017.

2. "Nationality," website for Kingdom of Belgium Foreign Affairs, Foreign Trade and Development Cooperation, specifically the pages "Born in Belgium," https://diplomatie.

belgium.be/en/services/services_abroad/nationality/being_granted_belgian_nationality/born_in_belgium; and "Born to a Belgian Parent," https://diplomatie.belgium.be/en/services/services_abroad/nationality/being_granted_belgian_nationality/born_to_a_belgian_parent.

3. Marco Martiniello and Andrea Rea, "Belgium's Immigration Policy Brings Renewal and Challenges," Migration Policy Institute, October 1, 2003, http://www.migrationpolicy.org/article/belgiums-immigration-policy-brings-renewal-and-challenges/.

4. "Molenbeek St-Jean," Brussels Institute for Statistics and Analysis, 2016, http://statistics.brussels/figures/key-figures-per-municipality/molenbeek-st-jean#.WconnEyB104; Julia Lynch, "Here's Why So Many of Europe's Terrorist Attacks Come through This One Brussels Neighborhood," *Washington Post*, April 5, 2016, https://www.washingtonpost.com/news/monkey-cage/wp/2016/04/05/heres-why-so-many-of-europes-terror-attacks-come-through-this-one-brussels-neighborhood/?utm_term=.83240a70209b.

5. Sarah Teich, "Islamic Radicalization in Belgium," International Institute for Counter-Terrorism (ICT), February 2016, p. 24, https://www.ict.org.il/UserFiles/ICT-IRI-Belgium-Teich-Feb-16.pdf; Barbara Wesel, "Brussels' Great Mosque and Ties with Salafism," *Deutsche Welle*, November 21, 2015, http://www.dw.com/en/brussels-great-mosque-and-ties-with-salafism/a-18866998#.

6. Teich, "Islamic Radicalization in Belgium," pp. 24, 26.

7. "Saudi and the Brotherhood: From Friends to Foes," *Aljazeera English*, June 23, 2017, http://www.aljazeera.com/news/2017/06/saudi-brotherhood-friends-foes-1706 23093039202.html; "Morsi's Visit Brings Back the History of Saudi–Muslim Brothers Ties" [in Arabic], *Alsharq Alawsat Newspaper*, July 18, 2012, http://archive.aawsat.com/details.asp?section=4&article=685584&issueno=12277#.Wct2s9MjEWo.

8. Lorenzo Vidino, *The New Muslim Brotherhood in the West* (New York: Columbia Univ. Press, 2010), pp. 26–27; Ian Johnson, *A Mosque in Munich: Nazis, the CIA and the Rise of the Muslim Brotherhood in the West* (Boston: Houghton Mifflin Harcourt, 2010), pp. 182–83; Manea, *Regional Politics of the Gulf*, pp. 123–24; "Saudi and the Brotherhood: From Friends to Foes."

9. Lynch, "Here's Why So Many of Europe's Terrorist Attacks"; Ryan Heath, "The 12 People and Ideas That Ruined Molenbeek," *Politico*, November 18, 2015, http://www.politico.eu/article/attack-on-paris-molenbeek-dirty-dozen/; Teun Voeten, "Molenbeek Broke My Heart," *Politico*, November 21, 2015, http://www.politico.eu/article/molenbeek-broke-my-heart-radicalization-suburb-brussels-gentrification/.

10. Heath, "The 12 People and Ideas That Ruined Molenbeek"; Voeten, "Molenbeek Broke My Heart."

11. Voeten, "Molenbeek Broke My Heart."

12. Bibi van Ginkel and Eva Entenmann, eds., "The Foreign Fighter Phenomenon in the European Union: Profiles, Threats & Policies," *International Centre for Counter-Terrorism – The Hague* 7, no. 2 (2016): 25.

7. The White Man's Burden and the Mainstreaming of Islamism

1. "Islamic Relief Canada," Charity Intelligence Canada, https://www.charityintelligence.ca/charity-details/501-islamic-relief-canada; "Board of Directors," Islamic Relief Canada, http://islamicreliefcanada.org/about/bod/.

2. "UAE Sends Clear Signal on Fighting Terrorism," *Gulf News*, November 20, 2014, http://gulfnews.com/news/uae/government/uae-sends-clear-signal-on-fighting-terrorism-1.1415740; "List of Groups Designated Terrorist Organisations by the UAE," *National*, November 16, 2014, https://www.thenationalnews.com/uae/government/list-of-groups-designated-terrorist-organisations-by-the-uae-1.270037.

3. "Islamic Relief Worldwide (IRW)," NGO Monitor, http://www.ngo-monitor.org/ngos/islamic_relief_worldwide_irw_/; Samuel Gerber, "Islamic Relief: Not Welcome at UBS and CS," *Finews*, January 6, 2016, http://www.finews.com/news/english-news/21399-islamic-relief-charity-ubs-credit-suisse-postfinance-uk-hsbc-israel.

4. These are the al-Farouk Battalion in Homs, the Tawhid Brigade in Aleppo, the Suqur al-Sham in Jabal Zawiya, and the Ahrar al-Sham in Idlib. See Raphaël Lefèvre, "The Syrian Brotherhood's Armed Struggle," Carnegie Endowment for International Peace, December 14, 2012, p. 3, http://carnegieendowment.org/2012/12/14/syrian-brotherhood-s-armed-struggle-pub-50380; Magnus Norell, Aje Carlbom, and Pierre Durrani, "The Muslim Brotherhood in Sweden," report commissioned by the Swedish Civil Contingencies Agency, November–December 2016, p. 10.

5. See Vidino, *The New Muslim Brotherhood in the West*, pp. 183–86.

6. Elham Manea, "Women's March: Why Use the Headscarf (Veil) as a Symbol for Islam?," *Huffington Post*, January 24, 2017, http://www.huffingtonpost.com/entry/womens-march-why-use-the-headscarf-viel-as-a-symbol_us_5884a1ede4b0111ea60b971c.

7. "Federation of Islamic Organisations in Europe" [in Arabic], *Ikhwan Wiki*, https://goo.gl/u57S2R.

8. "About Us," Federation of Islamic Organisations in Europe (FIOE) website, archived at http://web.archive.org/web/20010607062629/www.fioe.org/about_us/about_us.htm.

9. Ann Kröning, "Van der Bellens Tag, an dem alle Frauen Kopftuch tragen," *Die Welt*, April 26, 2017, https://www.welt.de/vermischtes/article164022903/Van-der-Bellens-Tag-an-dem-alle-Frauen-Kopftuch-tragen.html. For the video of the president making these remarks, see Karl, "Austrian president Alexander Van der Bellen wants ALL women to wear a headscarf (subtitles)," April 26, 2017, YouTube video, 0:32, https://www.youtube.com/watch?v=JgoDXWhjjak.

10. Jamie Merrill, "NUS Motion to Condemn ISIS Fails amidst Claims of Islamophobia," *Independent*, October 15, 2014, http://www.independent.co.uk/student/news/nus-motion-to-condemn-isis-fails-amidst-claims-of-islamophobia-9796193.html. For the text of the motion and the division within NUS, see Harry Shukman "NUS Refuses to Condemn ISIS Terrorists…Because It's 'Islamophobic,'" *Tab*, October 14, 2014, https://thetab.com/2014/10/14/nus-refuses-to-condemn-terrorists-because-its-islamophobic-22191.

11. Manea, *Women and Shari'a Law*, pp. 11–34.

12. Bernhard Ott, "Viele Schweizer haben Angst, Kritik am Islam zu üben," *Der Bund*, August 26, 2017, https://www.derbund.ch/front/redaktion-empfiehlt/viele-schweizer-haben-angst-kritik-am-islam-zu-ueben/story/22154105.

13. Rafaela Roth, "Jacqueline Fehrs Islam-Streit auf Facebook," *Tagesanzeiger*, August 29, 2017, https://www.tagesanzeiger.ch/zuerich/region/jacqueline-fehrs-islamstreit-auf-facebook/story/16017053.

14. Ibid.

15. Ibid.

16. Archbishop Rowan Williams, "Civil and Religious Law in England: A Religious Perspective," lecture at the Royal Courts of Justice, February 7, 2008, archived at http://aoc2013.brix.fatbeehive.com/articles.php/1137/.

17. Quoted in Dominic McGoldrick, "The Compatibility of an Islamic/*Shari'a* Law System or *Shari'a* Rules with the European Convention on Human Rights," in *Islam and English Law: Rights, Responsibilities and the Place of Sharia*, ed. Robin Griffith-Jones (Cambridge: Cambridge Univ. Press, 2013), p. 55; Manea, *Women and Shari'a Law*, p. 91.

18. For more information on how Islamists view this, see Barry Rubin, ed., *Political Islam*, vol. 1 (London: Routledge, 2007), pp. 1–44.

19. Roth, "Jacqueline Fehrs Islam-Streit auf Facebook."

20. Lee Roden, "Debate Rages in Sweden over Muslim Brotherhood Report," *Local*, March 3, 2017, https://www.thelocal.se/20170303/debate-rages-in-sweden-over-muslim-brotherhood-report.

21. "About the MSB," Swedish Civil Contingencies Agency, https://www.msb.se/en/About-MSB/.

22. Norell et al., "The Muslim Brotherhood in Sweden," pp. 4, 21, 26.

23. Ibid, pp. 20–21.

24. "Undermålig forskning i svensk myndighetsrapport," *Religionsvetenskapliga Kommentarer*, March 2, 2017, http://religionsvetenskapligakommentarer.blogspot.ch/2017/03/debatt-undermalig-forskning-i-svensk.html.

25. Roden, "Debate Rages in Sweden."

26. Dr. Magnus Norell, a Swedish expert on terrorism and political violence, interview by author via Skype, August 7, 2017.

27. "Report on the Muslim Brotherhood in Sweden Causes Debate March," Eurel Project: Sociological and Legal Data on Religions in Europe and Beyond, March 2017, http://www.eurel.info/spip.php?article2751&lang=en. See also the MSB statement in Swedish: "MSB om förstudien Muslimska brödraskapet i Sverige," Swedish Civil Contingencies Agency, March 3, 2017, https://www.msb.se/sv/Om-MSB/Nyheter-och-press/Nyheter/Nyheter-fran-MSB/MSB-om-forstudien-Muslimska-brodraskapet-i-Sverige/.

28. Göran Adamson, *Populist Parties and the Failure of the Political Elites: The Rise of the Austrian Freedom Party* (New York: Peter Lang, 2016).

29. Göran Adamson, *The Trojan Horse: A Leftist Critique of Multiculturalism in the West* (Malmö: Arx Förlag, 2015), p. 11.

30. Ibid.

31. "Brown v. Board at Fifty: 'With an Even Hand': A Century of Racial Segregation, 1849–1950," Library of Congress, https://www.loc.gov/exhibits/brown/brown-segregation.html.

32. Manea, *Women and Shari'a Law*, p. 12.

33. Adamson, *The Trojan Horse*, p. 11.

34. "Malmö högskola rensade ut mångfaldskritiker: passade på vid nedskärning," Academic Rights Watch, July 17, 2015, http://academicrightswatch.se/?p=1670.

35. Aje Carlbom, "The Imagined versus the Real Other: Multiculturalism and the Representation of Muslims in the Sweden" (PhD diss., Lund University, 2003), https://lup.lub.lu.se/search/ws/files/4421698/1693275.pdf.

36. Norell, interview by author.

37. Alison Pargeter, *The Muslim Brotherhood: The Burden of Tradition* (London: Saqi Books, 2010), p. 133.

38. Ibid.

39. Vidino, *The New Muslim Brotherhood in the West*, p. 79; Pargeter, *The Muslim Brotherhood*, p. 116; Johnson, *A Mosque in Munich*, pp. xii, 89–191, 217–18; John C. Zimmerman, review of Sylvain Besson, *La conquête de l'Occident: Le projet secret des Islamistes, Terrorism and Political Violence* 20, no. 1 (2007): 141–42.

40. Johnson, *A Mosque in Munich*.

41. Without Borders Show, "Youssef Nada: The Financial Strategy of the Muslim Brotherhood" [in Arabic], pt. 2, *Al Jazeera Arabic*, October 9, 2006, http://goo.gl/yMfpBJ.

42. For the text of the document, see the appendix of Sylvain Besson, *La conquête de l'Occident: Le projet secret des Islamistes* [The Conquest of the West: The Secret Project of the Islamists] (Paris: Seuil, 2005). pp. 193–204.

43. Pargeter, *The Muslim Brotherhood*, p. 116.

44. Vidino, *The New Muslim Brotherhood in the West*, p. 79.

45. Zimmerman, review of Besson, *La conquête de l'Occident*, p. 142.

46. Ibid.

47. Ibid.

48. Ibid.

49. Ibid.

50. Ibid.

51. Pargeter, *The Muslim Brotherhood*, p. 117. She repeated the same sentence in the book's new edition of 2013.

52. Vidino, *The New Muslim Brotherhood in the West*, p. 79.

53. Ibid., p. 80.

54. "Undermålig forskning i svensk myndighetsrapport."

55. "Om Islamiska Förbundet," Islamiska Förbundet website, http://www.islamiska-forbundet.se/omif/.

56. "Federation of Islamic Organisations in Europe" [in Arabic], *Ikhwan Wiki*, http://goo.gl/u57S2R.

57. Mahmoud Aldebe, "Point of View: Swedish Elections and the Muslim Brotherhood" [in Arabic], *Akhbar (Danmarks Nyheder)*, September 17, 2010, http://www.akhbar.dk/ar/article2/1309-2010-09-17-09-35-09.html.

58. Ibid.

59. "Faisal Maulaw: The Jihadi Jurist" [in Arabic], *Ikhwan Wiki*, http://goo.gl/u57S2R.

60. "Facts about Migration and Crime in Sweden," Government Offices of Sweden, February 23, 2017, http://www.government.se/articles/2017/02/facts-about-migration-and-crime-in-sweden/.

61. Carlbom, "The Imagined versus the Real Other," p. 13.

62. Ibid., pp. 63–64.

63. Aldebe, "Point of View: Swedish Elections and the Muslim Brotherhood."

64. Johan Westerholm, Swedish investigative journalist, interview with author via Skype, August 28, 2017; Pascal Delwit, "European Social Democracy and the World of Members: The End of the Community Party Concept?," in *Social Democracy in Europe*, ed. Pascal Delwit (Brussels: Éditions de l'Université de Bruxelles, 2005), pp. 214–16.

65. Karen M. Anderson, "The Church as Nation? The Role of Religion in the Development of the Swedish Welfare State," in *Religion, Class Coalitions, and Welfare State Regimes*, ed. Kees van Kersbergen and Philip Manow (Cambridge: Cambridge Univ. Press, 2009), pp. 228–32.

66. Email Correspondence with Peter Weiderud, former president of Christian Social Democrats (2005–2015), October 29, 2017.

67. Sweden Christian Social Democrats, "Delaktighet, identitet & integration," report 4, 1999, p. 8.

68. Email Correspondence with Peter Weiderud, October 12 and 29, 2017.

69. Aldebe, "Point of View: Swedish Elections and the Muslim Brotherhood."

70. These are the al-Farouk Battalion in Homs, the Tawhid Brigade in Aleppo, the Suqur al-Sham in Jabal Zawiya, and the Ahrar al-Sham in Idlib. See Lefèvre, "The Syrian Brotherhood's Armed Struggle," p. 3; Norell et al., "The Muslim Brotherhood in Sweden," p. 10.

71. Sweden Christian Social Democrats, "Delaktighet, identitet & integration," p. 9.

72. Carlbom, "The Imagined versus the Real Other," pp. 91–92.

73. Ibid.

74. "Education in Sweden," official website of Sweden, https://sweden.se/society/education-in-sweden/.

75. Westerholm, interview by author.

76. Carlbom, "The Imagined versus the Real Other," p. 192.

77. Hans Ingvar Roth et al., "Tolerance and Cultural Diversity Discourses and Practices in Sweden," report, European University Institute, 2013, p. 54, http://cadmus.eui.eu/bitstream/handle/1814/27518/ACCEPT_WP5_2013-24_Country-synthesis-report_Sweden.pdf?sequence=1; Harriet Agerholm "Swedish Prime Minister Condemns Gender Segregated Muslim School Bus as 'Despicable,'" *Independent*, April 5, 2017, https://www.independent.co.uk/news/world/europe/swedish-prime-minister-stefan-lofven-gender-segregated-school-bus-boy-girl-disgusting-a7667981.html; "Stockholm School Criticised for Segregated Gym Classes," *Radio Sweden*, August 29, 2016, http://sverigesradio.se/sida/artikel.aspx?programid=2054&artikel=6505680.

78. Magnus Norell, follow-up email with author, October 13, 2017.

79. Former Swedish politician and civil society activist, interview by author via Skype, October 15, 2017.

80. Westerholm, interview by author.

81. Former Swedish politician, interview by author.

8. The Battle for Values and Norms in Europe and North America

1. For more about the history of music and dancing in Islamic civilizations, see Saad Zaghloul Abd al-Hameed, "Artistic Life" [in Arabic], in Said Abd al-Fatah Aashour et al., *Studies in the History of Arabic Islamic Civilization*, 2nd ed. (Kuwait: Zat al Slassel, 1986), ch. 6.

2. Arshad Alam, "Competing Islams," *Outlook India*, September 14, 2006, https://www.outlookindia.com/website/story/competing-islams/232494.

3. Tanya Basu, "What Does Islamophobia Actually Mean? A Brief History of a Provocative Word," *Atlantic*, October 15, 2014, https://www.theatlantic.com/international/archive/2014/10/is-islamophobia-real-maher-harris-aslan/381411/.

4. Robin Richardson, ed., *Islamophobia: Issues, Challenges and Action: A Report*

by the Commission on British Muslims and Islamophobia (Stoke-on-Trent: Trentham Books, 2004), p. 7.

5. Quote by Robin Richardson, in Basu, "What Does Islamophobia Actually Mean?"

6. A second use in print was found in the reviews of Quellien's book in academic journals and in a biography of Muhammad by Alphonse Etienne Dinet (1861–1929), a French painter and convert to Islam who lived most of his adult life in southern Algeria. His book was published in 1918. In the English version, the word *islamophobie* was translated as "feelings inimical to Islam"; see Robin Richardson, "Islamophobia or Anti-Muslim Racism—Or What? Concepts and Terms Revisited," Insted Consultancy, 2012, p. 3, http://www.insted.co.uk/anti-muslim-racism.pdf.

7. Edward Said, "Orientalism Reconsidered," *Race and Class* 27, no. 2 (1985): 9.

8. Richardson, "Islamophobia or Anti-Muslim Racism," p. 3; Samir Amghar, Amel Boubekeur, and Michael Emerson, eds., *European Islam: Challenges for Public Policy and Society* (Brussels: The Centre for European Policy Studies, CEPS, 2007), pp. 148–49.

9. Tariq Modood, "Muslims, Race and Equality in Britain: Some Post-Rushdie Affair Reflections," *Third Text* 4, no. 11 (1990): 131–32.

10. Former Swedish politician and civil society activist, interview by author.

11. Farid Hafez, "The Global Muslim Brotherhood Conspiracy Theory," *Bridge* (Georgetown Univ.), September 19, 2017, https://bridge.georgetown.edu/research/the-global-muslim-brotherhood-conspiracy-theory/.

12. Basu, "What Does Islamophobia Actually Mean?"

13. Pernille Ammitzbøll and Lorenzo Vidino, "After the Danish Cartoon Controversy," *Middle East Quarterly* 14, no. 1 (2007), 3–11, http://www.meforum.org/1437/after-the-danish-cartoon-controversy.

14. For more information on the Islamist role in the Rushdie affair, see Kenan Malik, *From Fatwa to Jihad: The Rushdie Affair and Its Aftermath* (Brooklyn, NY: Melville House Publishing, 2009).

15. Ammitzbøll and Vidino, "After the Danish Cartoon Controversy"; Elham Manea, "We Do Not Speak the Same Language!," in *The Cartoon Debate and the Freedom of the Press*, ed. Bernard Debatin (Münster: Lit Verlag, 2007), pp. 45–46.

16. Ammitzbøll and Vidino, "After the Danish Cartoon Controversy."

17. Elham Manea, "In the Name of Culture and Religion: The Political Function of Blasphemy in Islamic States," *Islam and Christian–Muslim Relations* 27, no. 1 (2016): 117–18.

18. Ibid.

19. Ibid., pp. 125–26.

20. Karin Heremans, headmistress of the Royal Atheneum, interview by author, September 21, 2017, Antwerp, Belgium.

21. Charlemagne, "Antwerp's Muslim Headscarf Row, the Story on the Ground," *Economist*, September 17, 2009, https://www.economist.com/blogs/charlemagne/2009/09/antwerps_muslim_headscarf_row.

22. Ibid.

23. Ibid.

24. Heremans, interview by author.

25. Charlemagne, "Antwerp's Muslim Headscarf Row."

26. Ibid.

27. Heremans, interview by author.

28. Charlemagne, "Antwerp's Muslim Headscarf Row."

29. "Essam el-Erian Talks about the Muslim Brotherhood's Role in Spreading the Veil" [in Arabic], July 20, 2019, YouTube video, 5:12, https://www.youtube.com/watch?v=PncUp-ojbZs.

30. Maajid Nawaz, "Maajid Tackles 'Feminist' Muslim Who Said She'd Burn in Hell If She Didn't Wear a Hijab," *LBC*, September 3, 2017, http://www.lbc.co.uk/radio/presenters/maajid-nawaz/maajid-tackles-feminist-muslim-hijab.

31. See Quran, surah 33, *al-Ahzaab*, verse 59, and commentary such as Rania Karim, "According to the View of the Majority of Scholars, the Ummah's Nakedness from the Navel to the Knee Is Like a Man" [in Arabic], March 1, 2014, YouTube video, 1:48, https://www.youtube.com/watch?v=wuFYL9v5000.

32. "Slavery in Arabia - 1964," January 24, 2014, YouTube video, 6:47, https://www.youtube.com/watch?v=emRVkisdbhc.

33. Moustafa Moaouth, *The Problem of the Woman's Clothes and the Problem of Wearing a Woman's Clothing—the Veil: A Review of the Evidence and Arguments* [in Arabic] (Cairo: Rouya for Publications, 2009), pp. 25–28, 72–73.

34. Elham Manea, *Ich will nicht mehr schweigen: Der Islam, der Westen und die Menschenrechte* (Freiburg: Herder Verlag, 2009), pp. 96, 98–103.

35. Ibid, pp. 162–64.

36. Hasan al-Banna, *The Muslim Woman* [in Arabic], ed. Mohammed Naser al-Deen al-Albani, 2nd ed. (Beirut: Dar al-Jeel, 1988), pp. 9–19.

37. Ibid.

38. Ibid.

39. Ibid.

40. Bojan Stula, "Diese Frau brachte den Fall Therwil ins Rollen," *Basellandschaftliche Zeitung*, April 26, 2016, https://www.basellandschaftlichezeitung.ch/basel/baselbiet/diese-frau-brachte-den-fall-therwil-ins-rollen-ich-denke-vielen-sind-jetzt-die-augen-aufgegangen-130226549.

41. Valerie Zaslawski, "Kein Händedruck trotz Rechtsgutachten," *Neue Zürcher Zeitung*, August 22, 2016, https://www.nzz.ch/schweiz/fall-therwil-kein-handschlag-trotz-rechtsgutachten-ld.112342.

42. Elham Manea "Die Verweigerung des Handschlags ist nur der Anfang," *NZZ am Sonntag*, April 10, 2017.

43. Andreas Schmid, "Aufsicht untersucht Moschee-Stiftung," *NZZ am Sonntag*, April 17, 2017, https://www.nzz.ch/nzzas/nzz-am-sonntag/geldfluesse-der-basler-koenig-faysal-stiftung-aufsicht-untersucht-moschee-stiftung-ld.14382; Joël Hoffmann, "König Faysal Stiftung und ihre Terrorfinanciers," *Basler Zeitung*, April 14, 2016, https://bazonline.ch/basel/stadt/Koenig-Faysal-Stiftung-und-ihre-Terrorfinanciers/story/26387393; "Niemand kann uns zwingen, Hände zu berühren," *Tages Anzeiger*, April 10, 2016, https://www.tagesanzeiger.ch/panorama/vermischtes/niemand-kann-uns-zwingen-haende-zu-beruehren/story/21674547.

44. Manea "Die Verweigerung des Handschlags."

45. Daniel Wahl, "Ein zu strenges Leben nach dem Koran: Eine Schwester der Basler Handschlag-Verweigerer musste vor ihrer Familie in ein Frauenhaus fliehen," *Tages Anzeiger*, April 23, 2016, https://www.tagesanzeiger.ch/schweiz/standard/ein-zu-strenges-leben-nach-dem-koran/story/15489305.

46. For more information, see Manea, *Women and Shari'a Law*, pp. 165–82.

47. "Girls Forced to Wear Hijabs in English Schools, NSS Reveals," *Secularism UK*,

September 24, 2017, http://www.secularism.org.uk/news/2017/09/girls-forced-to-wear-hijabs-in-english-schools-nss-reveals.

48. Amina Lone, British Muslim activist and former Labour councillor, interview by author, July 22, 2017, London; Amina Lone, follow-up interview by author via Skype, September 13, 2017; Iram Ramzan, "Amina Lone and the Shame of the Labour Party in the UK," *Sedaa*, August 27, 2017, http://www.sedaa.org/2017/08/amina-lone-and-the-shame-of-the-labour-party-in-the-uk/; Andrew Gilligan, "Labour 'Terrifies Black Women', Says Sacked Councillor Amina Lone," *Times*, August 27, 2017, https://www.thetimes.co.uk/article/labour-terrifies-black-women-says-sacked-councillor-amina-lone-mxd2w2lp5.

49. Lone, follow-up interview.

50. "C4 Survey and Documentary Reveals What British Muslims Really Think," Channel 4, April 11, 2016, http://www.channel4.com/info/press/news/c4-survey-and-documentary-reveals-what-british-muslims-really-think. For the full results of the survey, conducted between April 25 and May 31, 2015, see "ICM Muslims Survey for Channel 4," ICM Unlimited Polling, April 11, 2016, https://www.icmunlimited.com/wp-content/uploads/2016/04/Mulims-full-suite-data-plus-topline.pdf.

51. Dame Louise Casey, *The Casey Review: A Review into Opportunity and Integration*, Department for Communities and Local Government, UK Government, December 2016, pp. 10ff., https://www.gov.uk/government/uploads/system/uploads/attachment_data/file/575973/The_Casey_Review_Report.pdf.

52. Ibid., p. 9.

53. Necla Kelek, *Die fremde Braut: Ein Bericht aus dem Inneren des türkischen Lebens in Deutschland* (Munich: Goldman, 2006).

54. Ibid., p. 11.

55. Ibid., pp. 11–12.

56. For more Information see Manea, *Women and Shari'a Law*, pp. 120–35.

57. Indeed the first religious edict of the transnational Muslim Brotherhood arm for religious edicts—the Dublin-based European Council for Fatwa and Research (ECFR)—called on Muslims in Western democracies to follow Islamic law in their lifestyle and demanded that they "work hard" to get the states where they live to recognize "Islam as a religion, and…Muslims as a religious minority like other religious minorities." This recognition would include "full enjoyment of their rights, and ability to regulate their personal status such as marriage, divorce and inheritance" according to Islamic law. The ECFR is headed by Sheikh Yusuf al-Qaradawi, the spiritual leader of the Muslim Brotherhood movement, the one who said, if you remember, that Muslims will conquer Europe without resorting to the sword or fighting, but by means of *dawa* (proselytizing) and ideology. European Council for Fatwa and Research, *Resolutions and Fatwas* [edicts] *of the European Council for Fatwa and Research* [in Arabic] (Cairo: Islamic House for Distribution and Publication, 2002), p. 19; Sheik Yousuf al-Qaradhawi, "Islam's 'Conquest of Rome' Will Save Europe from Its Subjugation to Materialism and Promiscuity" [in Arabic], Qatar TV, July 28, 2007; video clip, translated and posted by MEMRI TV, the Middle East Media Research Institute, is available at http://www.memritv.org/clip/en/1592.htm.

58. "About Us," Islamic Shari'a Council website, http://www.islamic-sharia.org/aboutus/. See, for instance, Bangladesh Genocide Archive, *War Crimes File: A Documentary by Twenty Twenty Television*, http://www.genocidebangladesh.org/war-crimes-

file-a-documentary-by-twenty-twenty-television/. For more information on the Badr Squad, see for instance Husain Haqqani, *Pakistan: Between Mosque and Military* (Washington, DC: Carnegie Endowment for International Peace, 2010), pp. 79–80.

59. International Conference on Free Expression and Conscience, "Blasphemy, Islamophobia, Free Expression Panel," London, July 22–24, 2017; video available at Nano GoleSorkh, "Blasphemy, Islamophobia, Free Expression Panel," July 27, 2017, YouTube video, 1:20:55, https://www.youtube.com/watch?v=seJkIGV8urc.

Conclusion

1. Karima Bennoune documented this struggle in her highly acclaimed book *Your Fatwa Does Not Apply Here: Untold Stories from the Fight against Muslim Fundamentalism* (New York: Norton, 2013).

2. For the text of the 2015 Austrian Islam Law in both English and German, see "Islamgesetz," Bundesministerium Republik Österreich website, https://www.bmeia.gv.at/integration/islamgesetz/.

3. Austrian Islam Law, English version, § 6.12.2, https://www.bundeskanzleramt.gv.at/en/agenda/integration/the-austrian-islam-law.html.

4. Heiko Heinisch, Austrian historian and researcher on Islam, interview by author via Skype, August 2, 2017.

5. Manea, *Women and Shari'a Law*, pp. 147–48; Anya Hart Dyke, *Mosques Made in Britain* (London: Quilliam Foundation, 2009), pp. 5, 15–16; Change Institute, *Pakistani Muslim Community in England*, p. 39.

6. *Al Rashad on Raising Sons* [in Arabic], pt. 2, *Al Manara*, pt. 4, p. 22.

7. Ednan Aslan, "Projektbericht: Evaluierung ausgewählter Islamischer Kindergärten und –Gruppen in Wien," Institute for Islamic Studies, University of Vienna, 2016, p. 111, https://iits.univie.ac.at/fileadmin/user_upload/p_iits/Dateien/Abschlussbericht__Vorstudie_Islamische_Kindergarten_Wien_final.pdf.

8. Ednan Aslan, interview by author, Vienna, September 5, 2017.

9. "Strengeres Kindergartengesetz kommt," Wien ORF, November 10, 2017, http://wien.orf.at/news/stories/2877368/.

10. Sylvie Durrer, director of the Federal Office for the Equality of Women and Men (EBG), in a plenary meeting of the Federal Commission of Women Affairs, Bern, November 29, 2017.

11. Heremans, interview by author, September 21, 2017.

12. Elias Hemelsoet, policy advisor of the Flanders Community Education Board, video conference with author, October 5, 2016.

13. Ibid.

About the Author

Elham Manea is a writer, an activist, and a Privatdozentin (equivalent to associate professor) at the University of Zurich, where she specializes on the Middle East, women under Muslim Laws, and Islamism. She works at the Political Science Institute at the University of Zurich and as an independent consultant for government and international agencies. Her recent English-language publications include *The Arab State and Women's Rights: The Trap of Authoritarian Governance* (Routledge, 2011) and *Women and Shari'a Law: The Impact of Legal Pluralism in the UK* (I.B. Tauris, 2016).

Also from Telos Press Publishing

Screens of Power:
Ideology, Domination, and Resistance in Informational Society
Timothy W. Luke

The Crisis of Liberalism: Prelude to Trump
Fred Siegel

Anthropocene Alerts:
Critical Theory of the Contemporary as Ecocritique
Timothy W. Luke

Mastering the Past: Contemporary Central and Eastern Europe
and the Rise of Illiberalism
Ellen Hinsey

Germany and Iran: From the Aryan Axis to the Nuclear Threshold
Matthias Küntzel

Jihad and Jew-Hatred: Islamism, Nazism, and the Roots of 9/11
Matthias Küntzel

The Democratic Contradictions of Multiculturalism
Jens-Martin Eriksen and Frederik Stjernfelt

Free Radicals: Agitators, Hippies, Urban Guerrillas,
and Germany's Youth Revolt of the 1960s and 1970s
Elliot Neaman

Europe and the World: World War I as Crisis of Universalism
Edited by Kai Evers and David Pan

A Journal of No Illusions:
Telos, *Paul Piccone, and the Americanization of Critical Theory*
Edited by Timothy W. Luke and Ben Agger

The New Class Conflict
Joel Kotkin